In The Garden Devotionals

— — —

A Daily Walk and Talk With God

CANDIA CUMBERBATCH-LUCENIUS,
CERTIFIED HEALTH MINISTER

Printed in the United States of America

ISBN: 9798588226998

ISBN-13: 978-9798588226998

Rev. 2

Digital Inspirations

2402 Rambler Road

Wilmington, DE 19810

(302) 475-3013

www.Digital-Inspirations.press

ACKNOWLEDGEMENTS

To God be the glory, can never be stressed too much, because without Him I am nothing. I am and will forever be grateful to the Way Ministry that taught me God's rightly divided Word, and taught me how to understand, read, and enjoy reading the Bible. After taking several Biblical classes taught by the ministry, I felt led to write this book to encourage myself as well as others to spend time with and so we stay in fellowship with God.

Thankful to the many men and women who love God and faithfully stand for Him whose lives encourage me every day. For the love and support of my believing friends who I have been blessed to know and fellowship with over the years, I give God thanks.

I am thankful for my husband Jon, who supports, encourages, and assists me in making my writing and publishing dreams a reality. He has been extremely instrumental in helping with editing, and adding his digital skills to make the finished product an awesome work of art. Thanks Hon, I probably would not get so much done and have it look so amazing without your help.

For the love and support of my wonderful children and grandchildren, I give God thanks every day – Swanson, Makeeva, Jemini, Avelino, Saiah. Love and blessings to you all. Love and thanks as well to my mother - Mama, Mary

Cumberbatch for the foundation she laid in making sure we not only faithfully attended Sunday service and Sunday School, but Wednesday night Bible Study, Prayer Meeting, and Youth meetings every Friday. She taught us the Word and reminds us even today to put God first and pray. Love and thanks to my sisters and brother and their families we have come this far by faith. Last but not least, in loving memory of our dear brother Abraham Ralph – still miss him, looking forward to seeing him at Christ's return.

(Signature: Get intimate with the Heavenly Father by spending quality time with Him. Blessings, Candia)

About The Cover

The artwork on the cover of this book is a reprint of an original beautiful painting by Penny Scarboro of Art by Penny Elaine. It is used by permission and the original artwork, along with a reprint, is available on Etsy.com.

FOREWARD

Practicing the presence of God by spending time with Him in His Word is an essential and necessary part of a believer's growth and maintaining fellowship with our Heavenly Father as well as with each other in the household. God desires a close, intimate relationship with each of His children. Our daily walk and talk with God spending time in His Word is how we do that.

Picture yourself in a beautiful garden of many different types of flowers, beautiful green trees, lush foliage, and a clear path where you can literally walk and talk with God. Meditate on each verse, then go to the Word and read a few surrounding verses opening up your heart to get the message from the context.

Jesus Christ our example did just that as we read in the gospel of Mark.

Mark 1:35 And in the morning, rising up a great while before day, He went out and departed into a solitary place, and there prayed.

When He was sorrowful anticipating His subsequent arrest, sufferings, and crucifixion He went to a garden to spend quality time with His Father – God.

I trust these daily devotions will be a useful tool in helping us do that each and every day. Utilize the space on the pages to document your reflections, what blessed you about the days message and how you want to improve your walk and talk in fellowship with our Heavenly Father. Please share your thoughts with me at candia@atouchofnewhealth.com. I promise to try to respond to as many as I can.

Candia Cumberbatch-Lucenius
December 29th, 2020
USA

NOTES

NOTES

JANUARY

Friday January 1, 2021

Jeremiah 29:11 For I know the thoughts that I think toward you, saith the Lord, thoughts of peace, and not of evil, to give you an expected end.

As so many are feverishly writing down New Year's resolutions, they are focusing on the things they want to improve. I have long ago decided that these New Year's Resolutions were not for me. "Why?" you may ask. Because by the end of the first week in the year I have forgotten all that I painstakingly took the time to write out on New Year's Day. I find myself falling right back into the old habit patterns that I stated I wanted to change. Instead I have made a conscious decision that each day I will change or improve on one thing. One day at a time, learning to be flexible and to adapt if something is not working, has been more effective.

The year 2020 was a difficult one for so many with sickness and death at an all-time high around the world and many wondered when/if it would end. Plans had to be put on hold or cancelled, routines that were in place for years ended abruptly. Nothing seems sure anymore.

As we move into another year, it makes sense that our resolutions should include our relationship with God our Heavenly Father. God and His Word are the only constant, they have stood the test of time. Only God knows what lies ahead, so as we put our trust in Him, we can be sure that everything will be fine.

He wants only the best for us and is waiting on us to turn to

Him for that “unexpected end”. The Word encourages us to call upon Him and pray in verse 12. And as we lay our hearts out before God the blessings will follow.

Let us take some time to reflect on the past year and make a note of how we can improve our fellowship with God this year.

Saturday January 2, 2021

Deuteronomy 30:19 I call heaven and earth to record this day against you, that I have set before you life and death, blessing and cursing: therefore choose life, that both thou and thy seed may live:
20 (a) That thou mayest love the LORD thy God, and that thou mayest obey his voice, and that thou mayest cleave unto him: for he is thy life, and the length of thy days:

How many decided that they needed to write resolutions anyway? What do your resolutions look like today? Any different from what you would normally have done? Some may have made plans that the world will soon be back to life as we knew it pre-COVID. But is that what we really want? From what I remember life was quite chaotic, too busy to spend time with friends or family, running around trying to get things done, hardly any time for God, or to go to church. Schools were cancelling prayer and kids were being subjected to listen to teachers' opinions and views about life, God, the Bible.

It is clear that changes need to be made because life as we knew it was not working. God sets two choices before us – we have free will to make the right choice. God is our life and when we choose life in the right context - to obey God's Word, the result is blessings and long life. Consider ways you can make the choice to choose life the Word's way.

Sunday January 3, 2021

Galatians 3:28 There is neither Jew nor Greek, there is neither bond nor free, there is neither male nor female: for ye are all one in Christ Jesus.

As born-again believers we are all children of God and part of the ‘one body’. It is through what God accomplished by way of Jesus Christ that we are made all one in Christ. When the veil of the temple was rent, it symbolized the breaking down of the ‘walls’ that separated the Judeans and the Gentiles. Jesus Christ brought peace that reconciled us to God in one body.

We must see ourselves living peacefully coming together with the goal of moving God’s Word. There is so much division and fighting, back-biting and mistrust in the world. Everything Jesus Christ went through, his accomplishments that led to redemption, and freedom from sin was for all mankind, not a select few. Everyone has the same opportunity to be born-again, receive God’s gift of holy spirit and be as one in Christ Jesus. The Church has to be the solution to the world’s problems, but it can only be done as we unite and let go of the contentious behavior that divides God’s people.

Consider how we were made to be part of that ‘one body ‘and our role in moving God’s Word around the world.

Monday January 4, 2021

Psalms 84:11 For the Lord God is a sun and shield; He will give grace and glory No good thing will He withhold from them that walk uprightly.

God is our light (sun) and protector (shield). His grace (unmerited favor) is given to His children because He loves us. His glory (favor) is unconditional. God is light, so as we dwell in His presence we are always surrounded by that light – it is a light to guide and show us the way we should go; and a light that shields us from the darkness of the adversary.

Our response is to walk uprightly (according to the rightly divided Word so we can experience all that is good. God does not send harm, sickness or death on His children, but His hands (figuratively) are tied when our walk is off the Word. As soon as we turn our steps back to Him, He withholds no good thing from us.

Let us reflect on our spiritual walk and consider if it is in alignment with the truth of God's Word. Decide where we can do better.

Tuesday January 5, 2021

Jeremiah 15:16 Thy words were found, and I ate them; and Thy word was unto me the joy and rejoicing of mine heart; for I am called by Thy name, O Lord God of hosts.

What does Jeremiah mean? I am sure he didn't literally pick up a scroll and start munching on it. It is like Job states in chapter 23 verse 12, the Word was to him esteemed more than food. We feast on the Word, mull over it, mediate on it, retemorize it, until it is a part of us. As we nourish our bodies with meals to stay healthy and grow, so God's Word is our nourishment to allow us to thrive, stay healthy, strong and grow spiritually.

That is how we are covered, because the more we make the Word of God a part of our everyday life, the more we stay safe, healthy, and blessed.

How much of the Word have you assimilated/meditated on recently? We can make the decision to learn at least one verse a week going forward to boost our spiritual growth. That way as we meet people with questions, we are always ready with the Word-based answers. This is one way we can be a part of the solution to the world's chaos.

Wednesday January 6, 2021

Deuteronomy 10:12 And now, Israel, what doth the LORD thy God require of thee, but to fear the LORD thy God, to walk in all his ways, and to love him, and to serve the LORD thy God with all thy heart and with all thy soul,
13 To keep the commandments of the LORD, and his statutes, which I command thee this day for thy good?

God makes it so clear there is no room for confusion. We are to fear (reverence) the Lord, love Him, walk according to His Word and be of service. We show our love for God in our steadfast walk and service to His people. We always benefit from doing so - it is "for our good".

When we consider all God has already accomplished for us by way of His Son, Jesus Christ, that is the least we can do in return. This is not just a suggestion either, it is what God 'requires'. And God continues to shower us with His blessings every day, His compassions and mercy are new every day, they never run out. So, out of a heart of thankfulness and gratitude, we love God, walk according to His Word and share it with others.

Do we reverence God in our walk and service to Him? Where can we improve?

Thursday January 7, 2021

Joshua 1:7 Only be thou strong and very courageous,
that thou mayest observe to do according to all the law,
which Moses my servant commanded thee: turn not
from it to the right hand or to the left, that thou mayest
prosper withersoever thou goest.
8 This book of the law shall not depart out of thy
mouth; but thou shalt meditate therein day and night,
that thou mayest observe to do according to all that is
written therein: for then thou shalt make thy way
prosperous, and then thou shalt have good success.
9 Have not I commanded thee? Be strong and of a good
courage; be not afraid, neither be thou dismayed: for the
LORD thy God is with thee whithersoever thou goest.

We too can be strong and very courageous as we take a stand on the Word, not paralyzed by fear of the adversary's attacks. We do not waver or doubt but focus on what God can and will do for us because He promised. God is asking us to not turn away, but to meditate on His Word 'day and night', so we can have 'great success and be prosperous'.

Dealing with the unrest and unknown around the world may have left many with a sense of dread, fear, anxiety, and worry. Will things ever get better, will we ever feel safe, what is next? Even in those times, especially when we can see that things are beyond our control, we hold on to God's promises and trust in Him, knowing that He will come through for us.

God promises to be with us at all times, and as born-again

believers with Christ in us, everywhere we go God is with and in us. That is why we do not need to pray for God to go before, beside or behind us, He is already with us. Knowing this we can be strong, courageous, unafraid, not dismayed (alarmed or fearful.)

Let us consider what we have in Christ so we can be unafraid, bold, courageous and live without fear.

Friday January 8, 2021

Joshua 23:10 One man of you shall chase a thousand: for the LORD your God, he it is that fighteth for you, as he hath promised you.

God "has our backs" so to speak. He will fight for us. There is nothing we can do to protect ourselves that would be better than anything our God can do. Remember how He protected Daniel in the lion's den? These were ferocious, hungry lions, but they did not touch Daniel – only God could do that. In Acts chapter 9 when the Jews/Judeans were lying in wait to kill Paul, God instructed the disciples to help Paul escape by lowering him through a window in a basket. It is a promise, God will fight our battles for us – physically and spiritually.

Several years ago, the assistant manager on the unit where I worked went out of her way to make things difficult for me. It baffled me and my coworkers as we could not figure out why she was so antagonistic towards me. I began to pray believing God's Word that He would fight for me. After about one month she was unexpectedly transferred to a different department where we had no connection. Only God could pull that off. Once I realized that it was an attack of the adversary, I knew it was something I could not handle on my own and believed God to work it out.

Remember a time God got you out of a negative situation.

Saturday January 9, 2021

II Chronicles 7:14 If my people, which are called by my name, shall humble themselves, and pray, and seek my face, and turn from their wicked ways; then will I hear from heaven, and will forgive their sin, and will heal their land.

The past year was a year of terrible devastation and loss, sickness, and death through a pandemic. Many asked over and over again why was this happening, did God allow this, and why would He not stop it? God is light and in Him is no darkness at all, so sickness and death emanate from the author of death – the devil (Hebrews 2:14). God who is just, has to allow man by their own free will to turn to Him, away from their 'wicked ways', and pray for forgiveness.

God made the first move to save the world; He sent His Son Jesus Christ to redeem us from the adversary's destruction. He asks that we confess with our mouths Jesus as Lord in our lives and believe that God raised Him from the dead, so we can be saved. Instead, the world continues to reject him, turning away and ridiculing those who stand for Him. The more that happens the more leeway the adversary has to bring darkness, death, and destruction. How can we ask why?

What can we as believers do? We continue to speak God's Word and reconcile men and women back to God, reminding others that God is waiting with open arms to forgive and rescue those who come to Him. The ball in in our court.

Sunday January 10, 2021

Job 3:25 For the thing which I greatly feared is come upon me, and that which I was afraid of is come unto me.

In the Biblical class on the Way of Abundance and Power, we learn all about positive and negative believing. We learned that Job's negative believing caused him to lose everything. God was not trying Job, testing him, or making him suffer to pay for something he did, and in the same way God is not trying us by sending sickness or loss in our lives. Job's confession that the thing he greatly feared and that which he was afraid of, was what 'came upon him' tells us he understood what led to the devastation in his life.

The story of Job is about a real man who lived many years ago. He was persecuted because He was upright, righteous, walking and living for God and the adversary brought terrible loss and destruction in his life. Even a few of Job's friends thought he must be paying for something bad he did. But Job knew that was not the case; he stood fast, believing, and trusting God to turn things around, and God came through for Job. God gave back to Job double of all that He had.

What are the negative thoughts, negative believing that may hinder our progress? How can we change those to positive believing to get positive results in our lives?

Monday January 11, 2021

Job 27:6 My righteousness I hold fast, and will not let it go: my heart shall not reproach me so long as I live.

Previously we saw how Job's negative believing led to some terrible loss in his life. Thankfully, Job held on to his righteousness and never blamed God for any of the terrible things that happened even when his wife (who had also lost her 10 children), told him it wasn't worth it. He was not going to let disappointment break his heart.

This brings to mind stories of some who lost a loved one and in their grief question God about why it had to happen. Some even go as far as to turn away from God, breaking fellowship with the Father because of the erroneous belief that God 'took' their loved one. Others may have just received a diagnosis with a very poor prognosis, and their first reaction is anger directed at God, again because of the erroneous belief that God sent the affliction to try or prove them. These beliefs are contrary to God's Word that tells us that only 'good and perfect gifts' from God and that the author of death is the devil. Job recognized that and decided to hold fast to his integrity and stay righteous in God's eyes.

Consider how we too can hold fast to our righteousness in the face of heart break, sickness, and loss. The key is to spend more time in God's Word.

Tuesday January 12, 2021

Job 42:10 And the LORD turned the captivity of Job, when he prayed for his friends: also the LORD gave Job twice as much as he had before.

The true story of Job has already opened our understanding of the goodness of God as opposed to the badness of the devil (our adversary). Job had been attacked by the adversary and was afflicted with sickness, and lost all he had, including his 10 children. Because Job held on to the Word, refused to blame God and rebuked his negative speaking friends (miserable comforters), God turned things around for him. God rescued Job from the adversary's clutches (captivity) and gave him back double all he had lost.

No one is immune to the attacks of the adversary, but as we stand on the rightly divided Word and keep the negative confessions out of our hearts and mouths, God will bless us with more than we started with. We renew our minds to never blame God for the negative things that come up; we stay faithful, believing Him to turn it to positives and blessings.

List some Godly confessions and affirmations that can keep our believing positive.

Wednesday January 13, 2021

Psalms 12:6 The words of the LORD are pure words: as silver tried in a furnace of earth, purified seven times.
Psalms 12:6 (Contemporary English Version) Our Lord, you are true to your promises, and your word is like silver heated seven times in a fiery furnace.
7 Thou shalt keep them, O LORD, thou shalt preserve them from this generation forever.

God's words are pure, it has been tried and purified, and it still stands. No matter how many times people have tried to destroy it. God promises He will preserve (save) it from this generation and all future generations. There is nothing else that can make that promise. Unauthorized translations of the Bible were ordered to be burned as far back as the 1500's. God found a way to preserve His written Word.

Additional information can be found in writings about Martin Luther.

Consider how everlasting God's Word is and how it has stood the test of time. We have the Word of God in written form and electronically, at our fingertips twenty-four hours a day, 365 days a year. We cherish the words that bring life and wholeness to everyone who receives and believes it. God's Word is pure, His promises are true; He cannot lie, and does not change - that is why we can trust in Him.

Thursday January 14, 2021

Proverbs 3:5 Trust in the LORD with all thine heart; and lean not unto thine own understanding.
6 In all thy ways acknowledge him, and he shall direct thy paths.
7 Be not wise in thine own eyes: fear the LORD, and depart from evil.
8 It shall be health to thy navel, and marrow to thy bones.

We trust God completely and rely confidently on Him to direct our plans and decisions. Many times, relying on our own five senses does not produce the best results. God knows what is coming and He alone can see the future. Because He knows what is ahead, the direction He leads us to, will always be the best one. He removes road blocks, makes our path clear and smooth.

Several years ago, my husband was offered a job with great pay, benefits and opportunities for career growth; but it was in another state. I loved my job and did not want to leave. At that time, we did not live close to a fellowship where we could go to hear God's Word taught and have fellowship with like-minded believers, which was something we had been praying about for a while. As we prayed and believed together to make the right decision, God opened up a job in the new state for me. The pay was better than the previous job, and we had easy access to a Bible fellowship.

As we humble ourselves in reverence to God, recognizing and acknowledging Him as our Heavenly Father, trusting Him, and we stay away from evil we are refreshed physically, mentally, and spiritually. Then we can clearly see God's direction for our lives.

How can we get better at trusting God completely to direct our paths?

Friday January 15, 2021

Proverbs 13:24 He that spareth his rod hateth his son: but he that loveth him chasteneth him betimes.

Withholding discipline from a child does not prove that you love him/her. Many people in recent years tend to shy away from disciplining a child and categorize any form of disciple as “child abuse’. As born-again believers, our standard remains the Word of God and it is clear on the matter, going as far as to say that sparing the rod or not “spanking” a child just shows you hate him/her. If you love your child you want to make sure he/she is trained appropriately, reproved, and corrected with wisdom and love when they do something wrong or are disobedient.

Our responsibility as Christian parents is to teach our children and train them according to the Word of God. As we impart that knowledge to them, we are raising strong individuals who will stand for what is right and be productive in their communities. Children need guidance and direction and should not be left to alone to raise themselves. We reprove and correct wrong behavior to guide our children in the way that they should go.

Our standard is to accept the direction from God’s Word in raising our children.

Saturday January 16, 2021

Proverbs 16:7 When a man's ways please the LORD, he maketh even his enemies to be at peace with him.

Have you ever felt like no matter what you did, you could not please anybody? Your boss is upset, picking on you, and you are not sure why, your coworkers are complaining about you and your friends seem distant. You spend many a sleepless night trying to figure out what you did wrong. Then you remember a simple statement you made about something you thought was insignificant. “No, it cannot be that, can it?” you ponder. Maybe, because sometimes the adversary will use something really small and turn it into a huge problem. All of a sudden nothing is going right on the job or with your friends.

I remember a coworker who was not friendly towards me, would not speak to me and would not even respond to my greetings. It baffled me because I knew I had done nothing or said anything negative to her. My prayer every day that I worked with her, was for God to keep me peaceful so we could get the job done. Whenever we worked together, I tried to make the atmosphere fun, and light. One day, she called me aside and apologized for the way she had treating me, stating she disliked me because she was jealous of me, and it was nothing I had done. She continued to say that everyone seemed to like me, and I walked with my head up and appeared to be “stuck-up”. WOW!! That was it? With a laugh, I willingly forgave her, we became friends and were able to continue working well together.

As we continue to trust God, turn the situation over to Him, our worse enemy now wants to be our best friend, we may get an unexpected promotion and raise at work and the same coworkers all want to be on our team. The change may even seem unreal at first but remember that we have been praying about the situation and believe that God had a hand in 'our enemies being at peace with us'.

Even when you have no idea why there seems to be a problem, just give it to God and watch Him work on your behalf. Then list the blessings.

Sunday January 17, 2021

Proverbs 16:9 A man's heart deviseth his way: but the LORD directeth his steps.

As we journey through this life, we allow our heart, mostly our emotions to dictate our plans. Our decisions about relationships, jobs, finances, family, health are usually based on how happy they make us. Our happiness should not depend on what is happening in our lives, but unfortunately it does.

HAPPINESS is determined by our circumstances, including people; can change instantly depending on what is going on at any given time in our lives and is usually led by emotions.

JOY on the other hand goes beyond happiness; it is a quality of life not dependent on our circumstances and is not an emotion. We control it by our free will choice – we chose to live a life full of joy.

As we allow God to direct our every move, He establishes/ organizes and confirms each step we take better than we ever could.

Making plans for the next phase in your life's journey? Trust God to direct your steps.

Monday January 18, 2021

Deuteronomy 29:29 The secret things belong unto the LORD our God: but those things which are revealed belong unto us and to our children for ever, that we may do all the words of this law.

Over the years I have taken several Biblical research classes and still feel there are many unanswered questions about the Bible. I know many people who search every literary avenue to find these answers and try to explain certain things in life scientifically. My belief has always been, that there will be somethings that God just does not want us to know yet. He has revealed so much that He wanted us to know and teach to our children, but there will remain things that will be His secret until He wants to reveal them even if it is after the return of Christ.

Many Biblical scholars over the years have been able to prove that the Word of God fits with a "mathematical exactness and a scientific precision." So, what God has made clear to us is what we need to live the life He has called us to.

Consider what we know about how God's Word fits with a "mathematical exactness and a scientific precision."

Tuesday January 19, 2021

Ecclesiastes 12:1 Remember now thy Creator in the days of thy youth, while the evil days come not, nor the years draw nigh, when thou shalt say, I have no pleasure in them;

The best time to start a life of service to God is while we are young, when we have the strength and energy to give Him our best. The older we get, the less energetic we feel, and our interest and excitement lessens. Not that we do not want to continue to live for and serve God, but physically it may not be as feasible to do as much as we would like to.

The energy and vigor I had thirty and even forty years ago, is definitely not the same today. It was much easier to multi-task, to go out and speak the Word and to be of greater service. Sleep was easier to come by, so I always felt well rested. With the passing of time and changes in our lives' seasons, we seem to be slowing down and not able to accomplish tasks as quickly as we did previously. Now we work to train the youth, so they can give their lives in service to God while they are still full of energy and drive.

How can we continue to serve God, and what can we do now before "the years draw nigh?"

Wednesday January 20, 2021

Ecclesiastes 12:13 Let us hear the conclusion of the whole matter: Fear God, and keep his commandments: for this is the whole duty of man.

Our worship to God our Heavenly Father is filled with reverence, not fear as we acknowledge Him as the sovereign being and almighty. God asks that we keep His commandments and love Him – that is what He asks of His children. In summing up what God expects of His children, we worship Him and give Him praise that is due Him. The reason God created the earth is to bless man; the reason God made man was to worship Him.

Our duty and purpose is to serve, love, respect, and obey God which also includes loving others with the love of God.

Share how you worship God and keep His commandments.

Thursday January 21, 2021

Isaiah 1:18 Come now, and let us reason together, saith the LORD: though your sins be as scarlet, they shall be as white as snow; though they be red like crimson, they shall be as wool.
19 If ye be willing and obedient, ye shall eat the good of the land:

We have all made mistakes, poor decisions that were not pleasing to God or were off the Word. God is so loving and gentle; He beckons us tenderly to come talk with Him. No matter how badly we feel we've messed up, God is saying "come now, let us discuss this. You haven't done anything so bad that we cannot work it out." Whatever it is, no matter how bad it looks, it can be fixed, you can be washed clean. God already made provision for our sins found in 1 John 1:9, where He states He is faithful and just to forgive our sins and to cleanse us from unrighteousness or broken fellowship

We can always find the time to go to God humbly, pouring our hearts out to Him. It is our free will choice, we decide to go to God, and humbly ask for forgiveness so we can keep our relationship with Him sweet. He is willing and ready to "reason" with us and to forgive.

Friday January 22, 2021

Isaiah 26:3 Thou wilt keep him in perfect peace, whose mind is stayed on thee: because he trusteth in thee.
4 Trust ye in the LORD for ever: for in the LORD JEHOVAH is everlasting strength:

Keeping our minds 'stayed' on God requires renewing our minds on a daily basis, and not letting the negatives of the world take over our thoughts. Some days it takes minute by minute, hour by hour but it will literally keep us out of the 'soup' or from broken fellowship. We want and need that true, complete peace that only God can give. As believers we have the power of God in Christ in us, but we need to make a conscious effort to manifest it. "The key to releasing our inner power is the renewing of the mind; the key to the renew mind is the 'stayed' mind.

We remain committed, stay steadfast and focused on God and His Word, letting nothing take precedence. We fill our minds with God's truths and trust Him in every situation so we can experience "perfect peace". That peace is constant, and nothing can take it away as long as our minds are focused on God. The strength we receive from God is everlasting.

Consider the 'perfect peace' and 'everlasting' strength we have as we trust God and stand committed to Him and His Word.

Saturday January 23, 2021

Isaiah 33:6 And wisdom and knowledge shall be the stability of thy times, and strength of salvation: the fear of the LORD is his treasure.

With everything going on in the world – fighting, murders, protests, a pandemic, we can be confident in the knowledge and understanding of God's Word as our stability. We reverence and honor God for our salvation which continues to be our strength in the midst of the chaos.

Nothing in the world or the news can give us the firm foundation that we have in God. As we listen to the news or social media especially during a pandemic, a hurricane, tornado, earthquake, or fire, we can get more alarmed every second. We hear of the possible threats to our lives and what might happen, and everything sounds so dire. It becomes almost impossible to not just go into a panic mode from fear and anxiety and depression.

As born-again believers we know that God is our sufficiency and will keep us stable. By God's grace and mercy, we can be at peace always knowing that we are safe in Him.

Consider how year after year God's Word is stable and is the one constant that we can rely on.

Sunday January 24, 2021

Isaiah 35:8 And an highway shall be there, and a way, and it shall be called The way of holiness; the unclean shall not pass over it; but it shall be for those: the wayfaring men, though fools, shall not err therein.

God will always make a way for His people; it will be a clear path that directs our life. We are set apart for God's glory and our walk is one of holiness. Those who do not want to worship God will be not be part of that journey. We may even lose some friends dear to us as we continue on that path, but that just means that they are not meant to be on that part of our journey. Someone once said, "some people are in our lives for a reason, a season or a life-time". Not everyone will complete the journey with us.

As a people set apart to live for and worship God, our lives must reflect our walk.

It can be so easy to start wondering around both physically and in our minds, to allow ourselves to doubt God's Word, to be fearful about our future. No need for any of that. Our Heavenly Father will clear a path with no doubts, fears, or confusion for us. He has already declared us holy.

Monday January 25, 2021

Isaiah 43:7 Even every one that is called by my name: for I have created him for my glory, I have formed him; yea, I have made him.

God made man a three part being of body, soul, and spirit for His glory. First, He formed (yatsah) man's body out of the dust of the earth, then He made and breathed into man breath of life so he became a living soul (asah), and finally God created man's spirit (bara) in His very own likeness, so He could have full fellowship and communication with man.

God makes it clear in His Word why He went through so much to redeem man from the adversary's clutches after man sinned and lost his spirit connection with God. Man was lost, wandering around aimlessly with no direction; and life was a series of one disaster after another. God made a plan to send His Son Jesus Christ to buy back man's freedom from the adversary. When we believe and accept it we are back in fellowship with our Heavenly Father.

Our next move is to glorify God in our body, soul (mind) and spirit.

Tuesday January 26, 2021

Isaiah 43:25 I, even I, am he that blotteth out thy transgressions for mine own sake, and will not remember thy sins.

There is more than one place in the Word that God reminds us that He forgives us and forgets our sins. Psalms 103 tells us He removes our sins as far as the East is from the West. In Colossians 2:14, He blotted out our transgressions, nailing them to the cross.

God, through the accomplished works of His Son Jesus Christ, not only forgets our sins, but He also blots them out, completely expunged or erased everything that was against us. This means that when we were born again, we received full remission of sins, a one-time cleansing of all our sins.

Many of us allow our past mistakes to torment us forever, producing many sleepless nights. God says He has blotted out, erased, or wiped out our transgressions (sins) and will not remember them. So why do we remember them? As born-again believers, we are thankful for Jesus Christ's sacrifice for the forgiveness of our sins. Just as God does not remember our sins, we should forget them and leave them in the past.

Are you holding on to past mistakes that are keeping you from moving forward, from living an abundant life? Remember that God has blotted them out.

Wednesday January 27, 2021

Isaiah 40:31 But they that wait upon the LORD shall renew their strength; they shall mount up with wings as eagles; they shall run, and not be weary; and they shall walk, and not faint.

When we lost our brother several years ago, I was broken, sad, depressed. As much as I reminded myself that I am not supposed to "sorrow as them that have no hope," it was really hard. Just when I thought I was starting to heal from that sadness, I lost two friends who were very dear to me, and the pain and sadness enveloped me again. It took putting on a lot of the Word – sitting through a Bible class and the love, support, and encouragement from other special people in my life. The Word heals and God gives us the strength we need to keep moving.

Life with its many ups and downs, twists and turns can drain us mentally, physically, and spiritually. As we wait on God, not losing our trust in Him, looking past the situations in our lives to the hope of Christ' return, we will be strengthened, energized and renewed in our spirit. When we are weak, God is our strength causing us to pick ourselves up, dust ourselves off, walk and even run without getting tired or feeling faint. We will soar above the world's negatives as we trust God for the strength we need.

Thank God for renewing your strength so you can "mount up with wings as eagles, you can walk and not faint, run and not be tired" – physically nor mentally.

Thursday January 28, 2021

Isaiah 58:8 Then shall thy light break forth as the morning, and thine health shall spring forth speedily: and thy righteousness shall go before thee; the glory of the LORD shall be thy reward.

We do not always understand why we pray for hours, weeks, months and maybe years and only experience minimal or no change in a situation. As we look around, we may even see or hear testimonies of miracles others are having every day. The human tendency would be to question why me? And we may not get the answer to that either, but God is asking us to not lose faith in Him.

Are you or someone you know praying for healing? Does it look like you have been stuck in this spot for too long? Do not give up. This is a wonderful promise to claim to help build believing. Picture the first light of dawn breaking through the morning sky. One minute it is dark outside and suddenly the light floods the earth. You open your window or front door and the light just floods it. It is no longer dark; it is the break of a brand-new day. Everything looks bright and fresh. In the same way we can get the breakthrough to improved health. Remember your righteousness as a son of God and know that He is working and will come through for you. Picture that light flooding your body as you give praise and glory to God.

Friday January 29, 2021

Jeremiah 17:7 Blessed is the man that trusteth in the LORD, and whose hope the LORD is.
8 For he shall be as a tree planted by the waters, and that spreadeth out her roots by the river, and shall not see when heat cometh, but her leaf shall be green; and shall not be careful in the year of drought, neither shall cease from yielding fruit.

When we lose sight of our trust in God, and falter in our believing we are no longer looking past the present situation to the hope of Christ's return. When we allow what we can see by our five senses to block the promises of God we are like a tree that has lost all its leaves, and when the Fall changes to Spring, it stays dry and lifeless because it is in the middle of the forest with no water around and the sunlight blocked by even bigger trees.

Take a look at the trees near any body of water – a stream or river maybe. They are vibrant, the leaves a shiny green and as long as the water supply does not dry up, the roots spread out and there is always a fresh supply of fruit dangling from its branches. Those who trust and hope in God can boast of the same – vibrant, fruitful, and blessed.

Consider the many ways you are blessed because of the Word of God you know and your trust in God.

Saturday January 30, 2021

Jeremiah 20:9 Then I said, I will not make mention of him, nor speak any more in his name. But his word was in mine heart as a burning fire shut up in my bones, and I was weary with forbearing, and I could not stay.

When we are hit by a great loss, a grave diagnosis with a poor prognosis initially we are angry and may even say something like what Jeremiah says here. Maybe we have been speaking the Word and been ridiculed and rejected. We could maybe even decide to stop speaking the Word, and maybe say something like - "No one is listening anyway, they don't care; what's the point?"

When we develop that close, personal, sweet fellowship with our Heavenly Father and experience the many blessings He pours on us we cannot keep it to ourselves. We want to share our testimonies to everyone who will listen. The joy of having full sharing and open communication with God cannot be contained. You open your mouth and the words just flow out, like a river overflowing its banks.

Meditate on some of your testimonies that you can share.

Sunday January 31, 2021

Jeremiah 29:12 Then shall ye call upon me, and ye
shall go and pray unto me, and I will hearken unto you.
13 And ye shall seek me, and find me, when ye shall
search for me with all your heart.
14 And I will be found of you, saith the LORD: and I
will turn away your captivity, and I will gather you
from all the nations, and from all the places whither I
have driven you, saith the LORD; and I will bring you
again into the place whence I caused you to be carried
away captive.

God is always just a prayer away. No matter how long it has been since you last talked to Him, no matter what the situation God is waiting for us to come back to Him. When we turn to God whole heartedly, and pour out hearts to Him and confess our sins (broken fellowship), He bring us back into His inner circle (the household of believers), He will free us from whatever has us bound – sickness, fear, anger sadness, depression, any other chains that bind.

God invites us to "come boldly unto the throne of grace. That is because He does not hold our sins against us. We have been made righteous, justified by the accomplished works of Jesus Christ.

If you notice God does not have to go look for us, He never leaves us – we are the ones who break fellowship and need to pray and seek God.

Consider what chains may have you bound, where you have broken fellowship and remember God is waiting for you.

FEBRUARY

Monday February 1, 2021

Lamentations 3:21 This I recall to my mind, therefore have I hope.
22 It is of the LORD's mercies that we are not consumed, because his compassions fail not.
23 They are new every morning: great is thy faithfulness.

Thank God for His mercies to withhold punishment even when we deserve it, His compassions – understanding and empathy, and faithfulness – unfailing loyalty. It does not expire, not does it have a shelf-life. Every day we can wake up to a new day of all God has made available to us; we can ask His forgiveness, praise, and worship Him and be confident in the knowledge that He still loves us.

When I wake in the morning, before I even get out of bed, I like to lay quietly and remind myself of God's goodness. In the quiet of the day, I can bring to mind my thankfulness for waking up, being able to take a deep breath (some are not able to), for health, my family and life in general. Some days it is a lot deeper than that when I remember where God brought me from, how He stayed with me through some storms of life and helped keep my head above water.

Even when things are going great in our lives, we need God's refreshing to deal with the events/activities that may come up each day.

Whatever happened yesterday, the week before and so on is in the past and God in His merciful kindness has already forgiven and forgotten it all.

Let us consider some of God's merciful kindness, compassions, and faithfulness to us and how we can continue to walk worthy as His children.

Tuesday February 2, 2021

Lamentations 3:24 The LORD is my portion, saith my soul; therefore will I hope in him.
25 The LORD is good unto them that wait for him, to the soul that seeketh him.
26 It is good that a man should both hope and quietly wait for the salvation of the LORD.

Millions voted in 2020 to elect a president of the United States. On both sides people stated they were praying for their choice to be elected. For some of us we were just praying that God would allow the best person and their running mate to be elected. We trust that God knows what is best needed for His people at a time when so much is at stake. Our responsibility is to pray for our leaders so we can live a peaceful life in all godliness and honesty.

God is good always and everything He does for us is to bless us. God is basically all we have, He is our life and without Him life would have no meaning, so we put all our trust in Him, we wait on Him for the best of everything for us His children, even when it seems like it may not be what we expect. We keep moving and look past whatever the situation is in the world as we anticipate the hope of Christ's return.

God alone can see the future and knows what is best to allow us to live a peaceful life and continue to speak His Word. So, in whatever outcome we trust God fully. Let us consider the importance of God in your life.

Wednesday February 3, 2021

Proverbs 3:9 Honour the LORD with thy substance, and with the first fruits of all thine increase:
10 So shall thy barns be filled with plenty, and thy presses shall burst out with new wine.

Sometime ago, I heard a minister say that when he puts His tithe in the collection plate, He keeps his palms open upwards. When asked why he did that, he replied that he was proving God like it says in Malachi chapter three. He believed that as you give you receive, so he kept his hands open to receive the blessings he knew God would provide.

When we give back to God, we honor Him recognizing His love and goodness to us. Our tithe is the bare minimum that we give – it is one tenth off the top of our "first-fruits". When we do what we called 'abundant sharing', we are giving more than just the tithe. We are in a partnership with God as we give for the continued movement of His Word around the world, and He gives back to bless us so our needs are met. Everything we have is because God provides it in the first place. God gives us back more that we have room for. Our barns (bank account will be full) and our presses (cupboards) busting at the seams (so to speak).

Take a moment to consider how God has given you back double when you give your tithe with love.

Thursday February 4, 2021

Daniel 6:22 My God hath sent his angel, and hath shut the lions' mouths, that they have not hurt me: forasmuch as before him innocency was found in me; and also before thee, O king, have I done no hurt.

When Daniel was thrown into the lion's den for refusing to bow down and worship the king, everyone expected him to be torn to shreds by the hungry, ravenous beasts. Daniel believed God would protect him, and God shut the mouths of the lions, so they did not even touch him. Daniel told the king confidently that he knew God would protect him and even if God allowed the lions to eat him, he knew it was for a reason and He would still praise God to the end.

God is the same today and will do the same and more for us as we believe and trust Him. Do we have the same level of trust and confidence in God that Daniel had? Do we believe that God is willing and able to protect and save us in whatever situation we're in? Do we love and trust God to say that even if He does not, we will love and trust Him anyway? That is the commitment that God is looking for from His children.

Consider God's promise to protect and care for us as we believe and stand for Him. Let us be bold and confident to say that we will trust and believe God to do what seems impossible for us every time.

Friday February 5, 2021

Proverbs 17:22 A merry heart doeth good like a medicine: but a broken spirit drieth the bones.

Staying joyful no matter what, can promote healing.

Happiness is determined by our circumstances and can change depending on what is going on at any given time in our lives and is usually led by emotions.

For example, we may be happy as long as we are enjoying our job, if we get a promotion, and/or a raise. But if we work long hours and get passed over for a promotion, and maybe do not like our boss, we would be very unhappy. If we are in a relationship, maybe married, or have best friends we are happy once things are going great. If something is said or done that we do not like or hurt our feelings, we are no longer happy. What if we are dealing with health issues, are in pain or uncomfortable? It is definitely hard to be happy then

Joy on the other hand goes beyond happiness; it is a quality of life not dependent on our circumstances, it is not an emotion. We control it by our free will choice – we chose to live a life full of joy. So, if anything goes wrong in our relationships, even if it is a break-up, we can be joyful as we put our trust in God. If it is a health issue, we claim and hold on to God's promise of healing. That is how we can stay joyful and maintain a 'merry heart'.

Consider choosing to be joyful especially during health challenges and see God's healing goodness come to pass.

Saturday February 6, 2021

Proverbs 16:24 Pleasant words are as an honeycomb, sweet to the soul, and health to the bones.

I remember as a child, repeating over and over to myself this phrase, "sticks and stones can break my bones, but words can do me no harm." Children can be so mean to each other, and I was always bullied and harassed because I was usually the tallest in my class and because I preferred to keep to myself. Instead of losing my temper and lashing out, my mother suggested I use those words.

Later as I grew older, I learned that words can be just as harmful as when hit with a rock or pole. If those words are insulting, degrading or hurtful, they can cause mental stress, depression, and possibly worse. I had to change my phrase to "and be ye kind one to another", which I reminded myself of as I counted to ten, then counted backwards before I responded to whatever the situation was.

Kind words are like honey, sweet/nice to hear and can boost our spirits bringing healing both physically and mentally. We never know what people are dealing with in their lives, speaking kind words to them might be the difference between life and death. A kind word lifts one's mood, brings a smile to faces and healing to the body, both to the speaker and the one receiving. Consider that as you speak kind words to bless others you may be saving a life and you too are blessed.

Sunday February 7, 2021

Proverbs 16:32 He that is slow to anger is better than the mighty; and he that ruleth his spirit than he that taketh a city.

I remember a friend many years ago who was learning how to control her thinking and her tongue when she was verbally attacked. If someone was cursing her and calling her names she responded with "John 3:16". When I first heard it, I was stunned and asked her why she did that. She replied that because she did not want to use curse words, and she was trying to control her thinking and her mind, she reminded herself as well as the other person(s) that God loves all of us equally. I thought that was a unique and interesting way to handle it. It seemed to be effective since the opponents did not know how to respond and just walked away.

Controlling one's temper takes strength and dignity, and a renewed mind; it takes bringing our mind back to the Word and being meek and this is more powerful than the toughest warrior. Anyone can fly "off the handle" when something goes wrong, its human natures first and easiest response. It takes real inner strength to hold it in and control when and how you respond as well as what you say.

Consider your response the next time someone or something makes you angry.

Monday February 8, 2021

Isaiah 6:8 Also I heard the voice of the Lord, saying, Whom shall I send, and who will go for us? Then said I, Here am I; send me.

As born-again believers, we have been entrusted with the ministry of reconciliation and God is asking who will step up. Having free will, we have to make the decision to say, "here am I send me". We have so many opportunities to speak the Word and it does not necessarily mean going door to door. When we are out shopping, on the job, at an event where people are gathering, we can be ready to speak the Word. Our heart should be to listen and figure out where there is a need, then we can share how God's Word has the answers to meet every need.

God is really good at letting us know who to approach and start a conversation with. Even if there is no clear indication that we should say something, our rule of thumb should be to greet everyone we meet. We just never know who is searching, who is ready to receive the truth. Someone may have prayed for God to send someone to talk to them. People are out there searching, and we have the answers from God's Word. Again, someone may just need a hug and prayer. We can be ready to do that to bless as well.

Are you ready to answer God's call today? So many are searching and those of us who know the Word are the ones to take the message to them.

Tuesday February 9, 2021

Isaiah 45:6 That they may know from the rising of the sun, and from the west, that there is none beside me. I am the LORD, and there is none else.

This reminds me of the song by Eben called "You Are God All By Yourself." There is no other God beside the true God. Many have tried to give themselves that title. It never fits, because only the one true God created the heavens and the earth – all by Himself. He is Elohim, God the Creator, and deserves all glory, praise, honor and our full worship.

As the sun rising at the dawn of a new day, it fills my heart with awe and wonder at God's magnificent handiwork. The light of day emerges, the colors in the sky may be blue, grey, or orange as the sun peaks out. And again, at the end of the day as dusk begins to envelope the sky and the light of the sun is slowly fading away, I can see some God's masterpiece develop. God causes the sun to rise in the east and set in the west – He alone did that and no one else can.

We rejoice at the magnificence of our Heavenly Father, Creator of the heavens and the earth and consider the place He has in our hearts.

Wednesday February 10, 2021

Isaiah 49:15 Can a woman forget her sucking child, that she should not have compassion on the son of her womb? yea, they may forget, yet will I not forget thee. ***16*** Behold, I have graven thee upon the palms of my hands; thy walls are continually before me.

What a promise!! The analogy God sets before us is a woman may forget her own children that she gave birth to (hard to imagine, for most of us), but He will not forget us. To get our attention God is using a figure of speech '*condescencio'* talking about the palms of His hands. Many people have tattoos all over their body, but I have never seen any on the palms. Why? Because it is too painful – no one could endure it, but that is what God says He has done. And our face is continually (all the time) before Him; we are in His heart.

Using the analogy of a mother with her child, God is trying to make a point. You may have heard the phrase "protective as a mama bear" when referring to a mother and her young. They have a strong, almost indescribable bond and a mother may even give her life to protect her child. To describe His love for us in terms we may easily relate to, God is saying that even with that strong love for her child, a mother may abandon and/or forget that child, but He as our loving Heavenly Father will NEVER forget us.

Let us meditate on these truths; absorb the magnitude of God's love.

Thursday February 11, 2021

Isaiah 50:7 For the Lord GOD will help me; therefore shall I not be confounded: therefore have I set my face like a flint, and I know that I shall not be ashamed.

Many of us have some fears which can be debilitating preventing us from living our best lives. Maybe it is a fear of heights so you may never know what it would be light to climb to the top of the Empire State Building and experience that awesome view of the city. It may be a fear of flying, so one may never experience the joys of visiting other beautiful countries and being emersed in various cultures. What about the fear of failing an exam or at something else – a new job or a relationship for example. What happens? Nothing, because we do not try.

Because we have God's promise, we can be confident and not ashamed, confused but with determination we are steadfast on His Word. We know that His promises are true, and that we can trust Him, so we can face those fears and overcome as we remind ourselves that 'the Lord God will help me.'

Consider how confident we can be in the knowledge that God is always with us and is not only willing but able to see us through whatever the situation.

Friday February 12, 2021

Isaiah 54:17 No weapon that is formed against thee shall prosper; and every tongue that shall rise against thee in judgment thou shalt condemn. This is the heritage of the servants of the LORD, and their righteousness is of me, saith the LORD.

In life we will face many adversities. People may tell lies about us, slander our name and reputation. We may need to go before the principal, dean, pastor, or our boss to defend ourselves. Look at God's promise to His children – no weapons made to attack us will harm us and every lie against us will be refuted. What if one day we are called upon to defend our stand on God's Word? How would we handle that situation? The first thing to remember is that it is God's Word we stand on and He will give us the right words at the right time to give a reason of the 'hope that is in us.' God's Word never needs defending, so we answer with 'chapter and verse Then we allow God to be our defense attorney.

As children of the most High God, our victory comes from God and that is our inheritance.

Consider giving everything to God and trusting Him to do what He has promised.

Saturday February 13, 2021

Isaiah 55:6 Seek ye the LORD while he may be found, call ye upon him while he is near:

We have every opportunity to respond to God's call; now is the time while it is still available to do so. Just like the people in the days of Noah did not respond to calls to leave their sinful lives and go into the ark while it was available, we are encouraged to turn to God while we still have time. Once the doors were shut, the chance to do so was gone. We do not know when the door will be shut for us, so now is the time to respond.

God's Word tells us in 1 Timothy chapter two it is God's will that all men everywhere be saved and come to a knowledge of the truth of His Word. So, we as believers speak the Word to all. We make it available and those who are searching to know the truth will respond.

Consider your relationship with God; do you hear him calling on you? What will be your response?

Sunday February 14, 2021 –VALENTINE'S DAY

Ephesians 5:21 Submitting yourselves one to another in the fear of God.

I Corinthians 13:4 Charity suffereth long, and is kind; charity envieth not; charity vaunteth not itself, is not puffed up,
5 Doth not behave itself unseemly, seeketh not her own, is not easily provoked, thinketh no evil;
6 Rejoiceth not in iniquity, but rejoiceth in the truth;

Saint Valentine's Day – a day that people everywhere celebrate romance and love. Partners and spouses surprise each other with presents, dinner, candy, flowers and/or jewelry to profess their love. God's Word encourages us to submit to each other – it is not one sided, contrary to popular belief, in reverence to God as the head of the home. Because as we see in 1 Corinthians 13, charity (the love of God in the renewed mind) endures with patience and peace, it is kind, not envious and is humble. Charity is not prideful, haughty, rude, unmannerly, does not seek attention for itself and has joy speaking the truth.

The commitment to each other is to be salted and like-minded on the Word of God. When it seems really difficult to be our best, we go to the Word and let God guide our hearts and lives. With the same forgiveness God forgave us, we renew our minds taking it one day at a time to be kind, tenderhearted and forgiving. When the love and romance seem to have dwindled, we can still love with the love of God in the renewed mind in manifestations.

Consider your relationship, love life, or marriage, in relation to God's Word. How long do these acts of kindness last? Do you try to keep up or at least some of the romance throughout the year? Let us do our best to manifest the 'love of God in the renewed mind' with each other?

Monday February 15, 2021

Exodus 18:19 Hearken now unto my voice, I will give thee counsel, and God shall be with thee: Be thou for the people to Godward, that thou mayest bring the causes unto God.

When we listen, we receive the wise counsel we need to make the right decision. Leadership in the household is set in place so God's people are taken care of, they stand in the gap for us as ministers of God. When things come up, we go to our leadership for guidance. We will receive wise counsel from them because it is directly from the Word. As we take heed to the counsel given us from these men and women of God, we see God's hand of blessing on our lives.

God can direct our steps according to His Word as we are meek to receive Godly counsel and reproof if needed. We in turn can take what we've learned and pass this wise counsel on to others.

It is so easy to cry out to God when we are in trouble. Consider taking time to listen to what God has to say. Be reminded to be meek to receive wise counsel from God's Word.

Tuesday February 16, 2021

Psalms 1:1 Blessed is the man that walketh not in the
counsel of the ungodly, nor standeth in the way of
sinners, nor sitteth in the seat of the scornful.
2 But his delight is in the law of the LORD; and in his
law doth he meditate day and night.

Happy, prosperous, and favored are we when we decide to shun evil doers refusing to spend time in their company. We do not go to them for advice, because it will never be Word based. There will be those who scoff at the Word and mock you for your stand. They are to be avoided at all cost.

Peer pressure is real, and it does not just affect the young. Even in the workplace, there may be some who will try to influence negative behavior or entice us to do something wrong. It may be something as small as going out to lunch and being talked into taking an extra ten minutes. That is stealing time from your employer. Being coerced to cheat on an exam or on your timesheet on the job are both forms of stealing.

As believers we need to set an example by being the ones to stand up in the face of peer pressure and maybe even ridicule to say "no, this is wrong; I will not do it."

Instead take a stand, we learn to enjoy reading and studying the Word meditating on it day and night and sharing these truths to others. God sees and blesses us back for our stand on what is right. For further study consider reading the rest of the chapter.

Wednesday February 17, 2021

Psalms 16:8 I have set the LORD always before me:
because he is at my right hand, I shall not be moved.
9 Therefore my heart is glad, and my glory rejoiceth:
my flesh also shall rest in hope.

As we keep God always before us, we are reminded not to be afraid, shaken or moved. Feeling His presence with us keeps us confident, happy and we have restful sleep. These truths are not based on emotions, but on free will choice. As the Psalmist states we set the Lord before us, by keeping His Word in our minds, and hearts. There is no way a believer can experience the joy of true fellowship with God without spending time in the Word. The right hand is considered the hand of blessing, so with God at our right hand, we are sure to be continuously blessed. Consider practicing the presence of God by keeping His Word close.

Thursday February 18, 2021

Psalms 20:6 Now know I that the LORD saveth his anointed; he will hear him from his holy heaven with the saving strength of his right hand.
7 Some trust in chariots, and some in horses: but we will remember the name of the LORD our God.

I know there are many out there who are struggling with health issues, addictions, financial situations, and other negative situations. You may be feeling depressed, with an over-whelming sense of loss and loneliness. You may look around and those around you seem happy with not a care in the world. I want to say to you right now, "do not give up, God is waiting to hear you call on Him, waiting for you to be ready for His salvation. He will not force you or take control of your life but He will save you as soon as you make the decision to obey Romans 10:9.

As God's anointed, His chosen ones, we know He hears and will save us when we call on Him. We believe that "greater is He that is in us" and we trust in our Heavenly Father for deliverance. While others depend on and boast about all their weapons or defense mechanisms, we trust in God for our protection and safety.

Friday February 19, 2021

Psalms 18:1 I will love thee, O LORD, my strength.
2 The LORD is my rock, and my fortress, and my
deliverer; my God, my strength, in whom I will trust;
my buckler, and the horn of my salvation, and my high
tower.
3 I will call upon the LORD, who is worthy to be
praised: so shall I be saved from mine enemies.

We love Him because He first loved us. We know and can be confident that God loves us because He sent His Son Jesus Christ to rescue us from the clutches of the adversary that threatened to destroy us and keep us drowning in despair. He has gone through so much to allow His Son to suffer and die for us, rest assured that He will be with us to pick us up when we are at our lowest.

God is our strength; our rock and He promises to deliver us and protect us. As a shield He will literally block the attacks of the adversary as we trust Him. We can run to Him and feel safe and secure in His arms. All praise and glory go to God.

Spend some time in praise and worship for God's protection, because we know He does - even when we do not realize He has.

Saturday February 20, 2021

Psalms 18:29 For by thee I have run through a troop; and by my God have I leaped over a wall.

By our own strength we cannot get through every hurdle we have to face in life. As a kid I remember playing a game where one person ran into a line of other kids holding hands (forget what it was called), trying to break their hold. Most times it was impossible to get through, but the objective was to scan the line and look for the kid who looked the weakest. That is where you target. The rest of the team try to put a seemingly weaker person next to a strong one to make it more difficult for the opposing team to break through.

I did competitive high jump for my team in high school. It took a lot of training and precision, and consistent practicing, so I know leaping over a wall is no easy feat. That is why we do not rely on our own strength to conquer the hurdles we face in our lives.

When we are weak God makes us strong to get through anything – those walls of temptation, sickness, grief, broken hearts. We can burst through those walls and scale the highest mountain of whatever the problem is with God's help.

Let us acknowledge that with God we can do anything that may seem impossible.

Sunday February 21, 2021

Psalms 18:33 He maketh my feet like hinds' feet, and setteth me upon my high places.

As a deer climbs a mountain, she uses her front feet to test for loose stones then she knows exactly where to place her hind feet, so she does not slip and fall. The analogy is the "front feet" represents the Word, and as if we place our feet exactly where the Word directs us, we are in agreement with its truths allowing it to be our guide.

When I was about to graduate from high school, I had no idea what I wanted to do with my life. Several options presented itself and by graduation day I was still going back and forth in my heard. The one thought I kept going back to was that I really wanted to help others. What career should I choose to be able to do that? Until one day, it was as clear as day that I should be a nurse. What better way to help others than by caring for the sick? Today I am thankful I recognized that was what God called me to do. After 45 years, I can truly say, I had multiple opportunities and beautiful, rewarding experiences helping others.

Are we in agreement with and confess the truths in God's Word?

Monday February 22, 2021

Psalms 19:1 The heavens declare the glory of God; and the firmament sheweth his handywork.
2 Day unto day uttereth speech, and night unto night sheweth knowledge.

God's Word is written in the stars, where many over the years have seen revelation of things to come and God's plan. The sun, moon, stars and the whole heavens of planets show God's masterpiece and leaves us in awe of all its magnificence. Each day and night tell a story that if we take the time to study will open up a whole new understanding of all God's wonders.

As we often hear "slow down and smell the roses", how about taking time to slow down and enjoy God's magnificent masterpiece in the heavens.

Tuesday February 23, 2021

Psalms 19:14 Let the words of my mouth, and the meditation of my heart, be acceptable in thy sight, O LORD, my strength, and my redeemer.

As a kid, I remember playing with my friends in our yard or somewhere close to the house. We were usually within earshot of our parents who listened intently to what was going on, even if it did not look like it. One afternoon, we got excited about the game we were playing and one of the neighborhood children who had just lost started cursing and shouting that someone had cheated. I remember her mother calling her and saying if she heard those words again, she would wash her mouth out with soap. We giggled thinking it was funny, but also knew that our parents would literally do that.

There are somethings we may not want to repeat within earshot of our parents – words that may be derogatory, disrespectful, or rude. In the same way we want our words, meditations, every thought, and intent of our hearts to be always pleasing and acceptable to God our Heavenly Father and Redeemer, who is our strength. Since God is everywhere present, we know He not only hears everything we say, but He even knows what we are thinking. With that in mind, we need to 'reign in' those negative thoughts, and bring our thoughts back to the Word.

Wednesday February 24, 2021

Psalms 27:14 Wait on the LORD: be of good courage, and he shall strengthen thine heart: wait, I say, on the LORD.

So many times, we can feel lost, anxious, afraid, frustrated, and depressed. We feel like we have been waiting an eternity for the answer to our prayers for healing, a job, to be debt free, for a husband or wife. When that happens, do we give up, say God does not hear me, the answer will never come? Absolutely not! Our Heavenly Father wants us to be blessed, He always wants the best for His children.

When we go to God with our petitions, we must be patient. The answer is not always immediate, and it can sometimes be difficult to pray and wonder if God heard our prayer. Well yes, He always hears us, and once we pour our hearts to Him, we may need to stop and listen for the answer. So, we wait and not lose heart, but trust that the answer is coming, and we are never disappointed. God will give us the strength we need to endure as we wait.

Let us remember to take heart and wait, listening patiently for the answers from God.

Thursday February 25, 2021

Psalms 31:19 Oh how great is thy goodness, which thou hast laid up for them that fear thee; which thou hast wrought for them that trust in thee before the sons of men!

God is good all the time, and He has already given us so much. His mercies and compassions are new every day, so when we wake up, we know He is ready to bless us, and give us a fresh start. At the end of every day we can rest assured that He has got us covered; we sleep knowing that He is watching over us. God's Word is faithful, true, and tried and we can rely on every jot and title.

As we trust and reverence Him, there is so much that He still has is store for us. His abundance will be manifest for all to see. Every breath we take is a reason to give praise to our Heavenly Father. We inhale and exhale effortlessly and without giving it much thought, but pause now to give God thanks.

Let us consider some of the many things God has already blessed us with.

Friday February 26, 2021

Psalms 32:8 I will instruct thee and teach thee in the way which thou shalt go: I will guide thee with mine eye.

God's Word is our counsel, our guide teaching and instructing us in the right way. God knew everything we would need before we were born and planned for that. He made sure we would be fully equipped for whatever our adversary would through at us in an attempt to break us. II Peter states He gave us "all things that pertain to life and Godliness", by His divine power.

A specific section of the Word of God written before the 'Age of Grace' was written for our learning or so we can learn from the past mistakes of God's people. Then we have scriptures specific for our instruction so we know God's will for our lives, reproof for when we are not following those instructions, and correction to guide us back to the rightly divided Word.

Consider God's watchful eye (figuratively) guiding, protecting us and keeping us out of trouble as we trust His Word.

Saturday February 27, 2021

Psalms 34:1 I will bless the LORD at all times: his praise shall continually be in my mouth.

Continually does not mean twenty-four hours a day, but it does mean every day. When we wake up in the morning, our first thought should be of praise and thankfulness for another day. I have made it a habit to start speaking in tongues before I get out of bed, then I go down the mental list of things I am thankful for. The list may start with life, God's love for me and salvation, the ministry that taught me God's rightly divided Word, health, my family – husband, children, grandchildren, my mother, siblings, their children and grandchildren, extended family, the household of believers, our leadership, friends, a job. From there it might get more specific to include needs or other requests.

Can you see how easy it would be to praise God continually? Even in the midst of disappointment and troubles we can always find something to be thankful for. When we lost one of our brothers, our thanks and praise was for the time we had with him and how much of a blessing he was to us and our family and friends.

We are to give God praise always and bless His name. He is worthy and deserving of our continued worship and reverence.

Take a moment, pause and give God praise and thanks.

Sunday February 28, 2021

Psalms 34:7 The angel of the LORD encampeth round about them that fear him, and delivereth them.

Before a person is born again of God's spirit, God provides a guardian angel to be with those who believe and revere Him. The guardian angel makes his abode (so to speak) making that person his priority to protect and save them, deliver them when necessary. Because God handpicked us, predestinated those who would respond to His call, He has the fore knowledge of those who will need a guardian angel.

As born-again believers with Christ in us, we have God's gift of holy spirit in each of us and no longer need the guardian angel.

Consider all what God has protected you from (even things you may never have been aware of). I was heading out to run some errands and had planned everything I needed and where to go get them. I had even estimated the amount of time I would need to get it all done. After finishing up in one store, I got in the car and felt in my heart that God was directing me to go home. I sat still for a about a minute thinking of my 'to-do-list' and how much more I still had to accomplish. I started the car and headed home. On the news that evening I heard of a multiple vehicle accident in the area where I would have been headed. I thanked God for protecting me from that. Let us give God thanks for His gift of holy spirit in us.

MARCH

Monday March 1, 2021

Psalms 103:11 For as the heaven is high above the earth, so great is his mercy toward them that fear him. ***12*** As far as the east is from the west, so far hath he removed our transgressions from us.

As a young child, I would stare up into the sky and wonder what it would look like to see Jesus coming out of the clouds. I would think "we cannot even see the end of the sky". I would try to imagine Jesus walking down on clouds like a staircase. When I am traveling in an airplane, I look out of the window and see just clouds, the earth is not even visible. We are out there somewhere in the sky with no ground underneath. That is a long way up, or down – depending on how you look at it.

That is how merciful our God is, we cannot even see the end of His mercy; it is far beyond what we can measure. Now, think about the east where the sun rises and the west where it sets, the two never come together. When we confess our sins and God forgives us that is how far He removes them from us, so far that they don't touch us ever again.

Consider God's merciful kindness, his heart to forgive and forget our past sins and how much He loves those who respect Him.

Tuesday March 2, 2021

Psalms 38:6 I am troubled; I am bowed down greatly; I go mourning all the day long.

Psalm 38:22 Make haste to help me, O Lord my salvation.

Unfortunately loosing someone we love is a part of life. At some point in our lives we will experience grief, sadness, and heartbreak. Although we know to expect it, that it is inevitable when it happens the pain and grief can be unbearable. I can remember being in grief so painful, so heart-wrenching, it was like I was falling into deep hole, drowning and unable to get out. I wanted to be somewhere, but had no idea where, I wanted something and could not put it into words. I brought back to mind the words of the wife of one of our ministers "you need an overdose of the Word." So that is what I did, I sank into God's Word with tears in my eyes and a heavy heart. Then and only then, with the love and support of other dear loved ones did I begin to heal.

Are you or someone you know grieving, hurting or in mourning? Our hearts can be heavy at times – especially at the loss of someone close to us, a family member, or a dear close friend, maybe even the loss of a relationship. Depression may set in and we feel lost – mentally and spiritually. God is always faithful as we cry out to Him, to hasten to our side and bring healing to us.

Trust in God and His Word for that healing, stay thankful in everything, believing that the answer of peace is on its way.

Wednesday March 3, 2021

Psalms 42:1 As the hart panteth after the water brooks, so panteth my soul after thee, O God.
2(a) My soul thirsteth for God, for the living God:

In John 4:14 Jesus states that those who drink of the water that He gives will never thirst again. Another reference to that is found in John 7:38 "out of his belly shall flow rivers of living water," speaking of those who believe on Him. We long for the Word to satisfy our spiritual thirst. When we are born again, we are filled with holy spirit and bringing it into manifestation, it literally overflows from our inner being.

When I took a Bible class about thirty years ago, called Power for Abundant Living' was when I first felt that. It felt like I had taken my first deep, cleansing breath and was now able to be satisfied. So many are searching, their souls panting for something deeper, more fulfilling and struggle to accept that the answer is as simple as reaching out for the hands of our loving heavenly Father and accepting His words in Romans 10:9, when we can be then filled with the gift of holy spirit.

Consider God's gift of holy spirit which satisfies every longing soul.

Thursday March 4, 2021

Psalms 46:1 God is our refuge and strength, a very present help in trouble.

What is a refuge? One online dictionary describes it as a *"condition of being safe or sheltered from pursuit, danger, or trouble."* We can always feel that sense of being safe, we know that whatever dangers or troubles lie ahead, our God will cover and protect us. It is so reassuring that when we call out to God, He is right there when we need Him, immediately at our side to deliver us – "a very present help."

When we are weak, He strengthens us, we do not have to rely on our physical strength when life has beaten us down and we do not feel like getting up. Sometimes we keep struggling to do everything on our own and God is saying, "let me". He really wants to take over and help us prevail, all we have to do is surrender.

As we practice the presence of God, we are reassured that He will deliver us.

Friday March 5, 2021

Psalms 46:10 Be still, and know that I am God: I will be exalted among the heathen, I will be exalted in the earth.
11 The LORD of hosts is with us; the God of Jacob is our refuge. Selah.

God Almighty is everywhere present, so wherever we are, He is; and He promises to be our refuge, a stronghold, fortress, or a place of safety for us. We recognize Him in His rightful place – above all nations, supreme; and therefore we are assured that in His care is the best place to be.

As we wait to hear from God, we get quiet. Sometimes with all the loudness in and around us we might miss that still small voice. With believing we anticipate the answer is coming. God has a whole heavenly host of angels if needed to fight our battles for us.

Consider that it is in those 'be still' moments we get the answers of peace.

Saturday March 6, 2021

Psalms 51:1 Have mercy upon me, O God, according to thy lovingkindness: according unto the multitude of thy tender mercies blot out my transgressions.

Many Christians today live in mental turmoil, searching for peace and never fully being joyful, all because they go through life as if they are helping Jesus carry a cross. I have heard prayers like "God, please have mercy on me. I know I am a sinner, and I just pray that you hear my prayer, and please if it is your will." Are you struggling with knowing and believing that God has forgiven you? In His Word we are reminded of God's loving kindness. We have seen that His mercies stretch out so high up into the sky that they are immeasurable and sometimes we have a hard time believing or accepting His forgiveness. When we hold on to those things that torment us mentally, we have not accepted that we are forgiven.

Consider God's forgiveness – that it is a done deal in Christ and maybe it is you that has not been able to forgive yourself. Accept and receive God's forgiveness today so the peace of God can rule in your heart and mind.

Sunday March 7, 2021

Psalms 62:7 In God is my salvation and my glory: the rock of my strength, and my refuge, is in God.
8 Trust in him at all times; ye people, pour out your heart before him: God is a refuge for us. Selah.

God is the author of our salvation; He put everything in place and sent His "only begotten Son" for man's redemption. After Adam and Eve sinned and lost their spiritual connection with God, He knew He needed to make it so that mankind did not lose that spiritual connection forever. Adam's sin conferred his legal rights to the adversary, so God's plan had to be on firm legal ground to redeem man back. Jesus Christ's death and resurrection accomplished that.

Everything we have now is because of what God has done for us. We have been bought back and sanctified – set apart for Him. He delivers and protects us as we continue to trust Him and we are blessed as we open our hearts to Him in praise and thanksgiving. In God is our 'safe place'.

Meditate on all God has done for us and given us; everything we have in Christ.

Monday March 8, 2021

Psalms 73:28 But it is good for me to draw near to God: I have put my trust in the Lord GOD, that I may declare all thy works.

Have you ever felt so alone, as if you are the only person wherever you are, even if you are surrounded by a room full of people? What a scary feeling! That can happen when you are going through a painful situation – a break up or loss of a loved one. Everyone around is going about their business, the sun came out, but you are hurting and cannot seem to function. I remember experiencing that when we lost our brother. I was sad, crying, grieving, and for everyone around me was just “business as usual”. It was a feeling like no one cared or could care less that I had lost my brother who not just me, but everyone he met, loved. He was kind, loving, caring, fun - I missed him terribly.

It was only when I decided to spend more time in the Word that I started to heal, and not feel so alone, so isolated. Being close to God, basking is His presence is ‘good’ and refreshing. It is where I can feel safe and completely trust in Him. I can testify of His loving kindness.

Take time to practice the presence of God.

Tuesday March 9, 2021

Genesis 14:18 And Melchizedek king of Salem brought forth bread and wine: and he was the priest of the most high God.

(Jehovah-El – all powerful/Omnipotent}

God as Jehovah-El focuses on God as omnipotent, all powerful, denoting His strength and all His mighty works, as one who creates, as well as His wisdom (Job 36:5). Jehovah-El shows that God is both omnipotent (all-powerful) and omnipresent (everywhere present). He is not limited by time, space, or boundaries. God rescued the Israelites from Egypt and parted the Red Sea for them, saved Daniel and His friends in the furnace of fire, and raised Jesus Christ from the dead. There is no one no matter what they do, or how wealthy they are that can compare to the greatness of God.

Consider our God who is almighty, delivers His people and is the 'most High' - Elyon. Knowing that He is our Heavenly Father we can be confident as we walk and talk with Him.

Wednesday March 10, 2021

Psalms 86:15 But thou, O Lord, art a God full of compassion, and gracious, long suffering, and plenteous in mercy and truth.

There are so many examples in the Word of God's heart of love, forgiveness, and patience. King David documents several times of God's forgiveness towards him, knowing full well he did not deserve it. In the book of Acts, we follow the journey of Saul who later became known as Paul, who persecuted, had arrested, and even killed many who believed on or even spoke of Jesus. When he was confronted by Jesus and repented, God forgave him, and he became a wonderful apostle.

Have you ever felt that God would not forgive you, or that He is not even listening to your prayers? As a God full of compassion, God understands our every need and is patient, with mercy not quick to punish even when we deserve it. He is always ready and willing to forgive when we fall.

Consider as born-again believers we too can be compassionate, empathetic, understanding, and forgiving as God is towards us.

Thursday March 11, 2021

Psalms 100:5 For the LORD is good; his mercy is everlasting; and his truth endureth to all generations.

It cannot be stated enough how good God is, how He withholds punishment even when we deserve it. His merciful kindness is so vast, and His promises never expire – they are for generation after generation on them that serve Him. This life can be rough at times, when things just always seem to go wrong – relationships, jobs, our health, and we may experience loss of a loved one. How easy it would be to get discouraged and stay depressed because we may think why bother. The truth is we have an adversary and will experience negatives in life. No one is immune to his attacks.

Our confession must be steadfast that "God is good always, and always God is good." His Word is truth and has stood the test of time and will last through eternity. The adversary has made many attempts to get rid of God's Word, but it has proven indestructible.

We teach our children to love and serve God because His mercy, love, and promises are for them and their children.

Friday March 12, 2021

Psalms 103:1 Bless the LORD, O my soul: and all that is within me, bless his holy name.
2 Bless the LORD, O my soul, and forget not all his benefits:
3 Who forgiveth all thine iniquities; who healeth all thy diseases;

God has blessed us so much our response is to bring glory to His name. God knows as humans we may not be able to remember every single one of His blessings, so He asks that we simply not forget them all. The biggest blessings are that He sent His Son Jesus Christ to make forgiveness of sins available to us who believe and for physical healing. And for those we are eternally thankful. The two part to Jesus Christ's accomplishments makes us complete and we remember these every time we partake of the 'Holy Communion.'

Jesus' blood was shed for the remission or forgiveness of our sins and by His stripes physical healing was made available to us.

Saturday March 13, 2021

Ephesians 4:31 Let all bitterness, and wrath, and anger, and clamour, and evil speaking, be put away from you, with all malice:
32 And be ye kind one to another, tenderhearted, forgiving one another, even as God for Christ's sake hath forgiven you.

We get rid of any anger, temper, animosity and resentment, quarreling, loud brawling, contention, and slander which may include evil-speaking, gossip, abusive or blasphemous language, with any malice, spite, or ill will. These all lead to strife and violent behaviors. As one body in the household of God, we want to be like-minded, and build unity so the people are blessed, edified, and comforted. These negative behaviors only lead to division and strife, becoming a stumbling block and hindering others from coming to know the greatness of God's Word that we know and teach.

Instead we want to exhibit kindness to others, showing compassion, love and understanding. Growing up in a household of six, there was always some disagreement or argument with someone running to Mama with complains of who said or did something hurtful. Her response was to help us understand that we should be loving and forgiving. After each discussion we had to turn to each other and repeat Ephesians 4:32, while holding hands. And no, we did not necessarily enjoy it at first, but it grew on us over the years. It was the first verse we all learned and today is still a favorite of mine. As God in Christ has forgiven us, we also forgive one another, in our families, at work, our friends and in the household.

Consider what God has forgiven us for and how we too can be forgiving.

Sunday March 14, 2021

II Corinthians 9:8 And God is able to make all grace abound toward you; that ye, always having all sufficiency in all things, may abound to every good work:

God wants His children to experience all sufficiency in every category of our lives. If we are not, we are probably hindering God's abundance by our negative believing, allowing our circumstances to be dictated solely by our five senses. To enjoy the fullness of all God has for us, we get rid of all the negative thoughts of fear, worry, doubt and sickness. Instead we confess only positives and not accept what is manifested by way of the five senses. If we receive a poor diagnosis, we turn it over to God and confess His healing goodness.

Take a moment to absorb the enormity of that statement! God is able, He can and is willing to make all grace abound or have in large amounts (copious), so that we are completely satisfied with an adequate amount of all what we need, so we can excel in everything we do. Take a moment to get a clear mind picture of all this means.

Consider practicing positive confessions and shutting out all the negatives.

Monday March 15, 2021

Ephesians 4:29 Let no corrupt communication proceed out of your mouth, but that which is good to the use of edifying, that it may minister grace unto the hearers.

Anyone else remember as a young child saying, "sticks and stones may break my bones, but words can never harm me." The truth is sticks and stones can hurt us physically, but words hurt much deeper and have a much longer lasting effect. To kids many things said may seem "all in good fun" or they may consider some things "harmless pranks". I remember being made fun of because I was taller than the other kids in my class. It may not seem like much to most people, but to young girl trying to fit in, it was hurtful. It made me want to always slouch so I didn't feel like I was towering over everyone. When we were asked to line up, I was always in the back and still to bend my knees until I felt like I was the same height as the other kids. What about being teased if you are skinnier or heavier than others around you; maybe even shunned because your family was not as rich, and you never wore designer clothes? These are all situations where someone may feel ashamed, less than, and embarrassed. Many grow up with feelings of insecurity because they never grow out of these feelings.

Even as adults being judged because of the car you drive or even how many cars or houses you own, or maybe how you dress. Not knowing the others situation or circumstance we should show kindness. Several times I have invited someone to go shopping with me, ask them which things they like and offer to buy it for them because they took the time to go shopping with me. That way I was able to help them without seeming condescending and we shared a fun outing.

We never want to say anything bad or foul to hurt another person. What we say can have long lasting effects so let us choose to compliment with positive words and not negative. We want to speak only what is good and kind to build up, encourage and be a blessing.

Consider words of encouragement to bless and build others up.

Tuesday March 16, 2021

Ephesians 4:23 And be renewed in the spirit of your mind;
24 And that ye put on the new man, which after God is created in righteousness and true holiness.

Several years ago, I completed a Bible class called 'The Renewed Mind' and learned that "the renewed mind is the key to power". We learn to renew our minds minute by minute, day to day by spending time in God's Word daily. In Romans 12:2 we see that we are to be transformed by renewing our minds. God knows it is a process not an immediate or even overnight experience, but it will take work after we are born again to make that transformation from old behaviors to new. Another great point to keep in mind is that "the key to the renewed mind is the stayed mind." Once we renew our minds to the truth of God's Word, we have to keep our minds stayed/focused on these truths for spiritual growth and to experience the power we have in Christ.

As we speak in tongues much in our private prayer lives, we are equipped to renew our minds. We are born again, and God has clothed us in righteousness by Christ, so our thoughts are now Christ like and our actions/behaviors should be that of true holiness – ones set apart by God Himself.

Utilizing a phrase many of us are familiar with, "what would Jesus do?" we ask ourselves to determine if our actions are pleasing to God.

Wednesday March 17, 2021

Malachi 3:6(a) For I am the LORD, I change not;

When the children of Israel needed help, God rescued them from their oppressors and parted the Red Sea so they could escape being caught. When Daniel was thrown into the lion's den God protected him from being eaten alive. God promised Abraham and Sarah a son and when they thought it would never happen God worked a miracle and Sarah got pregnant when she was past ninety years old and Abraham was almost one hundred years old. Peter was arrested and thrown in jail for preaching God's Word; God got him out without any harm to his life. The Bible is full of countless stories of God coming through to protect, provide for and save people.

Since we know that God "changes not', we also believe that He is the same yesterday, today and forever, and we can rest assured that what He was able to do before He can do again. In recent years we have heard of or seen real life true stories of how God healed the sick, raised the dead, caused the blind to see and made the lame to walk. He is still performing miracles today.

Meditate on all God has done and that as we believe we can see those same results in our lives.

Thursday March 18, 2021

Malachi 3:10 Bring ye all the tithes into the storehouse, that there may be meat in mine house, and prove me now herewith, saith the LORD of hosts, if I will not open you the windows of heaven, and pour you out a blessing, that there shall not be room enough to receive it.
11 And I will rebuke the devourer for your sakes, and he shall not destroy the fruits of your ground; neither shall your vine cast her fruit before the time in the field, saith the LORD of hosts.
12 And all nations shall call you blessed: for ye shall be a delightsome land, saith the LORD of hosts.

When I was a little girl, I remember being so excited to drop my pennies into the 'offering plate' in church. I had no idea why I was doing it except that my mother told us we should tithe. Years later after taking a Bible class and reading a book called "Christians Should Be Prosperous", I finally got it. Giving back one tenth of what I earn to the movement of God's Word is "the basic law of prosperity". Hmm; how exactly does that work? God's Word tells us that God loves cheerful giver not one who gives grudgingly (2 Corinthians 9:7). As we tithe, we are proving God's promises to pour out blessings that we will not have room to receive.

Give back to the movement of God's Word puts us in a partnership with God as He promises as we give, we receive blessings that 'there will not be enough room to receive it.' What a promise! He promises to rebuke or prevent the adversary and anything he will throw at us; our farms and lands will be covered. People will notice and comment on our blessings, our friends will rejoice in our prosperity, wanting to try it out for themselves. I also learned about 'pushing the envelope' to give more – what we call "abundant sharing." We trust God to be our sufficiency.

Consider proving God and see how the blessings will be poured out..

Friday March 19, 2021

Philippians 1:6 Being confident of this very thing, that he which hath begun a good work in you will perform it until the day of Jesus Christ:

Sometimes in life as believers we are tempted to get discouraged. Things may not look as bright as they did, or maybe we are sharing the Word with others and it seems like no one is interested. This may lead to disappointments and feelings of hopelessness. We may question what and why we do what we do. This is a trick of the adversary who is trying to make us give up and become stagnant. We need to recognize these feelings of despair, sadness and weakness for what they are, and get our minds back in the Word.

As we renew our minds, we are convinced that the work God has started in us, He will continue until Christ returns. Our responsibility is to continue in faithful service to God with prayer and believing, remaining bold and courageous in speaking the Word.

We grow in grace and in our faithful walk one day at a time.

Saturday March 20, 2021

Philippians 1:27(a) Only let your conversation be as it becometh the gospel of Christ: that whether I come and see you, or else be absent, I may hear of your affairs, that ye stand fast in one spirit, with one mind striving together for the faith of the gospel;

Children sometimes act one way in front of their parents and in a totally different manner if their parents are not around. One 80's comedy that I enjoyed watching showed an episode that highlighted that behavior. These two teenage girls were part of a program to spent time with mentors and learn from them. In front of their parents, and their mentors they were so sweet and kind and respectful. As soon as they were on their own, their behavior became delinquent when they ended up shoplifting and tried to pin it on the adult mentors.

Each person is responsible to choose to live or behave in a manner worthy of our calling as children of God. Our conversation refers to behavior which we must line up with the truth of the gospel. Whether we are in the presence of other believers or leadership, our lives should be examples of who we are called to be – children of God. Then as a household we stand firm in one accord united in our believing.

As we first build ourselves up individually, we can bring others together in unity.

Sunday March 21, 2021

Philippians 2:3 Let nothing be done through strife or vainglory; but in lowliness of mind let each esteem other better than themselves.
4 Look not every man on his own things, but every man also on the things of others.

I am sure we have all witnessed or maybe we ourselves as children loved showing off, boasting. My family did not have much, so we never had the most fancy clothes, or shoes. We wore each other's hand-me-downs and wore them out. I remember being taunted many times for an outfit that was so outdated it looked like something my grandmother would wear. Myself and my siblings made the most of it and tried to join in the heckling to lessen the effect of the jesting. As we got older and things got better, I determined to never be that person who would tease someone else for having less than. Even as an adult to this day, if I know of someone struggling, my first impulse is to try to help in some way.

We have the mind of Christ as believers so we do not get haughty, thinking we are better than others but by free will choice we decide to respect each other with admiration and praise. We love with the love of God in manifestation in the household. We stay united in prayer and fellowship, steadfast on the Word sharing it and giving of our abundance with others.

We do not allow open doors for the adversary to drive a wedge between us in the household of faith. The love of God in manifestation reigns in our hearts.

Monday March 22, 2021

Philippians 2:10 That at the name of Jesus every knee should bow, of things in heaven, and things in earth, and things under the earth;
11 And that every tongue should confess that Jesus Christ is Lord, to the glory of God the Father.

There are many who do not believe in God and/or Jesus Christ. I have heard statements that we have been tricked into believing there is a God, that we are just following others blindly. Whether people believe it or not God created the heavens and the earth, He made man in His own image, and sent His Son Jesus Christ to die so we could be bought back legally from the adversary. Jesus Christ was pronounced dead and lay in a tomb for three days and three nights, after which God raised Him from the dead.

After God raised Jesus Christ from the dead, He was ascended into heaven and sat Him down at His right hand, above all principalities and earthly powers. The name of Jesus is one of great power and salvation, and everyone and everything will bow down at His name, worship and praise Him proclaiming Him Lord to the glory of God our Father.

Everything Jesus Christ did was to glorify God and instructs us to do the same.

Tuesday March 23, 2021

Philippians 2:15 That ye may be blameless and harmless, the sons of God, without rebuke, in the midst of a crooked and perverse nation, among whom ye shine as lights in the world;

Have you ever tried to look for something in the dark? Not very productive – I know, I've tried. It can also be very frustrating because I would keep bumping into things, grabbing something that I had no idea what it was, and wasted a lot of time. As soon as I turned the light on, everything was clear and right in plain sight was the object I had been unsuccessfully trying to find. That is what God's Word does for us. We live in a world shrouded in darkness and as we shed the light of truth from God's Word, everything becomes clear and we find exactly what we spend years trying to find. That is how I felt after taking my first Bible class many years ago.

When we become born-again, we are children of God and as such are children of light – I Thessalonians 5:5, because God is light. Our lives literally radiate the light of God so as we shine as lights, we illuminate the truths from God's Word. The light of life is found in God's Word and cannot be turned off. We are to be bold, courageous, and fearless as we speak the Word, knowing it is truth and it is life. That light will draw others to God out of a world perverted by the darkness of sin.

We are not required to be perfect, but without blame or above reproach and faithful.

Wednesday March 24, 2021

1 Corinthians 1:10 Now I beseech you, brethren, by the name of our Lord Jesus Christ, that ye all speak the same thing, and `that` there be no divisions among you; but `that` ye be perfectly joined together in the same mind and in the same judgment.

Growing up in a home with five siblings there was always disagreements and arguments about one thing or another. Since none of us had our own bedroom you can imagine how uncomfortable it would be to be in such close proximity and not happy with the other. It was not that easy to stay mad for too long, especially when our mother's way of handling these fights was to have us repeat Ephesians 4:32 to one another.

As believers we are born into God's family and become brothers and sisters in Christ. God desires that we come together as one body and be in agreement on the Word for the furtherance of the gospel. We are to be united with no divisions as we speak the Word with one purpose, being like-minded, and joined together in love. The decisions we make should be Word based and benefit the whole body of believers.

We come together in agreement, fully united when we teach or share God's Word.

Thursday March 25, 2021

1 Corinthians 1:30 But of him are ye in Christ Jesus, who of God is made unto us wisdom, and righteousness, and sanctification, and redemption:

Sometimes as a child, we had to careful when we came home after school hungry and looked for a snack before dinner. Because there were six mouths to feed and we did not always have a lot, we knew not to just walk in and grab anything we felt like. We were aware that maybe someone else might like a piece of that fruit. No matter how much we had, I can remember my mother putting part of the dinner aside for a neighbor and their children because she knew they were in need. Some children from other families may be allowed to just walk in and have whatever was available. In each case, the children knew and understood what was available; they knew their place in the family dynamic.

As children of God we know and understand our place in His family and our rights as His sons and daughters. We receive the wisdom of God and are given 'sonship rights' through Jesus Christ when we are born again of God's Spirit. We are made righteous – able to stand in the presence of God without the sense of sin guilt and condemnation, justified – free from sin and it's consequences, God has set us apart for heaven – sanctified us, we have been redeemed from the curse of the law, and have been given the ministry of reconciliation to help bring men and women back to God's Word.

These are our sonship rights and all we have in Christ.

Mediate on all God has given us in Christ when we confess Him Lord and believe God raised Him from the dead.

Friday March 26, 2021

III John 2 Beloved, I wish above all things that thou mayest prosper and be in health, even as thy soul prospereth.

In John 10:10 we read that Jesus Christ came that we might have life and have it more abundantly. Part of God's promise for that more than abundant life includes us being in good health and experiencing prosperity in our lives. Our health and prosperity is dependent on our believing God's Word and continuing faithfully in it. The Greek word pisteuō is defined as to "rely on, to be persuaded of" and "place confidence in." The root word pistis is to have a "firm persuasion" coupled with action.

We read in James 2:17 Even so faith, (pistis, believing) if it hath not works, is dead, being alone. Our believing must involve action, so to claim God's promise of healing we live without fear, or anxiety, do all we need to do by our five senses – eat right, exercise, drink enough water, get a good sleep, and abstain from indulging in things that are harmful to our bodies – alcohol, illegal drugs, and confessing what the Word says regarding physical health and healing wholeness. To claim God's prosperity in our lives we apply the principles of tithing and abundantly sharing as outlined for us in Malachi chapter 3.

God's desire is always perfect health and full prosperity for His children. We need to believe that and claim it, taking action, renewing our minds to what the Word says. If we are believing negatively, that is what will be manifested in our lives.

Consider putting off all negatives from your mind, confessing only the positives from God's Word to experience complete health and prosperity.

Saturday March 27, 2021

1 Corinthians 2:12 Now we have received, not the spirit of the world, but the spirit which is of God; that we might know the things that are freely given to us of God.

Before I fully understood God's Word, I would get anxious about things that 'might' happen. I would try to picture how to handle a situation and get so worked up, I would make myself sick from worry with headaches and upset stomach. Once I had the opportunity to study God's Word I realized that because I now have a relationship with God, my Heavenly Father I can give everything to Him knowing He will work it out according to His will. Before we are born again, we are people of body and soul with no direct connection to God. When we become born again, we receive God's gift of holy spirit. Now God has made it available for us to have direct communication with Him.

God's gift of His holy spirit is perfect and opens up the lines of communication because us and God. We are able to recognize the blessings He freely bestows on us by His grace.

We thank God that now He can communicate to us by way of His holy spirit in us, by which we can glorify Him, get prayers answered, pray perfectly and many more benefits.

Sunday March 28, 2021

1 Corinthians 15:33 Be not deceived: evil communications corrupt good manners.

We are all very aware of peer pressure and how it can cause us to do things we would not normally do. We deal with it as children, teenagers and even as adults. If one or more of the children did something like maybe skip a class because their friends were all doing it, I remember hearing my parents response "if your friends all jumped off a bridge would you do it to?" My habit was to never be influenced by friends because I needed to think for myself. Skipping class to go to a movie or the beach just did not make sense to me. I felt like it may be fun at the time, but the consequences would not be pretty. And I was right, I witnessed what the punishment was on several occasions – thankful not to be on the receiving end of it. As a matter of fact, I never even saw a movie until I was in my thirties.

We do not allow ourselves to be led astray by keeping company with those who only have evil on their minds and in their conversations. That will only destroy our good name and moral character. Consider keeping company with those who will build you up and that you in turn can build up as well.

Monday March 29, 2021

1 Corinthians 15:58 Therefore, my beloved brethren, be ye stedfast, unmoveable, always abounding in the work of the Lord, forasmuch as ye know that your labour is not in vain in the Lord.

It has been a joy of mine to hear and/or read about men and women who have stood for God for years, being committed to the movement of God's Word and help train others to do the same. We have many examples in the Bible such as Moses, Joshua, King David, Queen Esther, Ruth, the Apostle Paul, Peter, Dorcas and so many more. In more recent times many have heard of the evangelist Billy Graham, and Dr. Victor Paul Wierwille who started "The Way International" with a goal to get the Word over the world. Even today we still benefit from the hard work and tireless devotion of these great men of God and their families. So many ministers and leaders in the ministry where I fellowship, have continued the great work, committed to moving and overseeing the work of the Lord. I am so blessed to be learning from them and serving in a household of God with these great men and women of God.

As Christian believers we remain firm, not easily moved, or turned away from the truths of God's Word. We stay committed to continue faithfully in service to God because we believe that our work is not in vain and we will be rewarded for our faithful stand.

Know that your life has purpose, and that God has noticed your faithful stand which allows you to always have the victory in Christ and your reward awaits.

Tuesday March 30, 2021

1 John 1:5 This then is the message which we have heard of him, and declare unto you, that God is light, and in him is no darkness at all.

Just as we need a light when we enter a dark room so we can see where to go, we need the light of God's Word to see and understand His direction or plan for our lives. We read in Psalms 119:105: Thy word *is* a lamp unto my feet, and a light unto my path. Having a clear and true understanding of God's Word enables us to walk as God has instructed us, to shine as lights for Him in this world. God is light, and as His children, we are children of light.

Darkness cannot exist in the presence of God, because of the brightness of His light. Any darkness in our lives will separate us from God's love. We want to avoid breaking fellowship, so we stay in God's light, His love, and His presence.

Wednesday March 31, 2021

1 John 2:1 My little children, these things write I unto you, that ye sin not. And if any man sin, we have an advocate with the Father, Jesus Christ the righteous:

The word "sin" here refers to broken fellowship because when we sin, we are being disobedient to God's Word. We are encouraged to stay in full fellowship with God. When I went to church as a young child, one of my great fears was doing anything wrong that God might not like and that He would not like me anymore. It was never clear to me that I could ask for His forgiveness and it would be ok – that I would be back in good standing with my Heavenly Father.

If/when we do break fellowship or are not in alignment with God's will, we turn to God in the name of His Son Jesus Christ who is our mediator to help mend that fellowship. (I Timothy 2:5)

Just like we break fellowship in our earthly family when we disobey, lie, or go against the standards set by our parents, we break fellowship with our Heavenly Father when we disobey His Word. God, who is rich in mercy understands that we are human, so He made sure there was a way for us to come back to Him in repentance.

I John 1:9 If we confess our sins, he is faithful and just to forgive us our sins, and to cleanse us from all unrighteousness.

As children I am sure we can all relate to how happy we would be when our parents forgave us when we apologized if we disobeyed or did not follow instructions as expected.

Many times, we would be instructed to finish our homework before we played outside. My father was away a lot as a cop and Mama as a teacher might have to stay to teach an extra lesson or to oversee detention. On occasion we were caught outside playing after we lost track of time, and the homework was not done. And yes we had to face to consequences of our disobedience, but we were forgiven and reminded of verses such as Ephesians 6:1 Children obey your parents in the Lord, for this is right.

So much more our Heavenly Father is waiting with open arms, willing and ready to forgive us. Once we genuinely admit our wrong, confess and ask God to forgive us, God brings us back into fellowship with Him and our responsibility is not allowing the adversary to trick us again.

APRIL

Thursday April 1, 2021

1 John 3:20 For if our heart condemn us, God is greater than our heart, and knoweth all things.

For years I would let mistakes I made torment me. I questioned my decisions and judgements berating myself so much I would feel unworthy. I know of a friend who walked away from her marriage after several years of verbal and emotional abuse that turned volent. She knew she had to leave for her own safety and the safety of her children, but she felt guilty for many years not allowing herself to be happy again. She tormented herself with questions such as "Did I do the right thing; will the kids be ok; maybe we could have worked it out if I had stayed a little longer; I wonder if I made a mistake." After I took a class on Biblical research and learned that we are not to condemn ourselves, was the time I felt free and I was able to show my friend those truths as well which gave her peace of mind.

The Word of God tells us we are justified and righteous and that is what we believe. There is no reason to doubt the truth of God's Word; we have been released from the bondage of sin and no longer live in fear.

We can have confidence in God and His Word believing we are righteous in Him and live a life of victory.

Friday April 2, 2021 – GOOD FRIDAY

1 John 3:2 Beloved, now are we the sons of God, and it doth not yet appear what we shall be: but we know that, when he shall appear, we shall be like him; for we shall see him as he is.

The reality of a believer's life is that NOW we are the sons of God. When we are born again according to Romans 10:9, and we receive God's gift of holy spirit, there is no waiting period. NOW, are we the sons of God. This is the time many Christians around the world are observing Jesus Christ's arrest, His suffering, torture, and crucifixion – during what is called 'Holy Week'. God had previously reassured Jesus that He would raise Him up after three days and three nights in the grave, which I am sure He remembered and anticipated when He gave up His life for us on the tree.

Jesus' sufferings are sometimes too much for us to bear. Several people have tried to portray it in some movies such as "The Passion of the Christ," and our hearts fill will praise and gratitude for God and His Son Jesus Christ. The magnitude of all we are and have in Christ as sons of God we still cannot fully fathom. What we do know is that when He returns we will be like Him for, we will see Him as He truly is – a Son of God with power.

Let us claim it, live it, and believe it. Say it with me "I am a Son of God with all power!" (SOGWAP!!)

Saturday April 3, 2021

1 John 3:8 He that committeth sin is of the devil; for the devil sinneth from the beginning. For this purpose the Son of God was manifested, that he might destroy the works of the devil.

When Jesus was crucified, darkness covered the earth. It was the darkest hour in the history of man, and I am sure it hurt God's heart to see His Son suffer and die like that. All His followers who had been with Him during His earthly ministry felt defeated. This is who they thought was to be their earthly ruler and now He was dead. Can you imagine the confusion, the questions, even doubt about what was real or not? God cannot lie and as bleak as it seemed on that day, He was preparing to raise His Son up. We know that sin is of the devil because he tricked Eve and subsequently Adam to commit the first sin of man. For those who choose to remain in that state they are living in darkness.

In contrast, God sent His Son with the sole purpose of destroying the works of the devil. He saved us, legally paid the price in full to free us from the adversary's hold and our redemption was complete.

Let us consider the significance of what Jesus Christ did for us.

Sunday April 4, 2021 – EASTER SUNDAY

Luke 24:1 Now upon the first day of the week, very
early in the morning, they came unto the sepulchre,
bringing the spices which they had prepared, and
certain others with them.
2 And they found the stone rolled away from the
sepulchre.
3 And they entered in, and found not the body of the
Lord Jesus.
4 And it came to pass, as they were much perplexed
thereabout, behold, two men stood by them in shining
garments:
5 And as they were afraid, and bowed down their faces
to the earth, they said unto them, Why seek ye the
living among the dead?
6 He is not here, but is risen: remember how he spake
unto you when he was yet in Galilee,
7 Saying, The Son of man must be delivered into the
hands of sinful men, and be crucified, and the third day
rise again.
8 And they remembered his words,

The details of Jesus' arrest, torture, sufferings, and crucifixion are well known. Some chose to ignore it and pretend it never happened. For those of us called Christians this is a significant period for us because it brings to mind God's plan of salvation to redeem us from sin and its consequences. But we rejoice in the knowledge that Jesus did not stay on the cross or in the grave. Three days after being buried in a tomb, God raised Him up, He was ascended into heaven and now sits on the right hand of God.

Our lives and everything we do and believe hinges on the day Christ will return and we will all gather together to meet Him in the air.

Consider the enormity of the phrase "HE IS NOT HERE, HE IS RISEN," and what it has meant for generations over the years.

Monday April 5, 2021

1 John 4:4 Ye are of God, little children, and have overcome them: because greater is he that is in you, than he that is in the world.
1 John 4:18 There is no fear in love; but perfect love casteth out fear: because fear hath torment. He that feareth is not made perfect in love.

I like these two verses together because as God's children we can live a life free from fear because of what God accomplished for us by way of His Son Jesus Christ. We have a personal adversary and will face attacks and difficulties in life, but we are assured that because Jesus Christ overcame, and we can too. The power of God in Christ in every believer is greater than any attack of the adversary. So we live a life free of fear and doubt, trusting and believing in God's promises to be our refuge and strength in our time of need. When we allow fear and doubt to take over our thoughts and feelings, we are no longer trusting God to come through for us.

We love God, we know He loves us, and He is bigger than anything we can face in this life. In God's perfect love, there is no room for fear.

Tuesday April 6, 2021

1 John 5:2 By this we know that we love the children of God, when we love God, and keep his commandments.
3 For this is the love of God, that we keep his commandments: and his commandments are not grievous.

God so loved that He gave – God's love is directly related to His giving. What greater love is there than to give His only begotten Son to die in our place. We love God and show it by loving His people in our acts of kindness and giving. 1 Corinthians 13 details some attributes of God's love that we as believers should practice towards each other. The love of God in manifestations in the household is kind; is not envious; is not haughty or proud; does not think evil of others, rejoices with one another celebrating successes, is patient, forgiving and generous.

Even when there is a behavior that is contrary to the Word, we can still exhibit the love of God to individuals as we lovingly speak the truth to bring their thoughts back to the Word. We too must have a meek heart to receive reproof and correction if our actions are not lined up with the truths of God's Word.

We can always manifest the love of God, with kindness, patience, and speaking the truth to one another.

Wednesday April 7, 2021

1 John 5:14 And this is the confidence that we have in him, that, if we ask any thing according to his will, he heareth us:

For years I wondered if God heard my prayers. I would pray and never get any answers; it seemed I was even more confused about what I was praying about/for. When I was trying to make a decision about what I wanted to do with my life or the right job to take, the answers never seemed clear and I concluded I would have to figure it out. It was years later that I realized that my prayers were probably not exactly according to God's will. My first mistake was that I prayed to Jesus instead of praying to God in the name of Jesus Christ. The Word clearly states that "no man cometh unto the Father, but my me (Jesus Christ), in John 14:6; and that He is the only mediator between God and man – "the man Christ Jesus," – 1Timothy 2:5. As soon as I became clear on these truths and changed how I prayed, the answers were coming so fast, I could hardly keep up.

We are assured and have no doubt in God's willingness and ability to hear us and answer when we ask anything that is according to His will. If a prayer is not answered, we must consider whether or not our request is according to God's will.

Thursday April 8, 2021

1 John 5:20 And we know that the Son of God is come, and hath given us an understanding, that we may know him that is true, and we are in him that is true, even in his Son Jesus Christ. This is the true God, and eternal life.

Who does the Word of God say Jesus Christ is? In Matthew chapter 16 Jesus asks His disciples that question and when Simon Peter responded with "You are the Messiah, the Son of the living God," Jesus stated "Blessed are you, Simon son of Jonah, for this was not revealed to you by flesh and blood, but by my Father in heaven." It could not be any clearer than that. We believe Jesus Christ is the Son of God, who lived among men and at the end of His earthly ministry gave up His life to pay the ransom for man. While here on earth, He went about doing good, healing the sick, raising the dead, and making known His Father, God. We have a clearer picture of God's heart because of the life and ministry of Jesus Christ.

It has been said "tell me what you believe about Jesus Christ, and I will tell you how far you will go spiritually." How would you answer that?

Friday April 9, 2021

1 Peter 1:10 Of which salvation the prophets have enquired and searched diligently, who prophesied of the grace that should come unto you:

We have salvation by God's grace and live in the Grace Administration. The prophets of old talked about it searching carefully to fully understand salvation. The heavens declared the glory of God, and many were able to read God's message to man through the stars. The one thing that was not clear to the prophets was God's plan of salvation to the Gentiles. They did as much research as was available to them to prophecy of what was to come regarding the Grace Administration. We now get to live it and teach it to the next generation.

I Peter1:11 Searching what, or what manner of time the Spirit of Christ which was in them did signify, when it testified beforehand the sufferings of Christ, and the glory that should follow.

The prophets tried to learn all they could about what was being revealed to them concerning the coming of the Messiah, the sufferings He would endure and the glory that would follow. There were still some things that would remain a mystery to them until it was revealed to the apostle Paul which was that the Gentiles would be included in God's plan of redemption.

Saturday April 10, 2021

I Peter 2:24 Who his own self bare our sins in his own body on the tree, that we, being dead to sins, should live unto righteousness: by whose stripes ye were healed.

When the prophets prophesied about what was to come, they could only go as far as they had been taught that is that we would be healed by the stripes of Jesus Christ. Our salvation, our righteousness is a done deal, completed when Jesus Christ took our sins to the cross. His broken body signifies our salvation from sin, and His shed blood signifies our physical healing. Looking back to what God accomplished through Jesus Christ, 1 Peter chapter two states that "by His we ***were*** healed." It is no longer a work in progress but completely, complete.

Take a minute to fully understand the magnitude of what God did for us. He provided complete mental, physical, and spiritual healing for each one of us, by way of His Son Jesus Christ. What is our response to this amazing, exceptional sacrifice?

Sunday April 11, 2021

1 Thessalonians 5:16 Rejoice evermore.
17 Pray without ceasing.

There was a time many years ago, when I needed to be around lots of people or I would be miserable. When I was able to laugh, and joke and have fun I was at my happiest, but as soon as everyone left, I was almost to tears. I would talk to God, but it left me flat, wondering whether He had heard me. What a scary thought – to think that God is not listening to me. It was sad when no one was around, and I felt alone but feeling like God was not hearing my prayers made me feel so alone. I started just saying "OK God, I am waiting to hear from you; show me what you want me to know; help me understand your Word, and let me know you are hearing me; help me have a relationship with you."

The day I took a Bible class and learned the keys to the Word's interpretation, all my prayers were answered, I experienced true, inner happiness and joy – not dependent on whether people were around me or not. It was great to truly understand the meaning of "pray without ceasing."

We are asked to "rejoice evermore and pray without ceasing." Life is hard at times and we are not always happy depending on what is happening around us at any given moment. But having inner joy and peace as believers we can rejoice in all God has given us. We can look past the pain, hurt, sadness, and tears to all God has in store for us. Praying helps keep the lines of communication to our Heavenly Father open, where our joy lies.

Monday April 12, 2021

1 Thessalonians 5:21 Prove all things; hold fast that which is good.
22 Abstain from all appearance of evil.

For many years all I ever heard was we have to take things by "faith". That was a bit confusing to me because I felt like God wanted me to understand so much more. A few times in the Word it states God does not want us to be ignorant. So just taking things "by faith" may not be God's plan for us. I have learned through Biblical research and study to not just accept everything I hear about God and His Word blindly. I examine it against the truths outlined in the Word then hold on to these truths from the rightly divided Word.

We are instructed to stay away from anything that even remotely resembles evil in any shape or form because in that way we leave open doors for the adversary to attack. If unsure or unclear of a situation we choose to turn to the Word instead.

Tuesday April 13, 2021

1 Timothy 4:15 Meditate upon these things; give thyself wholly to them; that thy profiting may appear to all.

As I mentioned previously, I was raised in an Evangelical Christian church. As a child I can still remember learning Bible verses in Sunday School and Vacation Bible School. As a teenager we switched to Bible camps to fill up our summer vacation. These were some of my happiest times that I will forever treasure. It was at Bible camp I first learned how to memorize bible verses many of which I still remember to this day. Some passages I learned then and that are still very dear to my heart are Psalms 1, 19, 23, and many other Psalms; also included was Romans chapter 8 and 12, Ephesians chapter four. One of our teachers challenged us to put God first by refusing to have breakfast before we got to read the Word and spend time with God. It was called "No Bible No Breakfast." It was something fun that challenged us and instilled a habit to spend time with God first thing in the morning before we started our day which I still endeavor to do.

As we meditate on the Word, we immerse ourselves in the truth and make them a daily practice in your life. It will not only bless our lives but others as well as they witness our testimony. Consider how we can make the Word our own as we study it, memorize (retemorize) it daily and help others do the same.

Wednesday April 14, 2021

2 Chronicles 7:14 If my people, which are called by my name, shall humble themselves, and pray, and seek my face, and turn from their wicked ways; then will I hear from heaven, and will forgive their sin, and will heal their land.

Over the years we have seen so many bad situations come up around us – school shootings, deadly fires, storms, and several pandemics. We hear people ask why God would let these things happen. Some disasters are even referred to as "acts of God," and people are told to not question what God did to allow so many to die or be killed. God is love, good, and light and never wants people to be hurt. Hebrews 2:14 clearly states that the author of death is the devil, so all the destruction and loss of live is being orchestrated by the devil. So, some may wonder "where is God during these times?" God is just and legally cannot violate man's free will. When people have allowed the adversary to keep them bound by sin, they are giving him the authority to bring death and destruction to their lives. When people are ashamed to speak God's Word and instead bend to the pressures of not allowing public prayers in school God cannot take away that free will choice. God is not to blame for these disasters.

God is waiting with out-stretched arms to receive those who call out to Him in true repentance. When believers – those called Christians have broken fellowship from God, will be meek to renew the mind, turn away from a life of disobedience and turn back to God in true humility, He hears and answers. He not only heals us spiritually (forgive our sins), He also heals us physically of any medical issues. The choice is ours; let us return to God.

Let us consider where we may have fallen short and be meek to renew our minds to the Word.

Thursday April 15, 2021

2 Corinthians 2:14 Now thanks be unto God, which always causeth us to triumph in Christ, and maketh manifest the savour of his knowledge by us in every place.

In life we will face many difficult times and challenges and at times we may feel defeated and unable to handle all that is coming at us. We may lose a job, be faced with a difficult diagnosis, lose someone dear to us or go through a terrible heart break. One example in the Word of God is the apostle Paul who went through many dark times, being thrown in jail, beaten, stoned, and left for dead. When God raised Him up, he went back into the city and continued to speak God's Word. In Acts chapter 27 we read of a storm hitting the ship Paul was on, with violent winds, tossing them about. It was so dark and dreary; Paul tells of not seeing the sun or stars for days. Instead of giving up Paul prayed until God gave him revelation reassuring him that they would all make it out alive.

Because we are told that God will cause us to 'triumph' every time, we trust and believe God's Word that when difficult situations or challenges come up we will make it through by the grace of God. We are thankful that we always have the victory in Christ as He makes a clear path for us to move His Word. Our lives are like a sweet aroma that people will be drawn to, so as to get a better understanding of the Word that we share.

Friday April 16, 2021

2 Corinthians 3:18 But we all, with open face beholding as in a glass the glory of the Lord, are changed into the same image from glory to glory, `even` as by the Spirit of the Lord.

As a teenager (many, many, years ago) I hated looking at my face in the mirror because of acne. I'm sure many can relate – both men and women. For years I combed my hair from memory because I just did not want to have to see my face. It eventually cleared up (teenagers there's hope) and I felt comfortable looking at myself in the mirror again. There are other reasons someone may not want to look at themselves in a mirror. Have you felt so guilty about something wrong you did that you felt like you couldn't face yourself in the mirror? Some have told me of feeling that way when they cheated on a test or lied to someone close to them.

As children of the most-high God, we reflect His glory in our faces as if looking in a mirror and seeing a transformation day to day. Each day we become more like Christ and others see that light shining in and through us reflecting the gift of God's spirit in us. We are confident of God's forgiveness and can look at our reflection and see the light of God radiating to others.

Saturday April 17, 2021

2 Corinthians 5:17 Therefore if any man be in Christ, he is a new creature: old things are passed away; behold, all things are become new.

When man lost his spiritual connection with God after Adam and Eve's sin, man lived by his physical nature which was not always God's will. The Bible records many instances where God's face was turned away from man because of his sinful behavior. God cannot look at sin because His very nature is pure and holy. Man continually did wrong in God's sight and had to suffer the consequences of these actions – to name a few, the children of Israel, Lot, King David and others. After God put His plan of salvation in place, people then had the opportunity to be born again of God's spirit. Once that happens, we are to leave behind the negative, destructive, bad behaviors also called 'old man nature' that would separate us from God.

As believers in Christ we have put off the old man nature and are born-again of God's spirit. All our past behaviors are gone, forgiven, and forgotten by the Almighty God Himself, and we are changed, different in our lifestyle and habits. Because we are justified (just as if we never sinned), in God's eyes, it is like we are a new person altogether, everything is fresh and new in Christ. That is how God sees us, and that is how we should see ourselves.

Sunday April 18, 2021

2 Corinthians 5:20 Now then we are ambassadors for Christ, as though God did beseech you by us: we pray you in Christ's stead, be ye reconciled to God.

Every country sends an ambassador to another country to represent the citizens of that country who live there. For instance America has an embassy in the United Kingdom where an American ambassador is available to handle any issues that come up involving any American citizens in the United Kingdom, and in the same way, the United Kingdom has an ambassador in their embassy in America. These ambassadors represent the leaders of their country, speaking on their behalf as needed. They may negotiate deals or make decisions based on what the President or Prime Minister has already put in place.

We are Christ's representatives, sent by God to do/continue the works of Jesus Christ. Everything God wanted available to His children He authorized Jesus Christ to do. After Jesus Christ's death, resurrection, and ascension, we became His ambassadors to represent the absent Christ. In the gospel of John, we read that we can do the works of Jesus Christ and greater because He has gone on to His Father. We have been authorized to speak for God in the name of Jesus Christ. As such our mission is to appeal to people everywhere to be reconciled (brought back) to God.

Monday April 19, 2021

John 20:31 But these are written, that ye might believe that Jesus is the Christ, the Son of God, and that believing, ye might have life through His name.

I remember talking to a friend of mine some time ago about the Bible and was stunned when she mentioned that the Bible was not read in her church. I wondered how then was she able to learn about God's will for our lives? She stated they believed what the pastor told them. I thought, what a sad way to live – not truly knowing God's Word for oneself and just having to take someone else's word as the truth. That is not God's will for His children; He wants us to have a close intimate relationship with Him. How can we do that if we cannot read His Word and understand what He wants for us, how He wants to bless us?

The Word of God clearly states that He has given us everything "that pertains unto life and Godliness." The only way we can get that is by a daily study of His Word. God opened up His heart and gave revelation to holy men to write out everything He wanted us to know about and believe on His Son, Jesus Christ. It is in His name we have eternal life as we believe.

Tuesday April 20, 2021

2 Peter 1:20 Knowing this first, that no prophecy of the scripture is of any private interpretation.

No man can legally interpret the Word of God to say what he thinks it should say. Man's opinion has no place in the rightly divided Word of God. When we read a passage of scripture and it seems unclear, we read it again, do further research and in-depth study from the Word itself until it is clear. We also have a wealth of resources we can learn from – men and women who have already dedicated their lives to years of Biblical research, many of their works already in print and available to us. It is important to know and understand that none of the prophecies in the Word came from man's own thinking or will. The following verse clarifies that.

2 Peter 1:22 For the prophecy came not in olden times by the will of man, but holy men of God spoke as they were moved by the Holy Ghost.

These prophecies were not man-made, but holy men of God spoke what was revealed to them by direct revelation from God (Holy Spirit). That is how we know that the Word of God is the will of God. If we do not like something in there, we have to renew our minds because the written Word is a done deal and cannot be changed legally. Whether people believe it or not does not make it any less God's Word.

Wednesday April 21, 2021

2 Timothy 3:16 All scripture is given by inspiration of God, and is profitable for doctrine, for reproof, for correction, for instruction in righteousness:

There have been so many arguments and disagreements regarding the author and/or the authenticity of the Bible. Some argue it was written by men and therefore full of errors. Others state that since it was written by men, it is not to be taken literally and that not all of it is meant to be adhered to. The Bible tells us as plain as day that the true author of the Word of God is God. The subject of the Word of God is His Son Jesus Christ. We cannot pick one or two passages out because it does not line up with what we want to do and say because it was written by man it is not true.

God is Spirit and has no hands, therefore He could not physically write the Bible but gave revelation to the men who wrote it. All Scripture is God-breathed and is profitable for doctrine – to teach us right believing; for reproof or correction when we are not believing right and for training/ instruction in righteousness as we learn to live according to God's will. Wherever there seems to be apparent contradictions, we need to pay closer attention to the verse, read the context to grasp a better understanding and/or look elsewhere in the Word to see where it was used before. The Bible is God's Word from Genesis 1:1 to Revelation 22:21 and is our blueprint for life.

Thursday April 22, 2021

2 Timothy 1:7 For God hath not given us the spirit of fear; but of power, and of love, and of a sound mind.

One of my great fears is driving over tall bridges especially after dark. Well, guess what? One day I accepted a job position that required me driving over a tall bridge. I was excited about the job and did not think about it until I was headed home after my first day and yes it was dark. I stopped at the foot of the bridge and prayed, speaking in tongues, and reminding myself that God had not given me a spirit of fear, but had instead given me power, love, and a sound mind. I made it over safely and many more times after that.

Several years ago, when speaking to a young lady I had just met, I was able to reassure her with those same words when she had concerns including some fear and anxiety about raising special needs children. She has done remarkably well so far and sees God's blessings on her and her children as she trusts Him.

God gave us His gift of holy spirit, not to enable a cowardly attitude, but that of strength and boldness, love of and for Christ and a mind disciplined to the truth of God's Word.

Friday April 23, 2021

Genesis 22:14 And Abraham called the name of that place Jehovahjireh [that is, The Lord will provide]; as it is said to this day, "In the mount of the Lord it shall be seen."

Jehovah-jireh: The Lord sees and provides. The only place in the Bible where this phrase is used is in Genesis 22, but there are many examples of God our Father's love and care. God always provides for His children; He makes sure we have what we need because He is our sufficiency and knows even before we know what we need. He provided a way out of Egypt for His people, and a path on dry land through the Red Sea. While the children of Israel were traveling through the desert, they had no means of finding food or shelter and God saw their needs and provided. God provided the sacrifice for Abraham when he thought he would have to sacrifice his son – Isaac.

Growing up, there were times I remember my mother praying with us for God to provide because she had no idea where the next meal was coming from. I cannot remember one time we went to bed with an empty stomach – someone would drop off some food, a close friend of the family who was a fisherman provided us with fresh fish almost every day. At some point we grew vegetables – so we had great meals. I am convinced God provided each time. We have no doubt that as we continue to trust and rely on Him, God will provide our every need.

Saturday April 24, 2021

Acts 26:18 To open their eyes, and to turn them from darkness to light, and from the power of Satan unto God, that they may receive forgiveness of sins, and inheritance among them which are sanctified by faith that is in me.

There was so much misunderstanding of what God expected from His people, the world was dark, and people had started doubting their belief in the one true God. Jesus' life and ministry was what was needed to clear things up. It took even His death on the cross for one Roman soldier to acknowledge that this was indeed the Son of God. God's plan was to help man see and understand His heart and love.

Jesus came to give us a true understanding of God and His Word, that our eyes would be spiritually opened to see clearly what was previously confusing to man; and turn people from the darkness of this world to the light of God's Word. He rescued us out of the clutches of the adversary so that we could be born again reconciled to God and set apart in His family to receive an inheritance once we believe. That is our hope.

Sunday April 25, 2021

Acts 2:42 And they continued stedfastly in the apostles' doctrine and fellowship, and in breaking of bread, and in prayers.
43 And fear came upon every soul: and many wonders and signs were done by the apostles.

The believers in the first century church faithfully continued in the Word taught them by the apostles, they maintained fellowship – getting together with other believers to worship God, sharing meals, and praying together. They were filled with reverence and respect for God’s Word as they saw the signs, miracles and wonders that were done by the apostles. After the day of Pentecost there was a kind of spiritual awakening. People heard Peter preach of Jesus and helped them understand that it was of Him the prophets spoke of for many years. At last, they ‘got it’ and were ready to change their thinking. As soon as they did, their lives changed, they followed the apostle’s doctrine, never wanting to miss a fellowship and were like minded.

The lives and actions of the first century church believers is our example. We as believers in the Grace Administration can receive the same blessings and results that they did, as follow what they did. Stay in fellowship – not forsaking the assembling of ourselves together, breaking bread and daily prayer.

Monday April 26, 2021

Colossians 1:27 To whom God would make known what is the riches of the glory of this mystery among the Gentiles; which is Christ in you, the hope of glory:

In the Old Testament the prophets studied God's Word as it was written in the stars. They were perplexed for years regarding the mystery that seemed hidden from them. Job talked about it in chapter 26, calling it the "empty place". For many years God kept it a mystery so He could put His plan of salvation in place. The adversary had blinded the eyes of the Judeans and did were not receptive to the Messiah, rejecting and then crucifying Him. God's back-up plan from the beginning was to allow everyone, not just the Judeans to be part of His family.

Many years later, God revealed the mystery that He had hid from the beginning which was that when they believe, the Gentiles also would have the privilege to be born again of His spirit with Christ in each and every believer. In the book of Romans we learn that the reason God had to keep His plan a secret was to hide it from the 'prince of the air' – the devil; because if he found out he would never have allowed Jesus' crucifixion. By the time he found out that when someone becomes born again, he has Christ inside it was too late to stop it. The adversary would have much preferred to have Jesus Christ alive on the earth any day than to have millions and millions of believers all over the world with that power of Christ in each one.

What an honor and blessing is ours to be welcomed into God's family with Christ in us, the hope of glory.

Tuesday April 27, 2021

Colossians 2:8 Beware lest any man spoil you through philosophy and vain deceit, after the tradition of men, after the rudiments of the world, and not after Christ.

As a child I was full of questions about God and the Bible especially if a teaching was unclear to me. I remember our minister telling my mother I talked too much and asked too many questions. In my teenage years I decided to visit different churches to find out if they had the answers I was searching for. As far as doctrines they varied slightly but the answers were always the same – man made responses, and no one was able to prove it to me from the Word. I remained perplexed for years until as an adult I took a Bible class called 'Power for Abundant Living (PFAL).

We as Christians are warned not to be drawn away and listen to man's opinions and traditions. Our true standard is to always be the truth of God's Word. There are those who may know many facts about certain aspects of life and try to lead others to accept their reasoning. They are very sincere about what they teach, but if it does not line up with the truth of the Word, it does not make it right. One minister used to say, "sincerity is no guarantee for truth." Our question should be "what does the Word say?" I am thankful I have been taught the truth.

Wednesday April 28, 2021

Colossians 2:10 And ye are complete in him, which is the head of all principality and power:

Growing up, I had learned to trust God and that He provides as my sufficiency. But there were many times I felt as if I needed to try different things myself to prove that I could manage on my own. Even after I prayed, I would think, maybe I can try this method or go this place and see how that would work. Maybe I needed to dress differently, fast and pray more, or get baptized in water a second time – maybe the first one had worn out. I believed I was born again but had doubts at times wondering if what I did was enough.

Over the years, as I studied the Word more, I came to understand that I already have everything I need in Christ. According to Biblical usage, we are "completely, completely, absolutely complete in Him." When we become born again -Romans 10:9, we lack nothing and have every need met in every category as we are filled with the fullness of God through the power of Christ in us. This goes way beyond what we can even grasp by our five sense.

Thursday April 29, 2021

Colossians 3:15 And let the peace of God rule in your hearts, to the which also ye are called in one body; and be ye thankful.

Several years ago, I lived in a small town on a hill which was beautiful on a warm summer day, but a little nerve racking on a very windy or rainy day. Looking out from my upstairs living room window on one side I could see a row of ranch houses on the opposite side of where I lived with a valley between us. One day a hurricane hit, and it was a rough one – heavy rain and winds, even lifting the roof in several areas of our house. At the time my son was less than a year old and so we bundled up, huddled together in a corner of the house, surrounded ourselves with furniture and prayed. We were able to stay peaceful in the midst of the howling winds as we waited it out.

In the morning when it sounded like everything had died down, I opened the window and tears flowed down my face as I thanked God for keeping us safe. The houses on the other side of the hill were all flattened out – a mangled mess of wood, clothes, and furniture. Apart for the roof lifting in one or two places our house was still standing. We chose to let the peace of God be our standard, trusting Him to protect us and He did.

We stay thankful, as we have been called to do, and do not allow circumstances or people to steal our peace or joy. As we choose to let the peace of God rule in our hearts and lives, He always comes through for us.

Consider the many ways we can let the peace of God rule in our hearts and lives.

Friday April 30, 2021

Colossians 3:16 Let the word of Christ dwell in you richly in all wisdom; teaching and admonishing one another in psalms and hymns and spiritual songs, singing with grace in your hearts to the Lord.

As a young child we attended a small Christian Evangelical church in our town. I really enjoyed going to Sunday School where we learned new songs and stories from the Bible. Many of these songs and stories have stayed with me over the years and I am thankful for that foundation to learn about God's love. The Word that I have learned as an adult has opened my eyes even more to understand the greatness of all we have in Christ. God's heart is as we learn and gain wisdom from His Word is that we in turn share it with others.

We let the words that Christ taught during His earthly ministry live in our lives in abundance. As we do, we will be rich in all wisdom and understanding as we encourage and exhort one another to do the same. In praise and worship, we lift our voices in song rejoicing in all we have in Christ.

MAY

Saturday May 1, 2021

Ephesians 1:19 And what is the exceeding greatness of his power to us-ward who believe, according to the working of his mighty power,
20 Which He wrought in Christ when He raised Him from the dead and set Him at His own right hand in the heavenly places,

O what unlimited and immeasurable greatness is God's power that He gave to us when we believed. It highlights His greatness and strength. It is the exact same power God exercised when He raised Christ from the dead giving Him the most exalted seat at His right hand in the heavenlies. We are thankful that we do not need to face life's challenges by our own strength. As we have seen in the Word, we wrestle against "spiritual wickedness in high places." Because we have the powerful ability of God in us, we can stand against every evil attack of the adversary. We have this power in unlimited abundance as we believe according to God's Word.

Our response to all we have available to us directly from God by way of His Son Jesus Christ is to help others by sharing these truths overflowing from God's Word. The many resources provided in specific Bible classes open up so much detail that propels us to victory in our lives and spiritual walk.

Sunday May 2, 2021

Ephesians 1:3 Blessed be the God and Father of our Lord Jesus Christ, who hath blessed us with all spiritual blessings in heavenly places in Christ:

We are citizens of heaven and earth is not our final home. This is one of the great blessings we receive as children of God which we look forward to. Spiritually our home is a place in the heavenlies where we are seated with Christ. As citizens of a county where we live, we are given rights – to live there and work freely, to vote, health benefits, and to retire with some kind of social security or retirement benefits.

As citizens of heaven, we have sonship rights given to us when we become born again. Along with those five sonship rights of righteousness, justification, redemption, sanctification, and the ministry of reconciliation, we also have the right to prosper and be in health. We have the right to free and bold access to our Heavenly Father God and have been provided with a mediator, Jesus Christ to ensure that we do. We have the right to a victorious life as super conquerors.

All blessings, honor and glory go to God the Father of our Lord Jesus Christ. He has blessed us with Christ in us and given us His gift of holy spirit including every spiritual gift. There is no greater gift anywhere on earth or in the heavens.

Monday May 3, 2021

Ephesians 3:5 Which in other ages was not made known unto the sons of men, as it is now revealed unto his holy apostles and prophets by the Spirit;
6 That the Gentiles should be fellowheirs, and of the same body, and partakers of his promise in Christ by the gospel:

God had a plan that He would include the Gentiles in His promise allowing us to be an equal part of His promise and inheritance through the good news of Jesus Christ. For many years it was kept secret, a mystery it was called, until God revealed it to the apostles and prophets by revelation. Now we live in the 'Age of Grace' which was ushered in on the day of Pentecost. It began a time when not only the Judeans, but all people everywhere had the opportunity for the first time to be born again and belong to the 'one-body' of Christ.

Consider how big this is, to be fellow heirs of God's kingdom. We have God's gift of holy spirit, we are sons of God, not in the future but now, and we have direct access to our Heavenly Father.

Tuesday May 4, 2021

Philippians 2:5 Let this mind be in you, which was also in Christ Jesus:

In the household of God there is one standard we live by and that is the Word of God. As children of God born again of His spirit, we have Christ in us and therefore have the mind of Christ. Our responsibility therefore is to think, live, and love as Christ did. During His earthly ministry Jesus Christ fed the hungry, healed the sick, raised men from the dead, and forgave sins. We are to have the same attitude/behavior, purpose, love, mind, and humility which was in Christ Jesus: He is our ultimate example.

God has forgiven us, redeemed us, justified, and sanctified us, made us righteous, and gave us the ministry of reconciliation. Let our lives reflect the heart of God.

Wednesday May 5, 2021

Ephesians 4:25 Wherefore putting away lying, speak every man truth with his neighbour: for we are members one of another.

When we are born again, we belong to a body of believers who make up the body of Christ. As each of our physical bodies is one and has many different parts each with its own unique function, so are we as members of the 'one body' but with different functions. We are to work together to benefit the household and to support the continued movement of God's Word. We strive to keep unity, peace, and love in the household as we speak the truth lovingly to one another. If we see or suspect a behavior that is contrary to the Word of God, we lovingly reproof and correct to help bring others back to living the Word. Under no circumstances are we to be judgmental, instead with speak the truth with love.

Lies and deceit are tricks of the adversary and should have no place among us. God needs us to all work together in one accord to bring glory to His name.

Thursday May 6, 2021

Ephesians 4:28 Let him that stole steal no more: but rather let him labour, working with `his` hands the thing which is good, that he may have to give to him that needeth.

Most of us might think of stealing as taking something without asking from a store, a neighbor or even a friend and not paying for it. How about taking a box of printer paper from your job, or a stapler or boxes of paper clips, maybe boxes of rice or pasta if your job is a grocery store? How about going to work an hour late every day and leaving fifteen minutes early without getting permission? Yes. that would be considered stealing as well.

As believers we want to set an example and be a witness to our coworkers and employers. Our lives are that of honesty, integrity, and ethics. We do not want to follow the mainstream and do it because everyone else is doing it. I'm sure many of us can remember our parents' question "if your friends all jumped off a bridge would you jump too?" It may seem like a silly question but think about it. Do we want to follow everyone stealing products or time from our employer because everyone is doing it and we do not want to be the odd one? As believers the answer is an emphatic NO!

Friday May 7, 2021

Ephesians 5:1 Be ye therefore followers of God, as dear children;

Many children look up to admire their parents so much that they determine to be just like them. They even chose the same career path and set the same standards in their home for their children as they saw from their parents. Some girls want to dress like or cook as good as their mothers. Boys may grow up and choose fishing or hunting as a hobby. Whatever they decide, the goal is always to make their parents proud. Sometimes as teenagers they may rebel for a period of time, but usually as they grow older the changes appear to reflect the principles taught buy their parents. Some of us may look so much like one or both parents that people we never met may take one look at us and state that "you are the picture of 'so and so'".

As children of God our lives should imitate the example set by His Son Jesus Christ. People should be able to look at us, our lifestyles and behaviors, and know that we are followers of God.

Saturday May 8, 2021

Ephesians 6:10 Finally, my brethren, be strong in the Lord, and in the power of his might.

One of the many promises in the Word is that God will never leave us nor forsake us. When we are faced with challenges, some may seem too big for us; we may be tempted to give up when it looks like we are not able to cope. We are exhorted to be "strong in the Lord", and the power we have in us because of His gift of holy spirit. As born-again believers we never have to face any of life's challenges by ourselves. We are children of the most High God and in Ephesians chapter one we are told that the same power God used to raise Jesus Christ from the dead is in each and every one of us.

We are not alone and when confronted we stand our ground claiming God's promises and His protection. When the adversary comes at us with "you and what army?" We can be bold and fearless as we respond with "God is my refuge and strength."

Remember, our strength is not our own but from God. So, we rely on the power of God in Christ in us to stand against the attacks of the adversary.

Sunday May 9, 2021

Ephesians 6:12 For we wrestle not against flesh and blood, but against principalities, against powers, against the rulers of the darkness of this world, against spiritual wickedness in high places.

This means that our fight/competition is not a physical one, but instead it is a spiritual competition. It is against rulers, authorities and devil spirit powers overseeing the darkness in the world, against the spiritual forces of evil in the spiritual realm – basically the adversary and his devil spirits. The adversary will use people in our lives to hurt us in some way, then we get angry with that person leading to strife and division in the household. When we remember that our 'fight' is a spiritual one, we can start the healing process by forgiving and not holding grudges. That helps us move on with a light heart and keep the peace.

Let us consider that the only way we will win in this competition is with the Word, and with the power of God. We do not try to lash back at one another but instead go to God in prayer, go to the Word for answers of peace.

Monday May10, 2021

Exodus 23:13 And in all things that I have said unto you be circumspect: and make no mention of the name of other gods, neither let it be heard out of thy mouth.

We are to be careful not to use the name of any other gods, to speak their name in either blessing or cursing. False gods are idols and come in so many forms like our jobs, money, earthly possessions or even someone. The Word of God clearly states that the "love of money is the root of all evil," and it has been the downfall of many. To be clear having a lot of money is not a bad thing, but loving money and all it provides more than a relationship with God is what brings destruction.

It is easy to say we have no other gods, or we worship no other gods, but consider the form some of these gods can take. It may be a loved one, a job, house, car, a sports team, a spouse or even oneself. Some people have been known to miss a service or rush out before it is over to see their favorite sports team play, or spend hours polishing a new car, spending tons of money to make it look "just right," then they state they cannot tithe and abundantly share because they don't have enough money left.

Take time to identify if someone or something is becoming an idol in your life and renew your mind to the Word so your only object of worship is our Heavenly Father – God.

Tuesday May 11, 2021

Exodus 3:3 And Moses said, I will now turn aside, and see this great sight, why the bush is not burnt.

Moses had been taught God's Word and as an adult the Word was brought back to his mind as he contemplated God's plan for his life. He had been raised by Pharaoh's wife and had lived the life of privilege, but when he remembered where he came from and tried to defend one of his people he was attacked and had to run away to save his life. It was here while possibly wandering what God would have him do, that he heard that voice and saw the phenomenon of the bush on fire that did not burn. God had Moses's attention and was able to direct him to return to Egypt to do His will.

God can speak to us is so many different ways, and like Moses we need to recognize His voice and pay attention. The key is to stay in fellowship with our Heavenly Father, so we never miss God's plan for our lives.

Wednesday May 12, 2021

Galatians 5:16 This I say then, Walk in the Spirit, and ye shall not fulfil the lust of the flesh.
17 For the flesh lusteth against the Spirit, and the Spirit against the flesh: and these are contrary the one to the other: so that ye cannot do the things that ye would.

When we are born again our lives are renewed by our spiritual walk. We are not made perfect overnight; we are not transformed into a person who will never make another mistake. Our goal is to make a conscious choice every day to allow God's gift of holy spirit in us to build us up. Fulfilling the "lust of the flesh" means to fall back into the old habit patterns we were used to before we were born again. Some of these include, covetousness, lying, stealing, gossiping, hatred, and lusting.

Instead, we change our habits to walk by the spirit – speaking in tongues and communicating daily with our Heavenly Father, practicing the presence of God. As we do it is less likely we will fall back into our old man nature of sin and desires that are contrary to the Word.

Thursday May 13, 2021

Galatians 6:9 And let us not be weary in well doing: for in due season we shall reap, if we faint not.

Many situations in life can cause us to get tired to the point of weariness. As parents we love our children with everything we have, but sometimes it wears the body and mind down – getting up, making breakfast, get them ready and take them to school, make dinner, help with homework, clean, wash, get them ready for bed and all that while having a full time job outside of the home. It basically feels like you have two full time jobs. No wonder we feel worn out, weary, and with little or no energy at times.

But then, we may attend a recital, a play, a baseball or football game, they bring home their report cards, you are so proud, they hug you, tell you they love you and you say it back; your heart is so full of love, joy and pride and it is all worth it. You go to bed with a smile on your face and get up the next day to do it again.

Let us not lose heart and get tired of doing good; let us keep believing and serving God because it will be worth it in the end when we receive our rewards from God. Not only will we have eternal life, but we will be rewarded with the five crowns for our stand and commitment.

Friday May 14, 2021

Genesis 1:14 And God said, Let there be lights in the firmament of the heaven to divide the day from the night; and let them be for signs, and for seasons, and for days, and years:
15 And let them be for lights in the firmament of the heaven to give light upon the earth: and it was so.

God did not have to create light again since He had done so previously (in Genesis 1:1), that is why it says here "and God said". He now made these lights from the main light source that He created when He "created the heavens and the earth". All the lights in and around the heavens and firmament tell a story – things God wants us to know. All this was put in place for man to enjoy.

Consider Psalms 19:1 – "The heavens declare the glory of God and the firmament showeth His handiwork."

We can look up to the skies on a clear night and see millions of stars glistening there and the moon sometimes so bright it lights up everywhere looking like daytime. If we take time to study the stars, we can see the many constellations that God placed there. What beautiful handiwork! We take time to give God thanks for the beautiful earth He created for us to enjoy.

Saturday May 15, 2021

Isaiah 55:8 For my thoughts are not your thoughts, neither are your ways my ways, saith the LORD.
9 For as the heavens are higher than the earth, so are my ways higher than your ways, and my thoughts than your thoughts.

The way God thinks, and works is vastly different from us, because He is Spirit. To get a clear picture take a walk outside and look up into the sky. We cannot see the end of it, that is how much higher God's thoughts and actions are than ours. He sees into the future way past what our finite minds can comprehend

We make decisions based off of what is available to us via our five senses. We can understand what we can see, smell, touch, feel, and hear. God is not limited by senses as He is everywhere present, yet we may at times try to say what we think God may be saying. The only way to get that information is from His Word where He has said he gave us all things that pertain to life and godliness.

Our response is to trust that as our loving Heavenly Father, He wants the best for us always. As we let His Word direct us we can get a glimpse into His ways.

Sunday May 16, 2021

Genesis 1:27 So God created man in his own image, in the image of God created he him; male and female created he them.
28 And God blessed them, and God said unto them, Be fruitful, and multiply, and replenish the earth, and subdue it: and have dominion over the fish of the sea, and over the fowl of the air, and over every living thing that moveth upon the earth.

God is Spirit so the image He created in man is His spirit. Man had direct access to God by way of His spirit until Adam and Eve sinned and that connection was lost. Placing man in the Garden of Eden was the ultimate care for God's creation. He made sure the plants, vegetation and animals were cared for, and man had enough to eat when he needed it.

God made man to have fellowship with Him and immediately put His plan in place to one day be able to give His spirit back to man. That is what happens when a man or woman becomes born again (Romans 10:9), he receives God's gift of holy spirit, and once again God sees us in His likeness.

God is still the same, making sure our needs are met daily.

Monday May 17, 2021

Genesis 1:31 And God saw every thing that he had made, and, behold, it was very good. And the evening and the morning were the sixth day.

On the sixth day of creation God took a look around and was pleased/satisfied with everything. "It was very good" the Word says. God put this whole world together putting a lot of thought into each day. Day by day He had a plan to add to what was already in place, taking time at the end of each day to look around before He found it "very good".

On the first day God made light -Day and darkness – night and on the second day He made the firmament and divided the waters. On the third day, those waters were separated from the earth and called seas, the dry land earth, grass, herbs, and trees of all kinds were then added. God made stars, the moon to light the night, and the sun to light the day on the fourth day. The fifth day God made life to live in the seas – whales, fish, crabs, turtles, lobsters and more, including fowls for the earth. On the sixth day of creation, God made cattle, horses, elephants, giraffe and more and then He made man before resting. In His final act of creation, God made man "out of the dust of the earth' in His own image.

Consider the phrase "it (all God's creation) was very good". We are in no position to complain about anything God made. Instead we need to realize that we could never do or have done a better job. We may look in the mirror and not be too happy about our bodies but remember we are made in the image of God. Any changes may distort that perfect image. God said it was "very good"; let us be thankful.

Tuesday May 18, 2021

Psalms 42:11 Why art thou cast down, O my soul? and why art thou disquieted within me? hope thou in God: for I shall yet praise him, who is the health of my countenance, and my God.

There is no reason to get so sad or upset to go down into deep depression no matter what we face in life. Why do we let things get us so troubled and restless that we lose sight of all God has done for us? Yes, negative things will come up – some will be hard for us to deal with or even manage on our own. Our faith and trust in God helps us see past whatever the situation is, to the hope of Christ's return and all that God has in store for us. We have so many promises in God's Word that help us know and be confident in God's ability to see us through.

When we feel like we need a helping hand to confess positives and claim God's promises, we can lean on the love and support of the household of believers.

Jesus Christ as our example endured so much, looking past the cross in anticipation of better things to come. We too can look past life's difficulties to God's glory as we claim His promises.

Wednesday May 19, 2021

Hebrews 12:2 Looking unto Jesus the author and finisher of our faith; who for the joy that was set before him endured the cross, despising the shame, and is set down at the right hand of the throne of God.

Our believing originates in all Jesus Christ did for us, we stay focused on Him. Jesus Christ was fully aware of the sufferings that lay ahead for Him, and He repeatedly went to God in prayer asking if at all possible, to please spare Him. He was also aware, because He had been taught the Word, including the prophecies about Himself, that this was the only plan to legally be man's redemption. He decided to choose to give it to the Father with those famous words "nevertheless, not my will, but thine be done." At that point, Jesus was fully persuaded to make the choice to give up His life for mankind. He decided to not focus on the sufferings, and the cross and instead chose to look past all that to the glory that He knew would be available to Him at God's right hand, after it was all over.

Consider everything Jesus Christ endured – His humiliation, sufferings, and excruciating death on the cross to make sure we were freed from the adversary's clutches, and that salvation was made available to us. It humbles me, fills my heart with love and gratitude and urges me to share those truths with others.

Thursday May 20, 2021

Hebrews 12:3 For consider him that endured such contradiction of sinners against himself, lest ye be wearied and faint in your minds.

When we start to feel discouraged about speaking the Word and nobody wants it, or we get ridiculed for being a Christian, it may seem like we're all alone. We may even be targeted at our jobs and feel persecuted when we know we haven't done anything to deserve the persecution. Remember how much Jesus endured from His own people; consider that we have an adversary that will send people to attack us just because of our stand for God and His Word.

The biggest thing to keep in mind is that "this too shall pass." As we stand firm on our conviction and trust God, He not only stands with us, but He gets us through bigger and better than we could imagine.

Friday May 21, 2021

Proverbs 3:26 For the LORD shall be thy confidence, and shall keep thy foot from being taken.

It is comforting to know that God is always so near and that we have no reason to be anxious or fearful about anything in life. God is aware of everything we have to face; He even knows what is ahead – around every corner or even in the future. We can be confident that He will protect us from dangers (seen and unseen); He will keep us safe, reassure us and keep us peaceful. We can trust that He will prevent us from getting caught in the adversary's snare as we keep our minds focused on Him and His Word.

Our responsibility as believers is stay tuned in to the Word so we are sharp on everything we need to know. We already have our "helmet of salvation, because we know we are born again, and the sword of the Spirit, which is the Word of God." Now let us build our believing which is our shield and walk out with confidence in God's willingness and ability to protect us no matter what.

Saturday May 22, 2021

I Thessalonians 1:6 And ye became followers of us,
and of the Lord, having received the word in much
affliction, with joy of the Holy Ghost.
7 So that ye were ensamples to all that believe in
Macedonia and Achaia.

One of the things I learned many years ago was that people are always watching me even when I am not aware that they are. It made me a bit paranoid for a bit until I heard the lyrics to a song that went "you cannot please all the people all the time," That made me decide to stop being concerned about who was watching me and what they thought about me. Once I got a better understanding of God's Word, I understood that as a Christian people are watching you to understand your lifestyle.

Just like those believers in Thessalonica, people are drawn to what we share regarding God's Word by our lifestyle habits, our behavior, or how we treat others. A believer once said to me that she was so blessed being in the same fellowship with us that she never wanted us to move. I thanked her for such a sweet compliment, as I got a little teary. Our lives are to be these examples that people want to always be around us.

Sunday May 23, 2021 - PENTECOST

Acts 2:1 And when the day of Pentecost was fully come, they were all with one accord in one place.
3 And there appeared unto them cloven tongues like as of fire, and it sat upon each of them.
2 And suddenly there came a sound from heaven as of a rushing mighty wind, and it filled all the house where they were sitting.
4 And they were all filled with the Holy Ghost, and began to speak with other tongues, as the Spirit gave them utterance.

Pentecost began the birthday of the church and ushered in the beginning of the Grace Administration when it was made available for the first time ever for men and women to be able to be born-again, receive the gift of holy spirit into manifestation and speak in tongues.

All who believed from then until now have been called children of God and receive everlasting life by way of the new birth. Speaking in tongues is the proof that we are born again and on our way to heaven at Christ return and nothing or no one able to prevent that.

Monday May 24, 2021

Acts 2:7 And they were all amazed and marveled, saying one to another, Behold, are not all these which speak Galilaeans?
8 And how hear we every man in our own tongue, wherein we were born?
9 Parthians, and Medes, and Elamites, and the dwellers in Mesopotamia, and in Judaea, and Cappadocia, in Pontus, and Asia,
10 Phrygia, and Pamphylia, in Egypt, and in the parts of Libya about Cyrene, and strangers of Rome, Jews and proselytes,
11 Cretes and Arabians, we do hear them speak in our tongues the wonderful works of God.

That was the power of the gift of holy spirit in manifestations. All twelve apostles received God's gift of holy spirit and spoke in tongues. The apostles were Galilean and spoke Aramaic so the languages they spoke were unknown to them, yet people from everywhere heard them speak in their language and recognized it as speaking "the wonderful works of God." As each of us are born again, we receive God's gift No one is missed who believes to receive, confesses with his/her mouth Jesus as Lord in their lives and believes God raised Him from the dead. (Romans 10:9) It is available to every born-again believer. We do not let the adversary rob us of that blessing that is rightfully ours to claim, and we do not settle for less.

That is how powerful speaking in tongues is, in the private prayer life where it strengthens a believer spiritually and/or in a believers meeting where it builds up other believers in the church.

Tuesday May 25, 2021

Isaiah 42:6 I the LORD have called thee in righteousness, and will hold thine hand, and will keep thee, and give thee for a covenant of the people, for a light of the Gentiles;

God has called us and made us righteous in Christ. It was years before I fully understood the true meaning of what it is to be righteous. One definition I learned explains that it is given to us freely by God when we are born-again. It was a judicial decision that allows us to do what God asks of us in Hebrews 14:6 – go into His presence boldly, with no sense of being sinful, no feelings of guilt or feeling 'less than.' Of our own strength or merit, we would never be worthy enough but by God's grace we made acceptable to Him.

We can confidently place our hands in His for safe keeping and trust that we are always in His care. That is God's promise to us as we keep His Word. We let nothing cloud our minds and take away what God has freely made available to us.

We are righteous in Christ, we are God's children, God has called you and set us apart for Himself. To God be the glory.

Wednesday May 26, 2021

Isaiah 55:11 So shall my word be that goeth forth out of my mouth: it shall not return unto me void, but it shall accomplish that which I please, and it shall prosper in the thing whereto I sent it.

There are times difficult situations will arise in our lives. We may feel lost and scared and search every day for answers. It can be easy to get discouraged when the answer does not come as soon as we would like it to. Just remember God's words are never empty, His promises are always sure and trustworthy and brings to pass exactly what He wants it to do. His words will never return to Him lacking anything but will be prosperous – we will see the benefits in our lives. God tells us many times in His Word that He loves us, that He is our refuge and strength, that He will never leave us nor forsake us. We recognize any challenge in life as an attack from our personal adversary, we renew our minds by going to God's Word for answers and claiming His promises.

Rest assured that we can trust God's words and rely on His promises, no matter what the situation.

Thursday May 27, 2021

James 5:11 Behold, we count them happy which endure. Ye have heard of the patience of Job, and have seen the end of the Lord; that the Lord is very pitiful, and of tender mercy.

Job was a real man who suffered several unimaginable devastation and loss. He lost everything including his children, property, and his health. I imagine there were days Job did not want to get out of bed, maybe pull the covers over his head; he may not want to eat even because of the immense sorrow and pain he was going through. But he was strong believer; although he did not necessarily understand why he was being tormented he trusted that God would see him through it, which He did.

As Job was able to endure everything the adversary attacked him with, even more so us as born-again believers. We have God in Christ in us, sons of God with the power of the gift of holy spirit in each of us. As long as we can see past the circumstances and hold on to God's promises to see us through, He will always come through for us and we will be rewarded for our faithful stand.

Friday May 28, 2021

Job 1:22 In all this Job sinned not, nor charged God foolishly.

We saw previously that Job endured unspeakable sufferings through no fault of his own. The Word sates that he was "perfect (a mature/strong believer) and upright (honorable/honest), and one that feared (reverenced) God, and eschewed (shunned) evil." Job is basically the 'poster child' for believers everywhere. His full story is detailed in the book of Job and gives a clear picture of his sufferings and the devastation he went through. Job lost his 10 children, all his property, his health and all his livestock. Being one of the richest men of his day, that had to be devastating, yet the Word tells us Job did not sin by accusing God of sending these things to test Him nor did he curse God foolishly.

Job recognized his error in not completely trusting God by becoming fearful about what might happen to his family. (Job 3:25) He acknowledged where he fell short confessed his error and renewed his mind. Amazing integrity we can definitely learn from.

Saturday May 29, 2021

Deuteronomy 31:8 I the LORD have called thee in righteousness, and will hold thine hand, and will keep thee, and give thee for a covenant of the people, for a light of the Gentiles;

We have been called. This is so significant and yet so many do not fully grasp that and lose sight of it. God has called us and made us righteous in Christ. We are no longer just a person of body and soul but fully equipped with the power of God's gift of holy spirit. With God in Christ in each of us, wherever we are God is there with us. Do you get that? Do you see and understand the significance of that? Let us take a moment to let that sink in.

He will continue to guide and direct us, protect us every day (hold our hands, it says here). God is making a solemn promise to never leave His own. Wow!! What a great, big, wonderful God we have.

Sunday May 30, 2021

Isaiah 55:12 For ye shall go out with joy, and be led forth with peace: the mountains and the hills shall break forth before you into singing, and all the trees of the field shall clap their hands.

Several times in my life, after I lost my brother, my father, and two very dear friends of mine my heart and head were in a really sad, almost dark place. After some of reflecting on the truth of God's Word regarding the Hope, I felt alive again, thankful for what I have in Christ. We will go through rough times in this life and feel like we are alone in the valley but take a look at what God has promised us. By His mighty hand of blessing He will lead us out peacefully, full of joy that even the mountains and hills will rejoice with us and the trees will be clapping their hands cheering us on.

This is all figuratively of course, but what an awesome mind's picture to help us get through anything. Trusting that God is with us no matter how low we are and is waiting patiently to take our hand and lead us out of the valley of despair, hurt, and grief can get us through pretty much anything. Praise God!

Monday May 31, 2021

John 3:21 But he that doeth truth cometh to the light, that his deeds may be made manifest, that they are wrought in God.

Recently I was watching a television show where the main character was arrested, and he insisted he believed he was being framed and that he did not do it. Although all the evidence pointed to him, he knew that the truth would be revealed. He was getting frustrated when both the prosecution and his lawyer stated he would be found guilty and said he should take a plea deal. He however stood his ground refusing the plea deal until the truth came to light that he was indeed framed by someone who wanted him to get in trouble.

God's Word is truth, and it is the light that will lead others to God. As we stand on God's Word speaking the truth doing what is right—morally, ethically, spiritually, everything we do, and touch will be blessed and stand out as God's favor on our lives.

JUNE

Tuesday June 1, 2021

John 8:31 If ye continue in my word, `then` are ye my disciples indeed;
32 And ye shall know the truth, and the truth shall make you free.

For those searching it can be very confusing to figure what is truth in the world today. So many go from one denomination to the next trying to find the truth. There is only one place we can find the truth which has all the answers we need to deliver us and set us free. What do we need to be set free from? In the Bible we learn that we need to be set free from the power of sin in our lives. God's Word is our only true standard for truth; and is where we experience real freedom. We are indeed followers of the Lord Jesus Christ when we continue to focus our minds steadfastly on the Word, making it our own and renewing our minds to be obedient to the standards therein.

As we consistently set aside study time to meditate on the Word we build the knowledge of God's Word in our minds and lives.

Wednesday June 2, 2021

Psalms 119:89 Forever, O LORD, thy word is settled in heaven.
90 Thy faithfulness is unto all generations: thou hast established the earth, and it abideth.

God is faithful to His Word – whatever He says He will do He always does. From the beginning of time when Adam and Eve sinned, God told them if they ate of the fruit of the tree of the knowledge of good and evil, they would die. The adversary convinced them that they would "not surely die" but as much as it must have hurt Him to do so, God had to keep His Word. It was not a physical death but certainly a spiritual one where man lost his spirit connection with God. God promised the Israelites He would rescue them from Egypt, and He did. Just when Abraham and Sarah had started to give up any hope of having children – God showed up and yes, they had a son. Time and time again we see God coming through even when people have started to lose hope.

The word of God is firmly established forever and will endure throughout eternity. The earth is firmly in place just as God created it – never again to be made without "form and void" by the adversary. God is faithful to keep His promises to us, even to this day because He has not changed; this is for our children and grandchildren and their grandchildren, as we continue to trust Him and believe His Word.

Thursday June 3, 2021

John 10:10 The thief cometh not, but for to steal, and to kill, and to destroy: I am come that they might have life, and that they might have it more abundantly.

The adversary is likened to a thief who comes in stealthily to steal our joy, health, and happiness, to kill our bodies, families, and destroy our peace. The adversary's attacks are sneaky most times so hidden that we get caught in his snare before we realize what it is. That is why we are encouraged to stay sharp on God's Word; that is the only way we can be full prepared to recognize and 'defeat' these attacks.

In stark contrast Jesus Christ came that we may experience a life full of abundance, joy, and peace; to give back to us everything the adversary steals, kills and destroys in our live. This starts with our salvation, redemption, and justification. After that God promises us health and prosperity in this life and eternal life with Him. Not only is that life abundant, but more than abundant as we faithfully stand for God and His Word.

We are thankful to God for that more abundant life.

Friday June 4, 2021

John 14:6 Jesus saith unto him, I am the way, the truth, and the life: no man cometh unto the Father, but by me.

People have searched for the true way to God the Father for centuries. The read books, study religions, fast and pray and still are confused. It took me years to realize how simple the answer is and as that as soon as we understand and accept who Jesus Christ truly is, only then our search can come to an end. The answer is not in man – pastors, ministers, priests, or religious denominations. It is found only in the Bible, the Word of God. How can we trust that the Word is true? Simple; it is the "God-breathed Word". (II Timothy 3:16)

God has set it out so plainly in His Word and yet for years many Christians have by-passed the simple truth. Jesus Christ is the only way to our Heavenly Father – God, He is our route to the truth of God's Word, and our only hope of having a life of blessings.

Saturday June 5, 2021

John 14:27 Peace I leave with you, my peace I give unto you: not as the world giveth, give I unto you. Let not your heart be troubled, neither let it be afraid.

Back in the 1960's as a young child, I heard so many talking of trying to achieve 'world-peace'. There is a movie about a beauty contestant show whose platform was 'world-peace'. Everyone everywhere has been praying for it; some are troubled, have many sleepless nights due to worries over when and if we will ever see the end of wars and have 'world-peace'. In this verse Jesus Christ is reassuring His disciples that in spite of whatever is going on in the world, they can have peace in Him. Jesus Christ left perfect peace for His followers – a peace of undisturbed quiet. Nowhere on earth is that kind of peace available and yet we can feel safe in it knowing that we need have no fear or worry because it is the peace that comes from God.

The year 2020 has been a year of real turmoil for people around the globe – it was not limited to one country or island. Many families lost multiple loved ones. Many medical professionals reached their breaking point which we witnessed on the news almost daily. The 'experts' seemed confused and misleading as to how to handle the situation. Through all this, God's Word promises us peace, reassuring us even as Jesus did for His disciples thousands of years ago, we are to not "let our hearts be troubled nor be afraid." Because we can have that peace of God as we trust and rely on Him and His Word.

Sunday June 6, 2021

John 16:33 These things I have spoken unto you, that in me ye might have peace. In the world ye shall have tribulation: but be of good cheer; I have overcome the world.

This year I have heard so many pray for things to "get back to normal" because it is too hard to deal with an escalating pandemic and the many lives lost. It is so painful to hear on the news about the millions of lives lost. I always pause for a moment of silent prayer for the equally millions of families left behind to grieve. But the truth is we cannot be correct in asking for life to "get back to normal." What would that look like? For many it may be something like this – jumping out of bed, running out, jumping in our cars, rushing through a hectic day at work. Then on our return home, rushing through dinner, maybe the news, falling into bed, only to repeat it again. We might miss birthdays or some other milestone, too tired to go to church on "my one day off." Maybe the too busy lifestyle is not really what we want to go back to, but a life of God's peace even in the midst of the troubles.

God never promised us a life with no troubles "skies always blue" like the song says, but we can be peaceful as we deal with whatever comes our way knowing that we will overcome and be victorious. Jesus Christ paid the price and overcame even death and we know with Him on our side we can prevail.

Monday June 7, 2021

Mark 11:23 For verily I say unto you, That whosoever shall say unto this mountain, Be thou removed, and be thou cast into the sea; and shall not doubt in his heart, but shall believe that those things which he saith shall come to pass; he shall have whatsoever he saith.

Do you remember the story of Peter walking on the water to meet Jesus in Matthew chapter 14? This is not a normal, typical day activity; people just don't wake up one day and say, "looks like a nice day, the ocean is calm; I think I will walk on water today." It took some believing on Peter's part to trust that first of all he could walk on water and to trust that because He was with Jesus it would be a possibility. Peter stated, "Lord, if it be thou, bid me come unto thee on the water." Jesus replied simply 'come" and he did, but as soon as he lost sight of Jesus and got troubled by the rough waves, he started to sink.

Miracles still happen, most being in the realm of phenomenon, but they require our believing to come to pass. Jesus is telling His disciples that they could literally tell a mountain to move into the sea and they could make it happen. The key is to believe with no doubt to receive what we are asking for.

So, if we are believing for something big to come to pass in our lives – to be debt-free, pay off student loans, buy a house, be completely healed from a devastating diagnosis, or even just to find the right life partner, we believe God with no doubt and trust that we will receive what we ask Him for.

Tuesday June 8, 2021

Mark 11:24 Therefore I say unto you, What things soever ye desire, when ye pray, believe that ye receive them, and ye shall have them.

"Have you ever said a prayer and found that it was answered?" That is a line in a song by one of my favorite artists. Every time I hear these words, it makes me pause and think. OK now seriously! That is definitely not a question a believing believer would ponder. We would have questions if our prayers were **not** answered. The singer does not exactly answer her question, but the following line states "all my hope has been restored; I'm not looking anymore." That's more like it. Our prayers can be a request to our Heavenly Father for healing, protection, a job, or finances; but our prayers may also be an expression of worship or praise to our Heavenly Father.

God truly wants us to have the desires of our hearts. We are exhorted to ask with a believing heart when we go to God in prayer, and the promise is we "shall", absolutely have them. No matter how bleak the situation looks, we can be assured that God hears and **will** answer our prayer. We pray, believing that we already have it, and we will.

Wednesday June 9, 2021

Matthew 18:19 Again I say unto you, That if two of you shall agree on earth as touching any thing that they shall ask, it shall be done for them of my Father which is in heaven.

God puts emphasis on the number two in His Word. Two is the number for something being established or permanently agreed upon. The Word states in Ecclesiastes that two are better than one because if one falls the other one can lift him up and two in bed together will warm each other up, but just one person in bed alone will not be warm. When God instructed Noah to bring the animals into the ark, it was by twos and sevens. Jesus sent the seventy out by twos saying He gave them power "over all the power of the enemy: and nothing shall by any means hurt you." Going out by twos strengthens the work they are doing; as one is speaking the Word, the other is supportive, silently praying and/or speaking in tongues. If the adversary sends some attack, together they can withstand it by the power and presence of God. As we understand the significance of two praying together, we can appreciate God's reason for encouraging it.

We go to God to prayer in the name of Jesus Christ with our petitions. When two people come together and get like-minded when they pray asking anything, God promises it shall be done. Is there something you have been praying for and still have no answers? Call another believing believer to get like-minded and pray with you.

Do not stop praying. Know and believe that the answer is on the way.

Thursday June 10, 2021

Romans 12:3 For I say, through the grace given unto me, to every man that is among you, not to think of himself more highly than he ought to think; but to think soberly, according as God hath dealt to every man the measure of faith.

Sometimes as Christians we tend to get a bit haughty about who we are and how much we can do. It helps to remember that God's grace ensures us that He is not a respecter of persons. Because one has a long suit in hospitality, or singing, or even some may sound like they are more confident in their operation of manifestations in a fellowship or Bible study does not mean they were gifted with something more special than another. No one is more privileged than another, so we do not think we are better or deserve more than another. There is a Proverb that pride always comes before some disaster and haughtiness before failure, which means that having too much pride or arrogance will certainly destroy you. It is a reminder to stay meek and not allow pride to take over our thinking.

We stay humble knowing that we are all saved by God's grace through faith or believing in the name of His Son Jesus Christ. There is nothing we can do to merit God's forgiveness and love; no amount of money can buy us a place in His kingdom or a seat closer to His side. Instead we remain kindhearted manifesting the love of God.

Friday June 11, 2021

Philippians 2:2 Fulfil ye my joy, that ye be likeminded, having the same love, being of one accord, of one mind.

Parents of more than one child may relate to sibling rivalry, fighting, or arguments between the siblings. Growing up with five siblings I remember many occasions when our parents were like a referee when one of us would want them to see our point of view or agree with us instead of another. Even as a parent I remember having to work through disagreements with my own two children so they could come to a compromise. Then and still now as they are adults, it always warms my heart and makes me extremely happy when they work things out, when they are spending time together peacefully and when they are in agreement with no arguments.

Imagine our Heavenly Father looking to us His beloved children expecting to see us in agreement on His Word. One of the things that would bring 'joy' to the heart of God is to see His children working together in harmony. God wants us to continue in unity or togetherness, of the same mind, loving one another with the love of God in manifestations in the household. As believers our purpose should be the same – that of living and teaching the accuracy of God's Word.

Saturday June 12, 2021

Philippians 2:13 For it is God which worketh in you both to will and to do of his good pleasure.

God's will should be paramount in our hearts and lives and not our own. When a friend of mine was rushed to the emergency room with difficulty breathing and complications from having had polio as a child, the first impulse of the medical team was to decide that it was time for her to give up. My first thought on hearing these words was that it was not her time to go. But I then thought to myself, "who are you to decide that? If the specialist team of doctors think they were not going to be able to save her live, who are you to think that it is not her time?" I had only recently learned about the benefits of speaking in tongues and I immediately put it into practice. I literally had no idea what I should be talking to God about or what I should be praying for in this situation. It took about a minute for God to show me why He led me to that hospital, that department at that time in my life, showing what exactly I need to do.

After my initial stunned silence, I raced down the hall following the stretcher and the doctors as they wheeled her to the Intensive Care Unit. After praying with her and confirming that she truly did not want to give up, I sprang into action calling ministers and believers to start a session of 24/7 prayer and requested believers sit with her round the clock to pray and speak in tongues.

The end result was that she survived, spending several weeks in rehab, and then being discharged home. I could not have known what to do without God working in me. In this situation His will and pleasure was that my dear friend – His child survive this event. It brought glory to God because the medical staff including all the specialists recognized her healing as the hand of God on her life – a miracle.

Nothing we do is of our own strength, but through God who is effectively working in us to strengthen, energize, and build us up with the ability to fulfill the purpose He has for our lives.

Sunday June 13, 2021

Philippians 3:13 Brethren, I count not myself to have apprehended: but `this` one thing `I do`, forgetting those things which are behind, and reaching forth unto those things which are before,
14 I press toward the mark for the prize of the high calling of God in Christ Jesus.

We graduate from high school and some move on to a technical school or college and even on to a graduate level education. At some point, most people move on to a full-time career or a business having arrived at the level of education they feel they need for the role they will be in the rest of their lives. In our walk as born-again Christians, we never fully reach that point.

The apostle Paul realizes he would not be perfect overnight, stating "I count not myself to have apprehended: - "have not reached my goal of where I need or want to be", but…I press toward the mark/goal or his purpose He knows he was forgiven so he is ready to forget these past sins and move on. His goal was to focus on the purpose God had called Him to fulfill and even through the trials he faced he was able to look ahead to the rewards God promised would be his if he remained faithful.

What an example for us to follow! None of us can really say we have "arrived" spiritually, but we keep moving with the Word toward our goal – our calling from God until we get our rewards. We have been called to be followers of our Lord Jesus Christ and to continue the work He started here in His earthly ministry. Because we know God has made us justified, and righteous in Christ we do not let our past failures or mistakes hold us back, we leave them in the past without condemnation, and keep pressing forward by God's grace.

Monday June 14, 2021

Psalms 119:130 The entrance of thy words giveth light; it giveth understanding unto the simple.

When I first started to need reading glasses, I could not understand what had happened. I woke up one morning, picked up the Bible for my daily devotions and could not understand the words. I could see them, but everything seemed cloudy and unreadable. I remember going to a local pharmacy later that day to test out some over-the-counter reading glasses. As I tried reading the directions on one product, I was still incredulous not wanting to believe I really needed these glasses. Hesitantly, I picked up a pair of the ones with the lowest number and slowly placed them on my face, turned to the product I had tried to read previously and yes you guessed it, the words were as clear as day. Tearfully I had to acknowledge that it was time for these reading glasses, and I bought them.

Without the light of God's Word, we would all be stumbling around in the dark trying to find our way. That is how we were before God sent His Son Jesus Christ to shed the light on the truth of His Word to open the eyes of our understanding to spiritual truths. Just like with the glasses I could now see and understand what I was reading, with the Word of God we understand His heart and purpose for us.

We are thankful for God shining a light on His Word so we could better understand all we have in Him as our Heavenly Father.

Tuesday June 15, 2021

Philippians 4:6 Be careful for nothing; but in everything by prayer and supplication with thanksgiving let your requests be made known unto God.
7 And the peace of God, which passeth all understanding, shall keep your hearts and minds through Christ Jesus.

The story has been told of two mothers - one with only one child and the other with several. The one with one child never let him out of her sight, walking him to the bus stop and waiting till he got on, then waiting at the bus stop to walk him home. She talked about how fearful she was that he could get hit by a car and he was never allowed to leave the house without her. One day her fears came true – her child was hit by a car just as she turned away for a second. The other mother helped her children get dressed and stood at the door, prayed for their safety, and sent them off to school. These children were never in an accident and grew up healthy and well. Our fears, worries, and anxiety are negative believing that directly impact every aspect of our lives.

As a parent I would hear stories of violence in schools or accidents involving school buses due to driver's negligence, but I sent my children off to school trusting God to protect them throughout the day. With prayer and speaking in tongues whenever I thought about them throughout the day, I trusted God to watch over them. I understood that worrying about their safety would not keep anything from happening and I fully believed that God would protect them. That was the only way I could go to work and be peaceful. Even when my son was hit by a car, walking home from school God still had him covered because he had no broken bones. I truly believed that was of God.

God exhorts us not to be concerned or overly anxious about anything. Instead we go to Him in prayer and thanksgiving for everything and in everything, pouring our hearts out to Him. He will provide an undisturbed quiet as we focus on all we have in Christ Jesus, allowing us to stay peaceful no matter what.

Wednesday June 16, 2021

Psalms 36:9 For with thee is the fountain of life: in thy light shall we see light.

Growing up on an island I have enjoyed many beautiful natural waterfalls. The water cascading down into a river or pool below is a sight to cherish. The water coming from these sources flow out of rocks on the sides of mountains, and is refreshing, rejuvenating, and cleansing. As we walk through the forest it usually looks dark and overcast. The many trees and brush hide the light of the sunlight. We can always tell when we are getting closer to one of these waterfalls as we start to see a clearing in the distance as a stream of sunlight hits the path in front of us.

Like the waterfalls, our source of life is like a well spring overflowing from God. That is where our life originates, and it is refreshing and energizing when God who is light provides the light for our paths every day. As we walk through life searching for our purpose, maybe not even sure what we are searching for, our vision limited by our lack of understanding of God the Holy, we are in a spiritual fog of darkness. When we are introduced to God, the light of His Word and His presence clears everything up. We understand life, our purpose and our destination.

Thursday June 17, 2021

Philippians 4:8 Finally, brethren, whatsoever things are true, whatsoever things are honest, whatsoever things are just, whatsoever things are pure, whatsoever things are lovely, whatsoever things are of good report; if there be any virtue, and if there be any praise, think on these things.
9 Those things, which ye have both learned, and received, and heard, and seen in me, do: and the God of peace shall be with you.

The things that are praise-worthy, things that would help us build excellent morals and ethical standards in our lifestyle are the things we aspire to. The first is things that are true – that would encourage us to be truthful, to speak the Word in love. Next, we meditate on things that are honorable, that would make us deserving of respect and honor; things that are pure or Godly, from the Word of God. Then the lovely or beautiful things are those that encourage us to see the beauty in God's creation, in His children to see others as God sees them. Our words should be words to build others up, words of praise and complimentary so they in turn can do the same for another. Our lives should merit praiseworthiness, admirable, one that others can look up to and help showcase our righteousness in Christ.

All these things and more we have already been taught and need to bring back to our minds and build in our behavior so we can be at peace with God and ourselves.

Friday June 18, 2021

Ecclesiastes 11:7 Truly the light is sweet, and a pleasant thing it is for the eyes to behold the sun:

One of my most favorite times of the day is daybreak, even before the sun comes up and I get to see the first light of day. What a pleasure and absolute lovely feeling, and as the sun starts to rise over the horizon and its warmth start to spread sometimes it is hard to take my eyes off its beauty. Just imagine if we went to sleep and the sun never came up in the morning, going days in darkness where it always looks like night. I know there are some places where people actually experience that, and I think how sad that they do not get to see the sunlight for days. They probably struggle to get out of bed on these days. Then one day they awake to light streaming in through the windows. They probably jump out of bed, singing and excited to get outside.

Before we were introduced to God's Word, that is how we were basically – just walking about day after day shrouded in darkness. Our lives consisted of doubt, worries, fears, and we were never truly happy. Then one day we are introduced to the truths of God's Word, things become clear, we can see and understand everything so much better. How wonderful!

Saturday June 19, 2021

Philippians 4:13 I can do all things through Christ which strengtheneth me.

(Amplified Version) I can do all things [which He has called me to do] through Him who strengthens and empowers me [to fulfill His purpose—I am self-sufficient in Christ's sufficiency; I am ready for anything and equal to anything through Him who infuses me with inner strength and confident peace.]

Are you getting ready to write an exam, interview for a new job, hike up a mountain or something else? Are you thinking, "there's no way I can do this? I'm not smart enough, brave enough or even strong enough." God's Word reassures us that we don't need to be because we are enough in Christ. All our weaknesses, fears, doubts, feelings of being less than, were nailed to the cross when Jesus paid the price for us. As our sufficiency, God in Christ, in us, is all we need to succeed in anything.

This verse says it all. Nothing is impossible with God on our side, with the power of God's gift of holy spirit infusing us with that inner strength and confidence we can do.

Sunday June 20, 2021

Philippians 4:19 But my God shall supply all your need according to his riches in glory by Christ Jesus.

In 2 Kings chapter four is the story of a woman whose husband had died. A man showed up stating that her late husband owed him some money and since he was no longer around to pay it back, he would take her two sons to work for him until the debt was paid off. She called Elisha a prophet of God and explained the situation. After asking what she had available she replied just a jar of oil, to which he told her ask around and collect as many empty jars as you can. When the jars were all filled, he told her she could sell the oil and make enough money to pay back her husband's debtors.

The Bible has many such stories of God supplying the need at the right time. He is still the same and still supplies - we have no need to worry about where even the next meal is coming from, what we will wear or whether He will take care of us.

God in Christ bountifully supplies our every need from His immense riches.

Monday June 21, 2021

Proverbs 1:23 Turn you at my reproof: behold, I will pour out my spirit unto you, I will make known my words unto you.

God's Word provides reproof/warnings and corrections when we are not following the standards outlined there for us. The Epistles are written for that purpose as we read in II Timothy 3:16. We are given the doctrine of what God expects from us in the books of Romans, Ephesians, first and second Thessalonians; reproof is provided from first and second Corinthians and Philippians, when we make mistakes and are off the Word; then we receive the correction and instructions on how to get on track from Galatians and Colossians.

When we break fellowship, God wants us to own up to our mistakes, acknowledge where we went wrong and of our free will choice turn back to Him. He is always willing and ready to forgive and restore us back to good standing with Him.

As born-again believers we will not lose the gift of holy spirit that God has placed in each one of us like they did in the Old Testament. But when we are not in alignment with God's Word, we are missing out on that sweet fellowship with our Heavenly Father as well as maybe losing our future heavenly rewards if we consistently stay out of fellowship.

Tuesday June 22, 2021

Proverbs 6:23 For the commandment is a lamp; and the law is light; and reproofs of instruction are the way of life:

So many times, we have seen religious doctrines changed or amended to justify people's lifestyles. One of the most glaring contradictions is from Romans chapter one where God's Word is very clear on His dislike for the homosexual lifestyle. God is love and loves all people; He did not differentiate when He sent His only begotten Son to die for the world. He however, mentions several behaviors that are not acceptable to Him, and one is clearly documented in Romans where it reads, "for even their women did change the natural use into that which is against nature:

And likewise also the men, leaving the natural use of the woman, burned in their lust one toward another; men with men working that which is unseemly, and receiving in themselves that recompence of their error which was meet."

We cannot change what the Word of God says just because we do not like it. The true standards still remain, and God's Word shines a spotlight on these truths.

God's Word is like a lamp that shines a light on man-made legalisms, and doctrines pointing out the errors, highlighting what God wants us to know, and helping us see the right path to take. If unsure of a teaching, doctrine, or standard, consider checking the source and comparing it with the truths of the Word for accuracy.

Wednesday June 23, 2021

Psalms 25:9 The meek will he guide in judgment: and the meek will he teach his way.

The book of Acts documents the life of a man called Saul who persecuted the church of God. His sole mission was to capture, imprison, and kill people who followed Jesus. He stood by and watched as a young man named Stephen was stoned to death just because of His stand for God. When Saul was confronted about his actions by Jesus Himself, he was meek to repent and change his whole lifestyle and behavior to reflect what God wanted him to, even changing his name to Paul. This is the same Paul who became a great apostle of Jesus Christ and wrote several of the epistles for us.

Likewise, we as believers are meek when we are confronted with mistakes or when our lives are not in alignment with God's Word. As we stay humble to the truths of God's Word, to accept the loving reproof and correction we receive, He will open it up to us, so we learn everything we need to navigate this life to live that more abundant life He has promised us.

Thursday June 24, 2021

Psalms 27:1 The LORD is my light and my salvation; whom shall I fear? the LORD is the strength of my life; of whom shall I be afraid?

Just as shining a light into a dark rook allows us to see where we need to walk and to find what we are looking for, God's Word lights up world for those who chose to believe. The light of God's Word illuminates the hiding places of the adversary so we can put on all the Word we need to defeat his attacks. Being sly and cunning is one way the adversary hides his true intentions to trick God's children into falling into his traps.

We may be spending time with friends or family and some things may be said or done that are contrary to God's Word. If we are not vigilant, we may be blinded by the darkness around us. We go to God's Word to find the truth regarding the situation in question allowing it to shine and dispel the darkness. God has already provided our salvation, so we are confident in our righteousness. With God as our strength we have no need to be afraid of the adversary's attacks. God's banner is ever present over His children.

Friday June 25, 2021

Psalms 37:5 Commit thy way unto the LORD; trust also in him; and he shall bring it to pass.

The Word of God is full of promises for us to claim because He wants us to enjoy a more abundant life. As parents we always want the best for our children, so we set rules and standards for them to follow. Having lived life we know and understand the many pitfalls that can snare children so easily. We encourage our children that we love them, and they can trust that we want them to be safe and happy. We help them understand what can happen, how they could get hurt if they do not follow the standards we have in place. For example, letting them know it is unsafe to go swimming alone until they are older, because if they need help someone is there. Or we may instruct them to only use the designated path to and from school instead of trying to dash across the railroad tracks which could be dangerous. As we remind them of our love and care for them, they develop more trust in us and are obedient to our rules.

God truly wants to give us our hearts desires because He loves us and wants the best for us. He only asks that we trust Him completely and surrender our all so He can put His plans for us into motion.

Saturday June 26, 2021

Psalms 69:19 Thou hast known my reproach, and my shame, and my dishonour: mine adversaries `are` all before thee.

King David recognized and acknowledges his mistakes and sins. He is remorseful and trusting God to forgive him and protect him from his enemies. He lays it all out before God, and humbly pleads his case. When we make a mistake, we immediately turn to God to hear and help us. God knows and sees everything; He knows who our enemies are and how they attempt to disgrace us and mock us. We trust Him to move us past these attacks.

We may have enemies for simply standing on the rightly divided Word of God. Someone may be so persuaded and sincere of what they believe that they are angry with us when we show them from the Word, where they are off. Their sincerity does not change the accuracy of the Word and so we stand firmly on "what does the Word say?" We trust God to protect us from those worldly attacks.

Consider the truth that we wrestle not against flesh and blood so whatever comes our way is from the adversary. The only way to defeat the attacks of the adversary in our lives is by the Word of God.

Sunday June 27, 2021

Psalms 103:3 Who forgiveth all thine iniquities; who healeth all thy diseases;

God does nothing halfway and made provision for our physical as well as spiritual health. John 3:16 tells us that God sent His Son that "whosoever believes" will be saved and in Romans 10 we learn that once we confess Jesus as Lord in our lives we are saved/made whole spiritually. Jesus shed His blood for the remission/ cleansing or forgiveness of all our sins. At that time, we are born-again of God's spirit and filled with God's mighty power and made righteous.

In first Peter 2, we read that by the stripes of Jesus Christ we were healed. His body was broken for our physical healing. Even today when we partake of Holy Communion, we bring back to memory these truths. By way of what God accomplished for us through His Son Jesus Christ, we are forgiven of our sins – made whole spiritually and healed of our physical illnesses as we believe and trust Him.

Monday June 28, 2021

Romans 6:12 Let not sin therefore reign in your mortal body, that ye should obey it in the lusts thereof.

As a child, as soon as I made a mistake or disobeyed, I struggled with how I would tell my parents, not whether or not to tell them. I knew that the only way to get back into their good graces was to acknowledge my wrong and ask for forgiveness. The longer I put it off the harder it was to go to them and try to make it right.

As born-again believers we do not want to stay out of fellowship with our Heavenly Father. God wants us to know of His unconditional love and that His arms are always wide open to receive us when we repent. Just like children are afraid to go to the parents the longer they put it off, it gets harder for us to go to our Heavenly Father if we put off confessing our broken fellowship too long.

We are human/mortal beings and will make mistakes, breaking fellowship, but the key is to come back to right standing as soon as possible by "confessing our sins – broken fellowship". God reassures us that He is "faithful and just to forgive us our sins and cleanse us from all unrighteousness" I John 1:9

Tuesday June 29, 2021

Romans 6:14 For sin shall not have dominion over you: for ye are not under the law, but under grace.

As children we are aware that our earthly parents love us, and we are keenly aware of the punishment if we disobey, but sometimes we feel that because they love us, it is ok to go against their wishes. We might try to justify it by telling ourselves that they love us, and it will be just fine. My thinking was that although I knew they loved me and would forgive me after the initial punishment, I did not want to disappoint them.

In the same way, we know God's love is everlasting and unconditional, His gift of holy spirit is permanent, but that does not give us a reason to allow our minds to be clouded by the adversary regarding living in sin. We live in the Grace Administration where we have been saved by God's grace. Therefore, we are no longer under legalism and we should not allow sin to have control of our lives/actions. And especially not use the fact that we are under grace to allow us to remain in our state of broken fellowship.

Wednesday June 30, 2021

Psalms 33:11 The counsel of the Lord (God's Word) standeth for ever, the thoughts of his heart to all generations.

God gave His Word to man thousands of years ago written in the stars first then He gave Moses the ten commandments written on tablets of stone. His standards for man have not changed over the years because God is constant and does not change.

It is so comforting that all God's commandments come with promises. He led the Israelites to a land flowing with milk and honey and He promised their days would be prolonged as they kept His Word. We are promised God's protection, that He will be our refuge, our strength, and provider as we are faithful to His Word. In Ephesians chapter six God addresses children and promise them long life if they obey their parents. The same applies to us as we are obedient to our Heavenly Father.

When we rightly divide the Word of God, His heart and will for His children is made clear. We know the Word will never fail and remains unchanging, so His will from generation to generation is made known and is constant. We do not ever have to be confused as to what we are to do with our lives because the Word of God is our guide.

JULY

Thursday July 1, 2021

Romans 8:31 What shall we then say to these things? If God be for us, who can be against us?

Growing up with my three sisters and two brothers was always an adventure. Sometimes we would get into fights with each other or get angry with each other, but the anger never lasted too long. We joked about being too silly, because one of us would always do or say something funny that had us in stitches. In spite of our disagreements, we knew we had each other's back. If another child had an issue or problem with any one of us, the problem became all of ours. We felt like as long as we stuck together, no one could get to us.

As God's children, we are assured that He is on our side, He will fight our battles for us, He causes us to prevail against the attacks of the adversary because He is for us and never leaves us alone. We need have no concerns of how we will fight our battles, stand against those attacks because we know we are covered and that God 'has our back' as we stay faithful, trusting Him to see us through.

Friday July 2, 2021

Romans 8:37 Nay, in all these things we are more than conquerors through him that loved us.

Some people are born with physical impairments and others for example a soldier may return home having lost one or more of his/her limbs. We see their stories on the news about how they can run a race or play basketball sitting in a wheelchair. I admire these people because they help keep my mind grounded when I start to feel I cannot accomplish something I would like to do. Recently I watched a documentary about this person climbing one the highest mountains in the world. It was tough and he had to stop and take a breather more than once, but he remained focused on his goal to reach the top of that mountain, and he did it.

No matter what situations we face in this life, no matter how high or unclimbable the mountain (doubt, worry, fear, anxiety) in our lives may seem, we are confident that we are more than (super) conquerors through Jesus Christ our Lord, who loved us enough to give His life for us. Let us continue to claim that daily. We are what the Word of God says we are.

Saturday July 3, 2021

Romans 10:9 That if thou shalt confess with thy mouth the Lord Jesus, and shalt believe in thine heart that God hath raised him from the dead, thou shalt be saved.
10 For with the heart man believeth unto righteousness; and with the mouth confession is made unto salvation.

When I was about five years old, I remember an event which has become a bit fuzzy in my mind over the years. There was a really bright light from the sky shining down over our town. Several adults started coming together, some praying, some singing an old gospel song "when the saints go marching in." Somebody stated it could not be Christ's return because there were no angels and no trumpets. Then as fast as it appeared, it gradually got dimmer and disappeared from our sight. In my little five-year-old mind, I wanted to know what that meant. When I asked my mother, she said that Christ would return to take the born-again back to heaven with Him. My next question was "how do I get born again?" She replied that I needed to ask Jesus to come into my life, so I did.

These two verses hold the simple key to our salvation and after I took a Bible class it became very clear to me. So, my mother's answer was almost accurate, and I believe I was born-again then, but it is a two-part response. We confess Jesus Christ as Lord in our lives, and we believe in our hearts that God raised Him from the dead. The Word says we are then 'absolutely' saved. Our believing is the door to our righteousness and our confession by mouth ensures our salvation.

It's as simple as that; let us not complicate it and give God thanks for all He accomplished for us by way of His Son our Lord and Savior Jesus Christ.

Sunday July 4, 2021

Romans 12:2 And be not conformed to this world: but be ye transformed by the renewing of your mind, that ye may prove what `is` that good, and acceptable, and perfect, will of God.

The word 'conformed' is to be molded like or to comply with. So many Christians find themselves behaving a way that is socially or politically acceptable to the standards of the world or people they associate with. God's Word asks us to instead renew our minds by being transformed or changed in our actions, behavior, or character. To do this, we decide to know and understand God's Word, we recognize we have God in Christ in us, God's love is a real presence in our lives and that we have sonship rights legally given to us.

As born-again believers and sons of God, we have free will choice to not allow ourselves to get in agreement with the things of this world. Instead we change our thinking to the truths of God's Word so our character mimics what is good, perfect, and acceptable to God.

Monday July 5, 2021

Romans 13:11 And that, knowing the time, that now `it is` high time to awake out of sleep: for now `is` our salvation nearer than when we believed.

The year 2020 was unprecedented in my knowledge of worldly upheavals. The year started with a fast-moving virus that quickly became a pandemic. Millions died and were dying as more people became infected and the medical world seemed at a lost as to how to handle it. Businesses were shut down, people asked to maintain social distance and wear face coverings in public in an effort to curb the spread. Nothing seemed to be effective. Eleven months later, the pharmaceutical industry produced a vaccine (not without controversy) to get rid of or at least limit the spread of the infection. The world watched in anticipation as one of the leading political powers in the world went through a trying and roller coaster election.

Paying attention to biblical prophecies show us that we are living in perilous days leading up to the new chapter in God's plan. We do not face these challenges with fear or anxiety but complete trust that God will see us through whatever lies ahead. It is no time to get spiritually lazy, but to get up and move, speaking the Word with boldness as we prepare for Christ's return.

Tuesday July 6, 2021

II Corinthians 4:5 For we preach not ourselves, but Christ Jesus the Lord; and ourselves your servants for Jesus' sake.
6 For God, who commanded the light to shine out of darkness, hath shined in our hearts, to give the light of the knowledge of the glory of God in the face of Jesus Christ.

God called us to speak His Word. Whether people believe or not, it is still God's Word; we share the gospel of Jesus Christ and what is available in Him. Our responsibility is not to defend God's Word, but to speak the truth of the salvation we have in Christ Jesus. God's Word when rightly divided helps us understand that it is not about us, we did not write the book. God's Word was given by revelation to holy men of God and written for men and women who love God and want to know Him better.

As God commanded the light to shine forth dispelling all darkness in Genesis chapter one, when He said "let there be light", so He has called us to be the lights of this world to shine brightly and dispel the darkness in a dark world. We have no need to argue with those who do not agree because whether people believe it or not does not change the validity of the truth of God's Word.

Wednesday July 7, 2021

Acts 1:8 But ye shall receive power, after that the Holy Ghost is come upon you: and ye shall be witnesses unto me both in Jerusalem, and in all Judaea, and in Samaria, and unto the uttermost part of the earth.

When we are born-again, we all receive God's gift of holy spirit and the inherent power that comes with it. As Jesus Christ commissioned His disciples to be witnesses, we too are called to go out and share the truths of God's Word, to be witnesses of His power. The disciples were told to go to the "uttermost part" or the ends of the earth. There is no limit on how far we should go to speak the Word. Many great evangelists and ministers have traveled all around the world over the years to reach as many as possible with the gospel of God's Word, His Son Jesus Christ and salvation in His name.

Believers everywhere take the place of the absent Christ, and as His representatives it is our responsibility to be witnesses of all He has done for us and the power we have. We do not all have to travel all around the world, because we belong to a household with believers everywhere. Wherever we are, each believer speaks the Word in their communities.

Consider stepping out of your 'comfort zone' and reaching out to those you meet while shopping, at work, or at school.

Thursday July 8, 2021

Luke 24:32 And they said one to another, Did not our heart burn within us, while he talked with us by the way, and while he opened to us the scriptures?

That is the same reaction we will have when we get quiet and let God speak to our hearts. When we get a clear understanding of the Word and it comes alive for us, we become valiant for the truth. For many years, I had questions about God and His Word that never seemed clear to me. Every answer I was given led to another question, and I just became more confused each time. I visited several religious organizations believing I would eventually find the answers to my many questions.

One day I took a Bible class, and I literally felt my heart "burn within me." I had answers at last, and it was almost overwhelming. It was hard to believe that it was so simple and that it was right there in the Bible, which so many different theological preachers never were able to help me find. I never blamed them because I realized they showed me what they knew. One of the things I've come to realize over the years is that the phrase "you can only go as far as you've been taught," is so true.

Not too long after that I was offered the opportunity to take more advanced Bible classes which I turned down initially until one day I heard God speak to me. Later I realized it reminded me of when Samuel heard the voice of God. I heard Father say to me that after all my years of questions I now have an opportunity to get answers and why am I turning it down. With tears in my eyes, I immediately called the class coordinator and over the next year or two took more Bible classes up to the advanced level. To this day I still get that feeling every time I repeat one of these Bible classes.

Friday July 9, 2021

Ezekiel 48:35 It was round about eighteen thousand measures: and the name of the city from that day shall be, The LORD is there.

(Jehovah-Shammah – ever present). God is everywhere present so wherever we set aside as our place of worship, He is right there to bless. The psalmist's states that wherever he goes God is right there and he cannot hide from the presence of God. In Psalm 16 we read that God is always right there with us, which is more accurate for us in the Grace Administration. We are born again and have God in Christ in us, we have been given God's gift of holy spirit and everywhere there is a believer, God is right there. When God by way of Moses led the children of Israel out of Egypt, He promised to be with them and be a "very present help in trouble."

I am reminded of a joke about an elderly couple who were in love and they were trying to be together as much as possible. In his attempt to help their children understand what they wanted, the man stated, "I love her so much, everywhere she is, I at." The children understood and finally gave their blessings for them to get married. God loves us and "everywhere we is, He at."

We do not need to "take a number" when we need to spend time in God's presence. He is ready, willing, and able to respond and be there when we need Him. Get quiet and spend some time with your Heavenly Father who is right there, right now.

Saturday July 10, 2021

Psalms 27:4 One thing have I desired of the LORD, that will I seek after; that I may dwell in the house of the LORD all the days of my life, to behold the beauty of the LORD, and to enquire in his temple.

Many can relate to getting so attached to the home they grew up in they never want to leave home. When they graduate from high school, they attend a local community college so they can stay at home. After college they get a job in the same town so they can stay home and maintain their level of comfort. Even if the place is not the most comfortable, nice, or not even well furnished, it is home and that is where they feel most loved and welcomed. Our hearts desire as children of God is to spend eternity with Him. We anticipate the time when we can just sit in His presence and revel in His power and glory.

As an adult when I travel away from home for business or even if I am visiting family, I have such a hard time falling asleep the first two nights. I toss and turn for several hours, and nothing seems to help me get comfortable. Not so with being in God's house of worship, His temple. We want to be among like-minded believers fellowshipping together in praise and worship in the presence of our Heavenly Father.

Let your imagination take you on a trip to God's kingdom – our heavenly home. How much better and more fulfilling it will be to be in the very presence of God.

Sunday July 11, 2021

Genesis 17:1 And when Abram was ninety years old and nine, the LORD appeared to Abram, and said unto him, I am the Almighty God; (El Shaddai) walk before me, and be thou perfect.

Jehovah, El Shaddai (the Almighty God). With God Almighty no obstacles is too big. He bountifully supplies our every need as He is the same today. God made a promise, a covenant with Abraham He was determined to keep. Abraham was ninety-nine years old, his wife Sarah about ninety years and God remembered His promise to them that they would have a son. When God spoke to Abraham all He asked was that Abraham trust Him to bring that promise to pass. As El Shaddai the emphasis is God being Almighty and all powerful, and there is nothing too hard for Him to do. God also made a promise to the children of Israel to get them out of Egypt safely and lead them to the "promised land," and He kept that promise. There were times they doubted Him when with the five senses it looked almost impossible. God's repeated response was always "trust me and believe."

God asks us to do the same – trust Him with our whole heart and not to lean on our own understandings. As we do, He keeps His promise to bountifully meet our every need.

Monday July 12, 2021

Exodus 15:26 And said, If thou wilt diligently hearken to the voice of the LORD thy God, and wilt do that which is right in his sight, and wilt give ear to his commandments, and keep all his statutes, I will put none of these diseases upon thee, which I have brought upon the Egyptians: for I am the LORD that healeth thee.

(Jehovah-Ropheka/Rapha – the Lord that heals). God reminds His people many times in His Word, that "I am the Lord that heals you." He instructed the Israelites to kill the Passover lamb to atone for their sins and for healing thousands of years ago. In Psalms 105:37 we read "He brought them forth also with silver and gold: and there was not one feeble person among their tribes." I am sure there must have been some very elderly people in the group, some were probably not in the best of health, but God healed everyone, so they could make the journey.

For us in the Grace Administration, God sent Jesus Christ to be the symbolic 'Passover lamb' to atone for our sins and for our healing. His blood was shed for the remission of our sins, His body was broken and by His stripes we were healed. In thankfulness we go to God with believing hearts for healing, because He is the Lord that healeth."

Tuesday July 13, 2021

Exodus 17:15 And Moses built an altar, and called the name of it Jehovahnissi:

(Jehovah Nissi – my banner) A banner symbolizes the connection with someone like a flag or logo symbolizes what country it is connected to. God helped the Israelites win a battle, by telling them to hold up a banner; when they got tired and the banner started to fall the enemy was defeating them, but when they kept the banner held up high they prevailed. Afterwards Moses built an alter at that place and called it Jehovah-nissi.

There's a song I can remember singing in Sunday School as a child that I still remember when I think of God being our banner. It goes in part like this 'His banner over me is love; The Lord is mine and I am His, His banner over me is love

The Lord is mine and I am His, His banner over me is love,
The Lord is mine and I am His; His banner over me is love,
His banner over me is love!

God's heart is always full of unconditional love for His children. He holds us in high esteem and wants the world to know we are His beloved. Our flag, our banner is the love of God. How do we respond to God's love?

Wednesday July 14, 2021

Judges 6:23 And the LORD said unto him, Peace be unto thee; fear not: thou shalt not die.
24 Then Gideon built an altar there unto the LORD, and called it Jehovahshalom: unto this day it is yet in Ophrah of the Abiezrites.

Jehovah-shalom (Our peace): God is our peace, and God gives us peace. In God's Word we read of God promising to give His peace to David, when He promised to give him a son. In Numbers chapter six, God promises Moses to make his face shine on him, and be to him, lift up is countenance upon him, and give him peace *or* shalom.

True peace only comes from God, it is complete, whole and with it we have no lack. It cannot and does not come from anything or anyone on this earth. God says that as long as we walk according to His Word, we will always have an undisturbed rest/quiet. We will have nothing to fear because we will be confident in His promise to take care of us.

Thursday July 15, 2021

Revelation 3:20 Behold, I stand at the door, and knock: if any man hear my voice, and open the door, I will come in to him, and will sup with him, and he with me.

Jesus Christ came down to earth by the will of His Father, God to be the Redeemer for man. He lived on earth teaching only what His Father wanted Him to share and doing only God's will all the time. Jesus was tempted of the devil – Matthew chapter four, yet He never sinned – Hebrews chapter four. He was arrested, suffered unimaginable torture, and died to pay the legal price to get us back from the adversary. After being dead and buried for three days and three nights, God raised Jesus Christ up from the dead and ascended Him up on high to sit at the Father's right hand.

Now Jesus Christ is asking ever so gently as He knocks on the door of our hearts to give Him access. Many have not quite understood that He will never force His way in; it has to be our free will choice. He so desires an intimate relationship with us, as our mediator to the Father, as we go to God in prayer in the name of Jesus Christ spending quality time with us. Our response is to confess Him as Lord in our lives. Once we have done that, let us daily continue that precious, intimate relationship with our Heavenly Father through His Son Jesus Christ

Friday July 16, 2021

Psalms 23:1 The LORD is my shepherd; I shall not want.

Jehovah-Roi/Raah – The Lord as our shepherd makes sure our every need is met; we lack nothing as we stay within His will.

The word 'raah' is the Hebrew form of the word 'roi', which means shepherd. A shepherd is one who "tends to/ cares for or raises sheep". The primary duties of a shepherd are to take care of and protect his sheep; he takes them to areas plentiful in foliage so they can graze and near a brook or stream where they can get enough water to drink and stay hydrated. Another significant responsibility is to keep an eye out for danger such as prey or plants that may be poisonous.

In Isaiah 40:11 it talks about the Lord Jehovah protecting his people like a shepherd – "He will feed his 'flock' and carry His lambs in His bosom." That speaks to the heart of God for His children – His tender love and care, and protection. He 'gently leads' also denoting His hands-on guidance over the most vulnerable. The Word also talks about how the shepherd will go look for one lost sheep even if he still has ninety left – he makes sure that one is brought back safely

Ministers of God are like shepherd, taking care off, helping protect and guide them with counsel from the rightly divided Word. If one goes off, the minister/shepherd finds them, gently leads them back and helps them renew their mind.

Saturday July 17, 2021

Jeremiah 23:6 In his days Judah shall be saved, and Israel shall dwell safely: and this is his name whereby he shall be called, THE LORD OUR RIGHTEOUSNESS.

(Jehovah-Zidkenu/Tsidkenu – our Righteousness). God has made us righteous as He is, through the accomplished works of Jesus Christ. **Righteousness** is the God-given justification/freedom that enables a person to stand in the presence of God without any consciousness of sin, guilt, imperfections, or condemnation.

As born-again believers one of the main things to defeat us spiritually is if we do not understand and accept all what we have in Christ. The adversary causes us to let feelings of sin-consciousness burden us down and we do not believe that God has already made us acceptable to Him. Most times we read the verse John 3:16 and acknowledge that God sent His only begotten Son to die for us, and forget the second of the verse that states "whosoever believeth in Him should not perish but have everlasting life." Our redemption is complete, and we are free from the bondage of sin, justified (in God's eyes just as if we never sinned), and made righteous.

One writer makes it very clear by stating that righteousness is not dependent on anything we can do, no amount of penance or fasting, it is not "by the cross we bear, but by the cross that Jesus Christ bore for you." We give God thanks for all He did for us as our righteousness. Amen.

Sunday July 18, 2021

Exodus 31:13 Speak thou also unto the children of Israel, saying, Verily my sabbaths ye shall keep: for it is a sign between me and you throughout your generations; that ye may know that I am the LORD that doth sanctify you.

(Jehovah-Qadesh - Our Sanctifier). 1Corinthians 1:30 lists a few things we have in Christ given to us by God himself – "*God is made unto us wisdom, and righteousness, and sanctification, and redemption*." One of our rights as children of God is sanctification. When Jesus Christ paid the price to redeem (buy) us back from the adversary, God sanctified/set us apart for heaven, as His very own. In Romans 8:17 we read that we are heirs of God, and joint-heirs with Christ. As sons of God and heirs we are legally entitled to all that He has; we share our inheritance with our big brother Jesus Christ because we are joint-heirs with Him.

Part of what we will receive is our inheritance in the new heaven and earth. The adversary has no hold on us and cannot stop us from going to heaven or from receiving our inheritance. This is one of the reason's we can live a more than abundant life. We know that no matter what is going on here on earth, our place in heaven in assured and our inheritance is sure.

Monday July 19, 2021

I Samuel 1:3 And this man went up out of his city yearly to worship and to sacrifice unto the LORD of hosts in Shiloh. And the two sons of Eli, Hophni and Phinehas, the priests of the LORD, were there.

(Jehovah-Zebaoth/Tsaba – Lord of hosts). God's Jehovah titles help describe Him so we can understand who is. God is Spirit, so many times in the Word human characteristics are used when talking about Him so we can get a clear picture of what He wants us to know. The different names/ titles used in the Bible also give us a better understanding of who our God is. From Genesis to Revelation are documented the mighty power of God, also His tender heart of love, and He has remained the same from generation to generation as they remained obedient to His Word. Each generation was instructed to teach God's Word to their children.

God is almighty, all powerful and worthy of all our praise; He is with us at all times and is our refuge and strength. With God's holy spirit in us we can communicate with Him anywhere, anytime. We teach God's Word to our children instructing them to in turn teach it to their children.

Tuesday July 20, 2021

Psalms 23:2 He maketh me to lie down in green pastures: he leadeth me beside the still waters.
3 He restoreth my soul: he leadeth me in the paths of righteousness for his name's sake.

Jesus Christ is sometimes called "the Good Shepherd" and as such He takes care of, provides for, and protects us. Just as the shepherd leads his sheep to grassier areas so they can be well fed, so as we follow in the steps of Jesus Christ, God leads us to where He wants us to be so we can be nourished by His Word. It took many years, but I did find that place where I get nourished with the truths of God's Word in many different ways – from other believers, ministers, and Word-centered publications.

As we trust God and His Word, we are at rest, peaceful, and always prosperous, and He will keep us calm, soothing away our fears and drying our tears. Knowing that we are righteous is God's sight is so reassuring and comforting. God's presence gives us renewed peace of mind and by standing on His Word we are confident we are on the path that pleases Him, and brings Him honor and glory.

Wednesday July 21, 2021

Psalms 7:17 I will praise the LORD according to his righteousness: and will sing praise to the name of the LORD most high.

(Jehovah Elyon – the Most High)

The Lord most high is the Lord and deserves our praise and admiration and our praise and worship are forms of prayer. The following are examples of praise to God.

I Chronicles 16:25(a) "… For great is the LORD, and greatly to be praised…"

Psalms 103:1 Bless the LORD, O my soul: and all that is within me, bless his holy name.
2 Bless the LORD, O my soul, and forget not all his benefits:

Psalms 107:8 Oh that men would praise the LORD for his goodness, and for his wonderful works to the children of men!

Psalms 99:9 Exalt the LORD our God, and worship at his holy hill; for the LORD our God is holy.

Psalms 100 is full of praise and worship to God – we've even made it into a song.

Psalms 100:1-5 Make a joyful noise unto the LORD, all ye lands.
Serve the LORD with gladness: come before his presence with singing.
Know ye that the LORD he is God: it is he that hath made us, and not we ourselves; we are his people, and the sheep

of his pasture.
Enter into his gates with thanksgiving, and into his courts with praise: be thankful unto him and bless his name.
For the LORD is good; his mercy is everlasting; and his truth endureth to all generations.

He is seated on high in the heavenlies in righteousness.

Thursday July 22, 2021

Genesis 1:1 In the beginning God created the heaven and the earth.

(Elohim – the Creator) or the Supreme God. God created the heavens and the earth which was then made 'without form and void' by the devil – Lucifer, somewhere between Genesis 1:1 and Genesis 1:2. After, the Spirit that was God "moved upon the face of the waters.", God then began to put the earth back together for man.

The amplified version of Hebrews 11:3 read that "By faith [that is, with an inherent trust and enduring confidence in the power, wisdom and goodness of God] we understand that the worlds (universe, ages) were framed *and* created [formed, put in order, and equipped for their intended purpose] by the word of God, so that what is seen was not made out of things which are visible."

From Genesis 1:3 to Genesis 1:31 we read of God putting the world together by His words. Evolutionists would have us believe that things just went "kaboom" and there was everything and everybody or that God created apes and gradually they morphed into man. As Christians we believe that the Bible is the Word of God given by revelation to holy men.

Friday July 23, 2021

Psalms 119:160 Thy word is true from the beginning: and every one of thy righteous judgments endureth for ever.

God's Word is His will from Genesis 1:1 to Revelation 22:21 and is truth. We cannot pick what we want to believe and reject what we do not like. Over the years there has been some confusion of Jesus's birth. Religions have historically celebrated it on December 25th every year. After years of biblical research, we have been able to accurately pinpoint the birth of Jesus Christ to be on September eleventh. (Read Jesus Christ Our Promised Seed by Dr. V.P. Wierwille for further study.) Another topic surrounding Jesus' death mostly about when exactly He died and how long He was in the tomb causes no end of confusion in the Christian world. Years of biblical research has accurately proven that Jesus died and was buried on Wednesday and not Good Friday as we have been taught to believe for so many years. The prophecy stated that He would be in the grave for three days and three nights. (Read Jesus Christ Our Passover by Dr. V.P. Wierwille for further study.)

Our responsibility is to study the Word, so we get a clear understanding of those truths. Then we renew our minds, change our thinking to the truth so our lives line up with what God says and what God wants us to believe.

Saturday July 24, 2021

Psalms 23:5 Thou preparest a table before me in the presence of mine enemies: thou anointest my head with oil; my cup runneth over.
6 Surely goodness and mercy shall follow me all the days of my life: and I will dwell in the house of the LORD for ever

Several years ago, I enjoyed employment at a hospital and had a great relationship with everyone I worked with. One day, a new employee came in who was really rude and disrespectful to me. I knew I had done nothing to her and did not deserve that treatment, so I patiently waited to see an improvement, which did not happen. Many others reminded me I was her superior and could write her up or report her to the manager. I decided to pray instead, and one day she came up to me and asked if she could talk to me. I said sure, and we went into a quiet area where she apologized for her behavior and stated she thinks she was just jealous of me, of how everyone seemed to like me and I always seemed to be in a "good mood.' Then she said what I thought was a strange request at the time. She asked if I would allow her to be my friend. Of course, I accepted he apology and replied that yes, I would like it if we were friends.

Even when it feels like we are surrounded by enemies, or there are those who are against us, God is right there with us. He can make it, so they want to be our friends, even inviting us to stay for dinner.

We are God's anointed, He covers us with His protection, and we lack nothing. God is good to us and He does not pass judgement or punish us, even when we deserve it. As His children our place in the heavenlies with our Lord is reserved forever.

Sunday July 25, 2021

Psalms 37:25 I have been young, and now am old; yet have I not seen the righteous forsaken, nor his seed begging bread.
26 He is ever merciful, and lendeth; and his seed is blessed.

As our God and Heavenly Father, we can trust that God is truth and cannot lie. Thousands of years ago, He promised the children of Israel to protect them and provide for them as long as they kept His commandments. As Jehovah-jireh, the one who sees and provides He is aware of the needs of His children even before they know it and He takes care of it. When He led them out of Egypt, everyone from infant to aged got out safely. When they needed to get across the Red Sea, God parted it for them, when they were hungry, he provided meat and manna. God took care of them every step of the way.

God is still the same today – He does not change. From our youth to old age, He is with us. He provides for us, so we have no lack. That is God's merciful kindness to His children, who He makes sure stays blessed.

Monday July 26, 2021

Jeremiah 30:17(a) For I will restore health unto thee, and I will heal thee of thy wounds, saith the LORD;

The Bible tells us "every good gift and every perfect gift is from above" from God the Father of lights. One of the many gifts we Heavenly Father is that He does not want us to be sickly and has made provision for that. In Psalms 103 God specifically states that He heals all our diseases, and in III John:2 He wants us to be in health. In Jeremiah, the promise is He will not only heal but restore health as well. What a promise to hold on to and claim! God is definitely NOT sending sickness and suffering to test us or teach us a lesson.

Are you sick; is your health compromised by any disease? Have the doctors said, "it doesn't look good?" Put all your trust in God because He wants to see all His children healthy. He wants to stop the adversary's attack as he tries to steal our health. God's promise is to heal and to give you back your health. Can you claim that right now? Remember, God is in the business of healing.

Tuesday July 27, 2021

Jeremiah 33:3 Call unto me, and I will answer thee, and show thee great and mighty things, which thou knowest not.

Previously I mentioned how I tried several religious organizations searching for the truth about God's Word, asking questions but getting no answers. It was so frustrating, I had decided to stop going to church for a while, and spent my days asking God for direction. One day I said to a friend, "I am looking for somewhere to worship God with other Christians." She introduced me to a ministry that called themselves 'non-denominational' and I was immediately intrigued. All the other denominations had not been able to give me any clear answers. I visited and heard that theirs was a place for people "who loved God and His Word." After I took a Bible class, I found so many answers to my many questions and was so much closer to understanding God's Word.

God never turns His back on us, because He is a loving Father who cares for His children. All we have to do is call Him, reach out in meekness and repentance, God promises to answer, to show us how much He loves us and all He can do when we trust Him. I am thankful I never completely gave up in my search for answers from God.

Wednesday July 28, 2021

Zephaniah 3:17 The LORD thy God in the midst of thee is mighty; he will save, he will rejoice over thee with joy; he will rest in his love, he will joy over thee with singing.

God promised His people so many times that He would go with them; they would never have to face their enemies alone. He kept that promise every time. As born-again believers we are promised even more security than the Old Testament believers who had to depend on God putting His spirit upon them. When we do what God asks of us in Romans 10:9 we receive God's gift of holy spirit, He places His incorruptible/imperishable seed in us, and we are His children.

God Almighty is with us at all times; no matter where we go, He is in us and with us. There may be times we experience grief, heartbreak, sorrow, or loss and feel like we are in a dark place, God is still with us – He will not leave us. When we are happy, rejoicing in some victory celebration, God is right there to rejoice with us. He is powerful to save and protect us so we can rest confidently in His love.

Thursday July 29, 2021

Isaiah 46:4 And even to your old age I am he; and even to hoar hairs will I carry you: I have made, and I will bear; even I will carry, and will deliver you.

I had a conversation with an elderly person some time ago, who reminded me of that verse. She had been feeling sad and depressed for a while because all her children were adults and had not just moved out, but had moved thousands of miles away; her husband had died and even her neighbors had died and their children had moved away. One day during her devotionals she was talking to God about her loneliness, praying for help to get past those feelings, and He gave her that verse.

As I get older, I find myself referring to the words written here and making them personal to me. It brings me comfort and peace of mind to know that I can rely on and trust in God's presence in every season of my life. What a wonderful reminder that even in our old age, God is with us and promises to never leave us. He will see us through the tough times and deliver us; the lonely times and be our friend; the sad times and be our comfort and peace.

Friday July 30, 2021

Deuteronomy 5:7 Thou shalt have none other gods before me.

Self -explanatory. God, the Father of our Lord and Savior Jesus Christ is the one and only true God. Nothing or no one else should be above Him in our lives. We read in 1 John 5:21 Little children, keep yourselves from idols. Amen.

(The Amplified version reads) "Little children, keep yourselves from idols (false God's) - from anything and everything that would occupy the place in your heart due to God, from any sort of substitute for Him that would take first place in your life. Amen (so let it be).

It may be easy for us to say that God is first in our lives, and we do not worship any other gods or idols, it may not even be evident to us that we are; but as we see here that could be "anything and everything that would occupy the place in your heart" that should belong to God. Some examples in our lives of an idol or god are - relationships, loved ones, jobs/careers, money - we can get focused on amassing wealth, hobbies, your favorite sports team, favorite entertainer, actor, or actress. These would hinder our direct connection to our Heavenly Father.

"NO OTHER GODS BEFORE ME" is still relevant in our day and time. Maybe even more so as we live in the Grace Administration - since God sent His Son to redeem, reconcile and buy us back from the adversary.

Saturday July 31, 2021

Psalms 121:1 I will lift up mine eyes unto the hills, from whence cometh my help.

David talks about looking towards the hills for help; maybe because the temple where he would worship was on a hill. We do not know that for sure, but it seems implied. Our help definitely does not come from the hills or mountains. David goes on to clarify that his help comes from God the Creator of the heavens and the earth. In our own worship and prayer to God, we look up towards the heavens, not that we expect help from the heavens but figuratively we look up to where we believe Jesus Christ is seated at the right hand of God as our mediator and advocate.

We keep our eyes focused on God, who alone is our source of help; we trust His Word for answers. Even the mountains and hills will bow down at his presence and the oceans will cease to roar at His voice. That is the power of God Almighty.

AUGUST

Sunday August 1, 2021

Deuteronomy 5:11 Thou shalt not take the name of the LORD thy God in vain: for the LORD will not hold him guiltless that taketh his name in vain.

We love our earthly parents and would not disrespect them or their names. My maiden name is not short – actually has eleven letters, and I have kept it hyphenated to my married name, which is eight letters long. Sometimes it is too long to fit some computer screens and the bank has had to leave out a few letters at the end. Some people have asked me why don't I drop one – use my husband's last name or just my maiden name. I want to respect my husband and my marriage, so I keep his name, but I really love my maiden name given to me by my father at birth and I want to hold on to it. My father is no longer with us and it is a way of feeling close to him.

How much more God almighty, the Lord of hosts who is all powerful and loving, deserves our reverence and praise. Any misuse or careless disrespect of God's name is irreverent and disrespectful.

Monday August 2, 2021

Jeremiah 32:17 Ah Lord GOD! behold, thou hast made the heaven and the earth by thy great power and stretched out arm, and there is nothing too hard for thee:

God is the sole Creator of the heavens and the earth, done by His power and mighty arm. The book of Genesis details how by His power God framed the heavens and earth even after Lucifer made it "without form and void." When the devil rebelled against God and left heaven taking a host of angels with him, he destroyed all that God had put in place. That is how devastating his rebellion was.

After God put everything in place, He created man and woman to enjoy it. As we take a look around at the earth around us and absorb the magnitude of all God did during creation, we can honestly say, 'there is nothing too hard for Him.' We still see the beauty in God's handiwork as we enjoy the beautiful green of trees in the Spring and flowers blossoming in an array of color. The amazing blue skies, the sun, moon, and stars are breathtaking to behold. When stand at the edge of the beach and take in the rolling waves, clear, crystal blue waters and ivory colored sands, I marvel at all God has done to bless us. Now think about the human body – the intricacy of it, medical professionals and scientists are still trying to grasp all that went into putting it together. God did all that and more and is still to do all that we ask of Him.

What do you need – finances, a life partner, a job, a promotion, a car, a house, children, complete healing? There is nothing too hard for God – trust Him.

Tuesday August 3, 2021

John 17:23 I in them, and thou in me, that they may be made perfect in one; and that the world may know that thou hast sent me, and hast loved them, as thou hast loved me.

God is in His Son Jesus Christ and we have Christ in us, so we are made perfect in Him. In our own selves we will never be perfect, but by God's love and forgiveness we are righteous. Our perfectness is only in what we have in God in Christ in us. God's seed in us is incorruptible – it will not perish and in that we claim our redemption, our righteousness, our sanctification, our justification. Having been given the ministry and Word of reconciliation, we have the authority to bring men and women back to God. That is how we can be confident of the love of God towards us.

God loved us so much He sent His Son Jesus Christ to die for us to legally buy back all the devil stole from Him. His love for His Son never wavered and He was with Jesus every step of the way through His sufferings and death seeing Him through until He raised Him up and He was ascended to be with Him.

Wednesday August 4, 2021

Deuteronomy 28:1 And it shall come to pass, if thou shalt hearken diligently unto the voice of the LORD thy God, to observe and to do all his commandments which I command thee this day, that the LORD thy God will set thee on high above all nations of the earth:

The world has been attacked in the year 2020 and yes that is not the first time. Many have asked where is God in all this, is He hearing our prayers, will He answer, will He help us? God is a just God and legally cannot interfere and force anyone to do what they do not want to do. We have seen the standards of God's Word compromised over and over, prayers were taken out of schools, children have been allowed to be disobedient, not held accountable for their mistakes, or punished when it was merited, the family and it's values set in place by God Himself has been changed. How can we expect God to violate man's free will and do anything? He has already done His part – sent His Son Jesus Christ to redeem man, made salvation and forgiveness available, but the world has repeatedly turned their backs on God's free gift. We have no right to ask where God is, if we are not willing to return to Him and do His commandments as set forth in His rightly-divided Word.

As we obey God's Word and continually keep His commandments, He promises to reward us handsomely. Remember the story of Joseph who was sold into slavery by his brothers. Instead of being bitter, angry, or resentful he forgave and loved them and stood for God. He was later promoted to the highest office in the kingdom. That is what our God can do for us as we take a stand for Him.

Thursday August 5, 2021

Proverbs 16:24 Pleasant words are as an honeycomb, sweet to the soul, and health to the bones.

I went to check out at a grocery store near my home and noticed the sad look on the face of the cashier. She sullenly greeted each person and rang up their groceries as if doing everything as she had been taught but with no enthusiasm. The few people in front of me said hi and quietly completed their purchases and left. When I got up to her and she said 'hi and how are you' like she had done previously, I replied as cheerfully as I could, given her sour look. "I am well, thanks and how about you; how are you feeling today?" She took a few seconds, slowly looked up at me with tears in her eyes as she responded. "I'm not doing too well; but thanks so much for asking, no one ever asks me how I'm doing." I replied, "I am sorry about that; most people just want to get done and head home. I don't think it's about you." I asked her if she was tired and she explained that she was eight and a half months pregnant and was having discomfort and pain after being on her feet for so long. I suggested maybe it was time to go on maternity leave, and she agreed By that time, I was finished checking out and told her I would be praying for her. She thanked me again and I left. I saw her once after she delivered her healthy baby girl and this time her greeting was much more cheerful.

We never know what is going on in someone's life. Everybody, even me initially thought she was just a grumpy employee who did not want to be there. I am thankful God told me to speak to her. Kind, gracious words are sweet like honey; they give peace of mind and physical health. Wow! Just by speaking a kind word we bless someone by bringing a smile to their face, maybe brighten their day and help them maybe feel better about themselves. Not only that, but it also does the same for the one speaking the kind words.

Friday August 6, 2021

John 14:12 Verily, verily, I say unto you, He that believeth on me, the works that I do shall he do also; and greater works than these shall he do; because I go unto my Father.

That is a promise from God. As born-again believers with Christ in us and manifesting God's gift of holy spirit, we can do everything Jesus Christ did while He was here on earth. That includes, healing the sick, sight to the blind, and yes even raising someone from the dead. During Jesus Christ's earthly ministry, He went about doing good the Word says – He was hospitable – feeding the hungry, loving, kind to even those He knew didn't care for Him – the Samarian woman at the well. John chapter 4). He forgave those who arrested and tortured and crucified Him. These are all things we can practice as well in our Christian walk.

The greater works that are available to us is reconciling men and women back to God by way of the new birth and speaking in tongues. God's gift of holy spirit was not available until after Jesus was ascended into heaven. Remember in John chapter fourteen Jesus told His disciples that He had to leave, but the Father would send the Comforter (gift of holy spirit) who would guide them in all things. Look what God has entrusted us with! With His gift of holy spirit in each of us we represent the absent Christ to do all the works He did while He was here on earth to speak in tongues, and lead others to the 'new birth'. What a tremendous honor and privilege is ours.

Saturday August 7, 2021

I Timothy 2:5 For there is one God, and one mediator between God and men, the man Christ Jesus;

There has been so much confusion and misunderstanding about who Jesus Christ really is. Some use Jesus's name interchangeably with God, so they pray using "dear God and dear Jesus" in the same way. Contrary to what many still teach, Jesus Christ is not God but the Son of God – a man who lived on earth and was subject to the same passions/desires as we are; tempted but without sin – not yielding to the temptation. There are certainly some seemingly contradictions to this in the Word, but extensive research has been done to clarify those and we are confident is making the statement that Jesus Christ is not God.

He is our ONLY way, (John 14:6) our means to, our mediator between us and our Heavenly Father – God (I Timothy 2:5). There are so many other clear verses to help us understand all God has for us. We are thankful that God included those in His Word so we could rightly divide it. For further study, please see the great research work by Dr. V.P. Wierwille, 'Jesus Christ is not God.'

Sunday August 8, 2021

Psalm 107:1 O give thanks unto the LORD, for he is good: for his mercy endureth for ever.
2 Let the redeemed of the LORD say so, whom he hath redeemed from the hand of the enemy;

God is a loving merciful God. One online dictionary defines mercy as *"compassion or forgiveness shown toward someone whom it is within one's power to punish or harm."* God would be legally right to punish man for our sins and even those who crucified His Son. He instead showed mercy/compassion and love to those who do not deserve it. The book of Lamentations chapter three lets us know that God's mercies and compassions are new every morning. He never runs out so we can be assured that we will not wake up one morning and be out of "appeals" with God. God is good always and forever and we maintain a heart of thankfulness to Him for His love and kindness, never punishing us according to our sins.

God sent His Son, Jesus Christ to pay the price for our freedom from the clutches of the adversary and we can now claim one of our sonship rights of redemption. We have been redeemed, legally bought back and the adversary has no hold or rights to us.

Monday August 9, 2021

Psalms 107:20 He sent his word, and healed them, and delivered them from their destructions.
21 Oh that men would praise the LORD for his goodness, and for his wonderful works to the children of men!

I previously mentioned how someone told me after I lost my brother "you could use an overdose of the Word!" I love that phrase because it was very instrumental in my healing process on several occasions. After briefly thinking about it, I asked around to find out where a Bible class would be running and when. The closest was about one and a half hours each way from where I lived but I gladly signed up a four-week Biblical class and received that healing. God sent His Word and healed my heart because I was open to focus past the sadness and grief to the Hope of Christ's return where I know I will see him again. For that we give God praise for all He has given us.

No better therapy anywhere in the world. I remember having severe pain in my knees from arthritis. I prayed, read several verses from God's Word, and spoke to my knees reminding them that I was already healed in the name of Jesus Christ. Less than five minutes later, I was pain-free. As we give God praise and thanks that we are already healed through all He accomplished by way of His Son Jesus Christ, we keep His promises in our hearts and minds. The Word heals!

Tuesday August 10, 2021

I Peter 3:12(a) For the eyes of the Lord are over the righteous, and his ears are open unto their prayers:

What a comforting verse to know that God is always watching and listening, and He hears our prayers. He knows everything we need even before we are fully aware of what that is. If we are not getting answers to our prayers, we need to assess our hearts to make sure we are in fellowship with our Heavenly Father. What could be hindering our effective prayer life? Are we harboring any grudges, anger, resentment, envy, covetousness, or possibly hate in our hearts to anyone, especially another believer?

Mark 1:25 And when ye stand praying, forgive, if ye have ought (anything) against any: that your Father also which is in heaven may forgive you your trespasses. Let go of any resentments so your heart is ready to receive God's forgiveness.

As we stay faithful to God and His Word His promise is to always protect, keep a watchful eye, hear, and answer our prayers. How comforting is that? No matter what situation we are in, we are never too far from our Heavenly Father that He cannot hear and answer our prayers.

Wednesday August 11, 2021

Matthew 6:7 But when ye pray, use not vain repetitions, as the heathen do: for they think that they shall be heard for their much speaking.

Some religious organizations over the years have used, (some still do) what Christians affectionally call 'the Lord's prayer' in Matthew chapter six, as their go to prayer. They pride themselves on repeating it several times a day. The Word clearly shows us that Jesus used that prayer as an example to teach His disciples how to pray. It was never meant as a 'one-size fits all' prayer. We may need to pray for all the things mentioned in that prayer, at some time but that should not be our only prayer.

God does not want prayers that are superficial and void of emotion. We do not just pick up a book and read a prayer someone else wrote. It may not have the same meaning for you as it did for the person that wrote it. Each person is unique and special in their own individual way as is each relationship with God. Speak to God like a kid talking to His father. He wants to hear your heart, what you are feeling or experiencing at that moment.

Do not be afraid to pour out your heart to God; He asks that we 'come boldly unto the throne of grace'.

Thursday August 12, 2021

Isaiah 41:10 Fear thou not; for I am with thee: be not dismayed; for I am thy God: I will strengthen thee; yea, I will help thee; yea, I will uphold thee with the right hand of my righteousness.

What a beautiful promise of God's love; the amplified version says it even clearer.

Isaiah 41:10 (Amplified) 'Do not fear [anything], for I am with you; Do not be afraid, for I am your God. I will strengthen you, be assured I will help you; I will certainly take hold of you with My righteous right hand [a hand of justice, of power, of victory, of salvation].'

Because we have a human nature there will be times when fear sneaks into our minds. It may be a fear of failure, of what someone may do to us, fear of sickness, dying or even a fear of success. We may be getting ready to take an exam and get so paralyzed by fear we cannot even function or on the other side we have big plans to start a business or a new job and in the same way get so full of fear we never even try.

God's Word assures us that He has not given us a "spirit of fear, but of power, love, and a sound mind." (II Timothy 1:7) We remember those words, keep them in our minds and hearts and repeat them as often as we need to help us take that leap or even just that first step.

Friday August 13, 2021

Psalms 119:45 And I will walk at liberty: for I seek thy precepts.

There is freedom in following God's Word – we are free to live, free to give, free to serve, all by our free-will choice. Jesus Christ came to make us free from the bondage of sin and the legalism that enslaves so many. And we are reminded of this in John 8:36 If the Son therefore shall make you free, ye shall be free indeed. Let us claim it and walk out on that freedom as we live and speak the truth of God's Word.

So many things in our lives can keep us in bondage and we never feel free. God wants us to be released from all so we are free indeed. Let us take inventory of what is keeping us in prison in our lives so we can be set free. Is it a sin that you have been holding on to, something that makes you mentally torment yourself, things that make you worry or be anxious? Are you afraid of sickness and disease, especially because the doctors said, "it is hereditary?" Does that keep you awake at night worrying about being predisposed to a certain disease because someone in your family had it? It is time to let go of all these negatives and believe God's Word that you can be totally free, released from these prisons in your mind forever

Saturday August 14, 2021

Psalms 112:1 Praise ye the LORD. Blessed is the man that feareth the LORD, that delighteth greatly in his commandments.

Those who respect and reverence God are blessed. It is as simple as that – we love God, live according to the standards He set for us in His Word and we will be blessed. The righteous man is featured in an original poem.

Do you know you are mighty, highly blessed and favored?
Because of your reverence and faithful worship to God.
You love to read and study His Word and are not wavered,
So, His light overcomes all the darkness of the world.
You are strong, gracious, and compassionate with God's people,
You stay in right standing with God, not shaken by doubt.
Remaining steadfast, trusting, believing, and relying on God,
With no fear and boldly confident that He is sufficient.
Your wife is virtuous, more precious than rubies and gems,
And your household enjoys studying and reading God's Word.
With your business ethics, you treat others fair and are just,
You are truly righteous in God's eyes and never forget that.

Although written specifically to the 'righteous man', the words can be applied to anyone as we give praise and honor to God Almighty!

Sunday August 15, 2021

Psalms 91:14 Because he hath set his love upon me, therefore will I deliver him: I will set him on high, because he hath known my name.
15 He shall call upon me, and I will answer him: I will be with him in trouble; I will deliver him, and honour him.
16 With long life will I satisfy him, and shew him my salvation.

Psalms chapter 91 is said to have been composed by Moses when he finished building the tabernacle in the dessert for the Israelites. No matter what, those words are timeless and could fit in any situation for any reason. They are all promises we can claim as we trust God to protect us to rescue us and provide for us. There will be times we will lift our voices in praise to God Almighty and other times we just need to remember His promises to be with us and take care of us.

Whatever the situation, we can still give praise and worship to God because we believe His Word and thank Him in advance for doing what He has promised He will do. We love God because He first loved us, and He promises to deliver/save us. Our God always hears and answers when we call on him. We can live a long, fruitful, and prosperous life as we take a stand for Him.

Monday August 16, 2021

Psalms 127:3 Lo, children are an heritage of the LORD: and the fruit of the womb is his reward.

When I was expecting my son, my heart was so full of joy and anticipation. The previous year, I had lost my first pregnancy carrying triplets. The pregnancy was mismanaged from the start and it was heart breaking when it ended that way. The doctors were not optimistic that I could carry another child due to the complications surrounding the miscarriage. As I prayed and trusted God to work in the situation I remembered how God answered prayer for Abraham and Sarah even at their advanced ages. Having my son, was truly a blessing and an added blessing came just over a year later when I was expecting again. I remember telling everyone, I already have my son, this next one will be a girl. I got strange looks and "don't get your hopes up, it might be another boy." I would be thankful either way, but my heart was set on a girl, so I bought ribbons, and pretty dresses in pink and some yellow just picturing a baby girl. Thankful to say, God answered my prayers and received my second blessing.

Our children are a blessing from God and are His heritage. That is why we make an investment in their future. Yes, a great education is wonderful because it will help them in life here on earth. But God wants us to train them up in "the way they should go", teach them a true and accurate knowledge of the Word of God. That will be 100 times more beneficial to them than any college degree, because it is for all eternity.

Tuesday August 17, 2021

Psalms 116:1 I love the LORD, because he hath heard my voice and my supplications.

One of the things my husband and I share is to remember to thank God after our prayers are answered. My prayer goes something like this, "God, thank you so much for answering my prayer. I know it was you because I could not have done it by myself. And dear God, do you know how much I love you? Because I do – love you for how you take care of me." That is always such a special and intimate time for me to 'bond' with my Heavenly Father. Recently we were hosting one of our Bible classes in our home and according to the local weather we were expecting some bad weather with high winds, heavy rain, and maybe a tornado. A tornado!! We do not get tornadoes around here. About the time people were scheduled to start arriving we heard there were about five tornadoes less than three miles away headed in our direction. We prayed, and my husband went outside and spoke to the tornadoes demanding they leave our area in the name of Jesus Christ. A few minutes later it got really quiet and we found out the tornadoes made a u-turn and headed in a totally different direction. That was one of those times when I told God thanks and how much I loved Him.

No matter where we are, no matter what the situation, God hears and answers when we reach out to Him. How reassuring to our hearts to know how much God loves us and we love Him too for His love and care toward us.

Wednesday August 18, 2021

Psalms 116:5 Gracious is the LORD, and righteous; yea, our God is merciful.

God's grace and mercy are our stamps of approval from Him. We are living in the Age of Grace where God made it available for His children to be removed from the curse of the law. Jesus Christ said He came to fulfill the law which means that we are no longer bound by it. God has forgiven us our sins, given us His grace, and justified us. In God's eyes we are "just as if we never sinned." Can you imagine what that is like? God has acknowledged that "all have sinned" (Romans 6:23), but because of His great love He has not only forgiven us but put those sins "as far as the east is from the west."

We cannot hear it enough – how righteous God is, because it reminds us that we are righteous in Him. We have the honor to be able to stand in the very presence of God without sense of sin, or guilt or deficiencies because Jesus Christ paid for it all with His life. God gives us of His divine favor and withholds deserved punishment from His children. We give thanks and praise to Him.

Thursday August 19, 2021

Revelation 22:5 And there shall be no night there; and they need no candle, neither light of the sun; for the Lord God giveth them light: and they shall reign for ever and ever.

When God first spoke those words in Genesis 1:3 "let there be light", He was making light available for us throughout the Word. Even before the sun, moon and stars were created God spoke light into being. When the devil made the earth "without form and void", darkness took over and covered the earth. To start to prepare the earth so man could inhabit it, God had to get rid of all that darkness.

God is light and "in Him is no darkness at all." (I John 1:6). And in the new heaven and earth where we will be with Him eternally, He is preparing a place where His light will illuminate everything, and His brightness will never dim.

Friday August 20, 2021

Psalms 117:1 O praise the LORD, all ye nations: praise him, all ye people.

2 For his merciful kindness is great toward us: and the truth of the Lord endureth for ever. Praise ye the LORD.

God's Word is truth and contains all we need to set us free from all the doubts, worries, and fears that have for so long hindered us from moving forward. That is what the adversary does to keep God's children from trusting Him – the more doubt and fear fills our minds, the more we remain stuck in our past and cannot fully accept all we have in Christ. We see over and over again emphasized in the Word how merciful, kind and forgiving God is, and it lasts forever. Why are we as believers still skeptical about our forgiveness? Why are we still so full of doubt regarding God's willingness and ability to remove our sins "as far as the East is from the West?" I have heard some people confess negatives such as "I know God has forgiven me, but I am suffering now because He has to make me pay for some of the things I did that were wrong." Where in God's Word does it say that? That is an out and out lie from the devil himself.

Let us accept all God accomplished for us through the life, sufferings, death, resurrection, and ascension of His Son Jesus Christ. The Word of God tells us by the stripes of Jesus Christ we were healed; it is a done deal – already accomplished healed mentally, physically, and spiritually; and with His shed blood we have remission (forgiveness) of sins.

Saturday August 21, 2021

II Corinthians 3:5 Not that we are sufficient of ourselves to think any thing as of ourselves; but our sufficiency is of God;

Sometimes when trying to encourage others, I have heard people say, "trust yourself, believe in yourself." For many this has been how they were taught from their youth. From the time their parents teach them to accomplish certain tasks they may tell them something like they need to be self-sufficient and not to depend on anyone to get where they want to go in life. Sometimes young girls are taught to change the tires on their cars and more just so they may not have to depend on a guy to help them out. I am not saying that is a bad thing just that it may not be the right reason to do something.

To be sufficient is to have enough for what we need. As believers we can never have enough of what we need to live an abundant life without God. No matter how proficient we may get, we cannot do it without God. With Him we are completely complete to live a more than abundant life. Everything we will ever need, God has already provided. Let us continue to trust Him to take care of every aspect of our lives.

Sunday August 22, 2021

II Corinthians 12:9(a) And he said unto me, My grace is sufficient for thee: for my strength is made perfect in weakness.

Have you ever watched a marathon race? All along the way are people who are not participating in the race, but they are on the side lines shouting encouraging words and/or calling out someone's name telling them they can do it. Some have said that was what they needed to get them to push ahead, it gave them an extra burst of energy to keep going. I have never run a marathon, but I walk for exercise. It is so much better to do it with someone else, because we talk and laugh and share jokes and before we realize it, we have walked over two miles. I do not like to walk alone, but when I have to, or sometimes when I am on the treadmill and tempted to stop after fifteen minutes these help give me that extra strength to keep on going. I use God's Word in verse or song, listening to verses like " but they that wait upon the Lord shall renew their strength" (Isaiah 40:31) or listen to a song like "Push On Through It" by Way Productions.

By our strength alone we can do nothing, and when we have done all we know to do and think that we cannot go on, remember God's power and strength far out-weigh our weaknesses. What a blessing that by God's grace we can overcome anything, and that is all we need in life.

Monday August 23, 2021

Hebrews 12:14 Follow peace with all men, and holiness, without which no man shall see the Lord:

In a world so full of turmoil, strife, bitterness and anger, God wants us to be at peace with everyone we come in contact with. As Christians we have been sanctified, set apart by God to be holy as He is holy. Our lives must be examples to those in our sphere of influence. Whether it is at work or school or when we are out in the community, our behavior/actions must allow others to see Christ in us. That means when someone is having a bad day and lash out, we stay peaceful, speak in tongues and trust God for the right words to diffuse the situation, then respond with a smile. Maybe ask, "what can I do to help you? Or is there anything you need?" The response just might be surprising. Sometimes it may mean saying nothing at all and walking away from a situation or area to allow things to diffuse. Some discussions about religious doctrines or political issues can become heated very quickly and escalate into something heated, causing anger and even hatred to develop.

Our responsibility is to "follow peace", do whatever is necessary to bring calmness to the situation. Letting the peace of God rule in everything we do, can help heal someone's heart, including ours.

Tuesday August 24, 2021

Ephesians 1:4 According as he hath chosen us in him before the foundation of the world, that we should be holy and without blame before him in love:

Many of us were born into our families and have a father, mother, brothers, and sisters. We had no choice who would be part of our family and our parents did not decide who their children would be. We didn't even get to choose our siblings. Each family member is different and have their own personalities and character traits, we love one another because we are family. Others were adopted into a family and legally became the children of a mother and father which sometimes include brothers and sister. In these cases, adopted children were chosen and the parents decided to make them a part of their family.

As born-again believers we were chosen by God to be His children, to be part of His family. (1 Peter 2:9) At our physical birth we were all born without God's spirit but received it when we confessed Jesus Christ as Lord in our lives, believing that God raised Him from the dead. God hand-picked His children, adopted us legally and set us apart, so He expects us to mirror the example He sent for us – His Son, Jesus Christ. We love Him and live our lives blameless, (above reproach) to bring glory to Him.

Wednesday August 25, 2021

Proverbs 15:1 A soft answer turneth away wrath: but grievous words stir up anger.

There have been times when someone said or did something that hurt my feelings. The first response is usually to turn away and cry holding on to the hurt for as long as I can. This was never good because I would go on for a long time feeling sorry for myself, because I was misunderstood, or treated unfairly. Even if I tried to repress it, feelings of anger and resentment would creep in on occasion. Most people may decide to lash out instead, but that is never the right solution either. When we respond in anger, it stirs up more anger; so, we take a deep breath and take a moment before we say anything. I am sure many of you have heard the phrase "count to ten." I take it a little further with "count to ten then count backward from ten." That usually gives me enough time to compose myself and respond with kind words to diffuse the situation.

A friend of mine would respond with a Bible verse, which I thought was quite smart. If someone did or said something to her and she wanted to respond with something negative, she took a deep breath and said out loud any verse that came to mind. It might be "Thy Word have I hid in mine heart, that I might not sin against Thee" (Psalms 119:11) or "God so loved the world that He gave His only begotten Son" (John 3:16) or maybe "be ye kind one to another, tenderhearted, forgiving one another." (Ephesians 4:32). Let us try it next time we are in a similar situation and watch God bring peace and turn things around.

Thursday August 26, 2021

I Peter 3:15 But sanctify the Lord God in your hearts: and be ready always to give an answer to every man that asketh you a reason of the hope that is in you with meekness and fear:

Recently I had a conversation with a dear friend of mine who told me that when she travels particularly to a French-speaking country or island, she is always asked how she pronounces her surname. Then she would be asked why it was pronounced the way it was and for a long time she never had an answer. Sometimes people would even venture suggestions on how she should pronounce it because as they stated it was a French name and she pronounced it like an English name. One day she decided to do some research into the origin of her last name and learned that it was indeed of French origin and when the family relocated to an English speaking country, it had been translated to an English version. Since then whenever she is questioned, she can explain that to anyone who asks.

We give God first place in our lives which is His rightful place. We study the Word daily, retemorizing (memorizing) as many verses or passages as possible. We take the Bible classes made available to us and make use of the many research resources at our disposal. As we continuously practice the presence of God, and keep His Word in our hearts and minds, we will always be ready to respond with the appropriate Word when questioned regarding our stand, our beliefs or the accuracy of God's Word.

Friday August 27, 2021

I Peter 3:1 Likewise, ye wives, be in subjection to your own husbands; that, if any obey not the word, they also may without the word be won by the conversation of the wives;
2 While they behold your chaste conversation coupled with fear.

The marriage between a man and woman was designed by God after He created Eve for Adam. (Genesis 2:25) As believer wives, it is our duty to be obedient to our husbands who are the head of our homes. We submit to each other by proper arrangement according to the Word and what works best for our marriage and family. Marriage is not a "one size fits all" and should not be patterned after another one. One lady once said to me, "this is what I do for my husband and it works for us." I kindly reminded her that my husband and I were two totally different people and what worked for her marriage would not necessarily work for ours.

Another young lady and I were having a conversation regarding how to handle disagreements in the marriage. When I shared with her that our responsibility as believing wives is to be patient and faithful to the Word as it states, and allow our behavior to be a witness to win the unbelieving husband to the Word, she was quite indignant about what would be her husband's responsibility while was doing her part. My response was to leave that to God.

If you are in a relationship mentioned in the verse as a Godly wife (or husband) just do all you know to do, according to the Word, including praying for your spouse, speaking in tongues, and trusting God to work in the heart. There is nothing we can do that would be better than what God can do. TRUST HIM!

Saturday August 28, 2021

I Peter 3:7 Likewise, ye husbands, dwell with them
according to knowledge, giving honour unto the wife,
as unto the weaker vessel, and as being heirs together of
the grace of life; that your prayers be not hindered.
8 Finally, be ye all of one mind, having compassion one
of another, love as brethren, be pitiful, be courteous:
9 Not rendering evil for evil, or railing for railing: but
contrariwise blessing; knowing that ye are thereunto
called, that ye should inherit a blessing.

There is nothing more powerful than a believing couple – husband and wife standing like-minded on God's Word. The husband loves God, loves, and cherishes his wife, his wife is in subjection to him in a manner agreed upon by the two of them. He does not lord his authority over her but lovingly cares for, provides for, and protects her.

One young lady said to me, "you know, I believe marriage was made for Christian husbands and wives." She and her husband were going through some difficulties and she asked me over to pray with her. We went to God's Word for answers and prayed together. She was comforted by the Word, became very peaceful, no longer agitated and anxious, reassured of God's blessing on their home and marriage.

In a marriage the husband and wife remain compassionate with each other, humble, forgiving, kind, loving and most importantly stand in one accord with unity on the Word of God. There is no room for strife, anger, bitterness and fighting. These will absolutely destroy a marriage.

Sunday August 29, 2021

Philippians 4:4 Rejoice in the Lord always: and again I say, Rejoice.
5 Let your moderation be known unto all men. The Lord is at hand.

When we wake every morning our first thought should be of praise and thankfulness to God for allowing us to see another day. Whatever happened the previous day is in the past and we have another opportunity to live for God, speak His Word and practice our ministry of reconciliation. Life may be chaotic at times, and we may be unsure about what we need to do, what our next step should be, but with thankfulness of heart, we rejoice in the Lord always. The year 2020 was a year full of turmoil, heartache, sickness, and loss due to a pandemic. As the year comes to an end the medical world is promising that things will get better with a vaccine. As believers we trust God who alone is our sufficiency and rejoice in what we have in Him.

Let us give God praise today and every day; always keep that joyful heart no matter what, show kindness, and be gracious to all. Remember we do it to glorify our Heavenly Father.

Monday August 30, 2021

Psalms 119:1 Blessed are the undefiled in the way, who walk in the law of the LORD.
2 Blessed are they that keep his testimonies, and that seek him with the whole heart.

The story of Daniel is well known to many Christians around the world. As a teenager – approximately sixteen years old Daniel was one of many who were captured and held captive in a foreign land. He was strong and bold to stand for God in the face of adversity. He refused the food of the kings table, choosing to eat as God had instructed His people and he was blessed with a promotion. When faced with a decision as to his commitment to God, Daniel chose to continue to pray to God, three times a day as he had been taught from his youth. Even when threatened to be thrown into a den of lions he stood for God, and God protected him.

God's blessings are on them that live according to His Word, whose lives are an example of right living. When we take a stand for God and refuse to allow the world to distract us God is faithful to bless us with His favor and protect us. Let us make that commitment to be a testimony for our God.

Tuesday August 31, 2021

Psalms 119:9 Wherewithal shall a young man cleanse his way? by taking heed thereto according to thy word.
10 With my whole heart have I sought thee: O let me not wander from thy commandments.
11 Thy word have I hid in mine heart, that I might not sin against thee.

Some religious organizations have taught that we can do good, make sacrifices, and give money to the poor to make amends or atonement/compensation for sins or past mistakes. While these are all great things to do none of them will allow us forgiveness of sins or make us right in God's eyes. The only way to change our past lives and leave our sinful lifestyle in the past is to do it the Word's way. Nothing else is as effective. 1 John chapter one verse nine tells us that if we confess our sins, God is faithful and just to forgive us and cleanse us from all unrighteousness. That is how it is done – the only way; we go to God in the name of His Son Jesus Christ who is our mediator.

With meek hearts we go to God in full and genuine repentance, in prayer; we make time to read and/or study His Word every day. Our daily time with God strengthens us spiritually so we can know that we are walking in His will. Staying consistent keeps us strong to resist the attacks and temptations of the adversary.

SEPTEMBER

Wednesday September 1, 2021

Matthew 6:24 No man can serve two masters: for either he will hate the one, and love the other; or else he will hold to the one, and despise the other. Ye cannot serve God and mammon.

Imagine trying to work two jobs with the same hours on the same days every day? One boss is expecting some assignments done by a certain deadline. The other boss across town has also given you assignments all due at that same time. That would be impossible wouldn't it? Try as we might we could not effectively make both bosses happy. Maybe you might get a few assignments done for one of your jobs but the other one would not get done.

In the same way we cannot expect to live for God and make worldly decisions at the same time. Or maybe decide to take a stand on one truth in God's Word while ignoring another. There would always be conflict and confusion in our lives trying to please both the God and Father of our Lord Jesus Christ and at the same time trying to please the god of this world.

Our heart is to serve God with our whole being with everything we have, not halfway. Trying to be a Christian only on Sundays, or special occasions is not enough to build us up and help us grow in our walk for God. By our free will choice, we make God our Heavenly Father first in our lives before anything or anyone.

The decision must be clear and distinct in our head as well as in our lives, so we can have a life more than abundant.

Thursday September 2, 2021

John 14:1 Let not your heart be troubled: ye believe in God, believe also in me.
2 In my Father's house are many mansions: if it were not so, I would have told you. I go to prepare a place for you.
3 And if I go and prepare a place for you, I will come again, and receive you unto myself; that where I am, there ye may be also.

Our homes are a haven of rest for us, where we can be ourselves without being anxious. As a child I loved playing outside with my siblings and other neighborhood children. Most days we were allowed to stay out until it started to turn dark and the streetlights came on. Soon after it started going dark, I remember we would all be nervous about being away from home in the dark and did not feel safe anymore. I was one of the first to start running towards home. Once I stepped into the house, I felt less anxious and safe again. As an adult whenever I travel away from home, it is usually a day or two before I can have a restful asleep and am always so happy to be back home.

There is a song that goes, "this world is not my home, I'm just passing through." Jesus Christ promised His disciples that He would leave to prepare a home for them in one of his Father's many mansions, and those words still apply to us in the Grace Administration. As God's children we are heirs to all that is His, and joint heirs with Christ. Our spiritual home is not on this earth but where we will spend eternity with God and His Son Jesus Christ. We believe in the Hope of Christ's return when we will be caught up to meet Him in the air and live eternally with Him in the place He has prepared for us with our Heavenly Father – a home where we will never have tears, only peace and joy.

Friday September 3, 2021

Matthew 6:25 Therefore I say unto you, Take no thought for your life, what ye shall eat, or what ye shall drink; nor yet for your body, what ye shall put on. Is not the life more than meat, and the body than raiment?
26 Behold the fowls of the air: for they sow not, neither do they reap, nor gather into barns; yet your heavenly Father feedeth them. Are ye not much better than they?
27 Which of you by taking thought can add one cubit unto his stature?

It is human nature to be concerned about where the next meal is coming from, what we will wear to church on Sunday, do we have enough saved up for our retirement. It is reassuring to know that God has us covered. I remember many times when I had no idea where the next meal would come from or even what the next meal would be. God provided every single time as only He could – maybe a friend would invite me to dinner, or someone would show up with money they owed me that I had forgotten about. Over the years these verses have been such a blessing and I share them with others I see them being blessed as well.

Several years ago, we were believing with our adult daughter for a good working vehicle so she could get back and forth to work and to be able to drop off and pick up her kids safely. One day we were at a meeting and ran into a gentleman we had not seen for a while. He asked if we or someone we knew needed a car – it was in great shape, low mileage and at a price within our budget. God meets the need every time and at the right time.

Take note of the analogy of how God takes care of the birds, “fowls of the air”. They have not a care in the world, but they always have enough for what they need. As children of God, He thinks of us as more precious than the birds, so He will make sure we are fed and clothed. We just need to trust Him.

Saturday September 4, 2021

I Peter 5:2 Feed the flock of God which is among you, taking the oversight thereof, not by constraint, but willingly; not for filthy lucre, but of a ready mind;

As a nurse I heard the phrase many times that "nurses eat their young." It meant that older nurses were not very kind or helpful to new, younger nurses, even bordering on harassment sometimes making it so difficult that the new nurse would buckle and quit under the stress. After being victim to such behavior by an older nurse in my first three years, I determined to never treat another nurse in that manner and never did; actually going out of my way to go the extra mile which was greatly appreciated. Being taught to be respectful to those older to me and those in senior positions I just took everything they did quietly and it took years for me to speak up and tell them that I would no longer accept or tolerate their harassment.

We count it a great privilege when we get to be a mentor or to 'under shepherd' a young believer, new in the Word. We welcome them with the love of God, teaching them with encouraging words so they can grow in their spiritual walk. By free will choice we lovingly and with kindness are always ready to serve, not for attention or looking for what we can get out of it. Our hearts are meek and with thankfulness to God we joyfully take care of and lead His people whenever we are given the opportunity.

Sunday September 5, 2021

Matthew 6:33 But seek ye first the kingdom of God, and his righteousness; and all these things shall be added unto you.
34 Take therefore no thought for the morrow: for the morrow shall take thought for the things of itself. Sufficient unto the day is the evil thereof.

We have previously seen from the Word that we do not concern ourselves about our needs for the future. We do ourselves an injustice when as Christians we lay awake at nights worrying about how we will feed our family or how we will pay our bills. Worrying about what might or might not be never solved any problems. Instead we put God first in everything, remember we are righteous in Him and trust Him. He in turn will supply our every need "one day at a time".

When the Israelites left Egypt, they had no idea what or how they would feed their families. Remember they were in a wilderness, or desert with no food or plants around. God send down 'manna' (bread) from heaven and even provided meat. Each twenty-four-hour period we give our need to our Heavenly Father to provide and every time He comes through. I exhort you if you have never done it, to just give God a try, put your trust in His ability to take care of your every need – no matter what it is. There is nothing too hard for God.

Monday September 6, 2021

I Peter 5:5 Likewise, ye younger, submit yourselves unto the elder. Yea, all of you be subject one to another, and be clothed with humility: for God resisteth the proud, and giveth grace to the humble.
6 Humble yourselves therefore under the mighty hand of God, that he may exalt you in due time:
7 Casting all your care upon him; for he careth for you.

We go to school to learn and expect our teachers to teach us what they know, what they have specialized in. Teachers are trained professionals who master specific subjects and are usually experts in their field of work. For example, a mathematics teacher loves working with numbers, has been trained and is fully qualified to teach the subject. When I started training to be a midwife, I enjoyed it so much I would stay up late at night just reading the textbooks. By my second month, the tutor was calling me her assistant and I graduated top of the class. For many years afterwards, I had the privilege to teach and train younger, student midwives which I thoroughly enjoyed.

God has His ministers in leadership positions to oversee His household of believers. They are in a position to care for the spiritual aspect of our lives helping us mature fully in our walk. Our duty is to be meek to learn from them, to trust that they have our best interest at heart according to God's Word. In humility and love we remain obedient, and are always ready to serve as needed trusting God to take care of our every need.

Tuesday September 7, 2021

Psalms 119:36 Incline my heart unto thy testimonies, and not to covetousness.
37 Turn away mine eyes from beholding vanity; and quicken thou me in thy way.

We live our lives one day at the time and need to renew our minds daily, maybe even minute by minute, to the Word. Now, honestly I do not covet 'things', for example I don't get envious or jealous of someone's new car(s), or their house(s), but I might want to be their size or be able to fit into a beautiful outfit like they are wearing or maybe have my hair grow as fast theirs. So, I renew my mind – I look at pictures of myself when I was slimmer, and my hair grew fast and with a smile I tell myself that there will be changes with age and I accept it. And then I give God thanks that I have no major health issues and my hair is healthy. The key for me is to focus on the Word of God and confess what it says about me. I am no less a son of God with Christ in me because I look different than I did 30 years ago. That helps me keep my mind from vain thoughts.

God's Word exhorts us to not covet and turn our eyes away from being vain. We are able to do that by keeping our minds focused on the Word.

Wednesday September 8, 2021

II Peter 1:3 According as his divine power hath given unto us all things that pertain unto life and godliness, through the knowledge of him that hath called us to glory and virtue:
4 Whereby are given unto us exceeding great and precious promises: that by these ye might be partakers of the divine nature, having escaped the corruption that is in the world through lust.

Everything relating to this life that we need to be a success God has made available to us. Let us consider that for a moment. God alone created the heavens and the earth, He formed man out of the dust of the earth equipping him with soul life. As the author of life God has provided everything we need for that life.

Whatever comes our way, and we are not sure how to handle it, we have access to God's Word where we can find the Word we need for that specific situation. As we build our knowledge in the Word, our understanding about these matters grow deeper. It has been said there are over 900 promises in the Bible. As born-again believers and children of God, we can claim any and all of them at any time to get desired results.

Thursday September 9, 2021

Philippians 4:11 Not that I speak in respect of want: for I have learned, in whatsoever state I am, therewith to be content.
12 I know both how to be abased, and I know how to abound: every where and in all things I am instructed both to be full and to be hungry, both to abound and to suffer need.

In the early years of our marriage, my husband and I struggled financially as we worked to build our new life together. He had moved from the state he lived in to join me and was searching for a job; with one income it was not always easy to make ends meet. I was pleasantly thankful for how we navigated our finances whether we had a little or much. We made little things into a fun event – like staying home to watch a movie or going for a long drive. Once he got a job and we settled into more of a routine we were able to eat out more and take trips. We never complained or fought over money no matter how much we had – we just thanked God and worked it out. Our main decision which we stuck with was to always give back to God in tithe and abundant sharing, and God always blessed us back.

The apostle Paul had become a changed man; he went from persecuting Christians to becoming a man of God. He was no longer this arrogant man full of anger and hate but a man who wanted to carry out God's will as he had learned to do. He was now living a humble life satisfied with whatever situation he was in, not complaining but accepting whatever was available to him at the time, trusting God to meet his need. As believers we remember that God is our sufficiency and we trust Him to take care of us and meet our needs no matter what the situation.

Friday September 10, 2021

Isaiah 61:1 The Spirit of the Lord GOD is upon me; because the LORD hath anointed me to preach good tidings unto the meek; he hath sent me to bind up the brokenhearted, to proclaim liberty to the captives, and the opening of the prison to them that are bound;
2 To proclaim the acceptable year of the LORD, and the day of vengeance of our God; to comfort all that mourn;

That is what Jesus had to say about His purpose for being here on earth. This passage is talking about Jesus Christ's earthly ministry, and as those who take the place of the absent Christ, it is our ministry as well. The Word tells us in the gospel of John that we are to do the works of Jesus Christ and 'greater'. We speak, teach, and preach the Word to those who have a heart to receive it, we can bring healing by our 'gifts of healing', whether it is a physical, mental or spiritual healing. And we bring deliverance to those enslaved in the bondage of sin.

As fully instructed believing men and women of God our mission to continue to carry out the works of Jesus Christ to preach, heal those whose hearts have been broken, to tell others of the freedom available in Christ, and showing them from God's Word how they can be free from whatever 'prisons' have them bound. God has given us everything we need to succeed as we walk out in boldness with confidence to do God's will.

Saturday September 11, 2021

Malachi 4:2 But unto you that fear my name shall the Sun of righteousness arise with healing in his wings; and ye shall go forth, and grow up as calves of the stall.

Through many years of research theologians and students of the Bible have been able to pinpoint this date as the date of Jesus Christ's birth. This is very easily fact-checked and although for years we have not broken tradition but continue to observe December 25th as His birthday we are fully aware that it is not. (For further study, read Jesus Christ Our Promised Seed by V.P. Wierwille). Keeping that in mind today, as we honor and revere the name of God, His goodness shines on us.

One promise in God's Word to His children is that our healing will be quick and complete so that we will be up running and jumping with no pain or complications. When God heals, He leaves no doubt that whatever the ailment was, it is completely gone. Are you in pain – physically or mentally, and you see no end in sight? Maybe even the doctors are unsure of the next steps to help you. No need to despair because God is just a prayer away, healing is available as we trust Him.

Sunday September 12, 2021

Psalms 71:3 Be thou my strong habitation, whereunto I may continually resort: thou hast given commandment to save me; for thou art my rock and my fortress.

In the Old Testament are many stories of walls around cities that not only keep those inside safe and keep them from leaving but was also meant to keep the enemy out, like in the story we read of the famous wall around the city of Jericho. Our parents built a fence around our yard to keep us from leaving without permission and anyone who needed access had to call out from the gate to be let in. These are all designed for the safety of those inside.

God puts a wall of protection around His children, so that nothing can harm us. We need never be concerned with having to fight our battles. For protection from those who would want to harm us we call on our Heavenly Father to save us. If we find ourselves in a situation where physical harm seems imminent, God will step in and be our protector. We call out to Him, speak in tongues, and trust Him and He will stop the hands of our attackers.

We are continually in need of spiritual protection from the wiles of the adversary and God will be a stronghold. In these cases, we go to God in prayer with the Word of God as our sword and believing is our shield.

Monday September 13, 2021

I Peter 5:8 Be sober, be vigilant; because your adversary the devil, as a roaring lion, walketh about, seeking whom he may devour:
9 Whom resist stedfast in the faith, knowing that the same afflictions are accomplished in your brethren that are in the world.

We are to stay alert and aware of the adversary's attacks. He is stealthy and comes around in different ways without showing his true self. Several ways the adversary may attack are by using our own minds to make us doubt and question the accuracy of God's Word. He may also use people – friends or family to hurt us and make us angry and unforgiving or he may cause destruction in our environment - fires, hurricanes, earthquakes, tornadoes – that people have erroneously called "acts of God", to make those who are affected turn their backs on God in anger.

When we trust our Heavenly Father completely, we are firm, unshaken in our believing that He loves us, only wants the best for us and will never cause any kind of harm to come to us. Only good and perfect gifts come from God who is the Father of light (James 1:7).

Tuesday September 14, 2021

Psalms 65:11 Thou crownest the year with thy goodness; and thy paths drop fatness.

When we closed out the year 2019, we had no idea what was coming. With resolutions on our minds we headed in as usual determined to make it a good year. Before we knew it everything was in disarray – we suddenly found ourselves in the midst of a raging pandemic, claiming lives in every town and country around the world. It has been rough both in the physical realm but also mentally it has been difficult for many to handle. As we come to the end of 2020, there is still so much uncertainty, so much fear and anxiety coupled with worries and doubts about our future. The world has put all it's hope in various vaccines to "save the world".

As Christians we strongly believe that God Almighty is our sufficiency. God's Word assured us that as we trust Him and allow Him to direct us, our lives will be crowned with His goodness. What a promise!! We cannot lose the grip on our believing now, for it is the time to get stronger in our commitment to God and His Word. We have lived a year and witnessed what the adversary can do when people allow him access into our lives, homes, schools, businesses, and countries, turning their backs on God. We can overcome the invisible enemies of viruses and pandemics and the destruction they bring.

God has promised that our year will be filled with His goodness, and our paths will be covered in riches. Let us claim it, a year filled/crowned with 'goodness'. God cannot lie, let us believe that what He has promised He will bring to pass for us, in the powerful name of Jesus Christ.

Wednesday September 15, 2021

Psalm 31:24 Be of good courage, and he shall strengthen your heart, all ye that hope in the LORD.

What another amazing promise to claim as we heard into another year of uncertainty. We have no need to fear, no need to be anxious, or worried but as God says in His Word, we are courageous. In spite of being beaten down by the rough times we had to endure, in spite of maybe feeling too weak to continue the fight, we know we can rely on God's strength to get us through. As we look at the life of our Savior and big brother Jesus Christ, I am reminded of the song, "God has not promised us skies always blue, flower strewn pathways all our lives through." We know tough times will come because the enemy is still working to defeat God's people, but as we stay strong, not allow our minds to waver but stand firm on God's promises we will be victorious. Jesus may have felt defeated as He faced the darkest days in history when He carried the weight of man's sins, was crucified and gave up His life to save us, but He focused on the promise of God that He would be resurrected and be seated at the right hand of God. That is what kept Him going.

The song continues that He will provide "strength for the day." We look past everything negative happening now, to God's promise to strengthen our hearts as we hope in Him. Our steadfast hope remains the return of our Lord and Savior Jesus Christ.

Thursday September 16, 2021

II Thessalonians 1:11 Wherefore also we pray always for you, that our God would count you worthy of this calling, and fulfil all the good pleasure of his goodness, and the work of faith with power:
12 That the name of our Lord Jesus Christ may be glorified in you, and ye in him, according to the grace of our God and the Lord Jesus Christ.

In life there are many occasions for try-outs and although I never was in one I think I can understand the level of excitement and anxiety when for instance beautiful young ladies line up and perform in front of judges expected to be picked or chosen to win a crown of Ms. America or whichever country they represent. They walk out proud eager to represent their country. I imagine it is the same thing for national football players being recruited from college to play on a national team. Based on what I have seen on television, it is so much excitement to be picked for one of the major teams. These players are also very excited to represent their teams, their states/towns, their coaches, and their managers.

Likewise, we have been called, handpicked the Word says even before the foundations of the world to carry out the work that Jesus started in His earthly ministry. Our calling is to be ambassadors/representatives of Christ. Because we've received God's grace, we are to walk worthy "in a manner of equal value to" that calling so we can exalt and glorify the name of the Lord, and that our lives are pleasing to Him. Are we excited to answer that call, and say "here am I God?"

Let us walk out each day with our heads held high, proud to represent our Lord and Savior Jesus Christ and to bring glory to our Heavenly Father who hand-picked us.

Friday September 17, 2021

II Thessalonians 2:16 Now our Lord Jesus Christ himself, and God, even our Father, which hath loved us, and hath given us everlasting consolation and good hope through grace,

17 Comfort your hearts, and stablish you in every good word and work.

God's heart for His children is always to give. From the beginning God gave man a beautiful place to inhabit in the 'Garden of Eden.' Then thousands of years later when He put His plan of salvation in place, he again gave His only begotten Son to die for us. God gives us His mercy and compassions which are new every morning. Every day God withholds punishments we deserve and gives us His unmerited grace/favor. God forgives our sins, removes them from us as far as the east is from the west and never remembers them.

Just when we think that He has given all He can God, by His grace and love has given us the promise of the Hope of Christ's return to look forward to, so we hold fast to that through the adversary's attacks, through sufferings, heartaches and/or loss. We can look past the pain to the light of our victory in Christ as it brings comfort and strength to our hearts so we can keep moving and sharing the Word.

Saturday September 18, 2021

I John 5:14 And this is the confidence that we have in him, that, if we ask any thing according to his will, he heareth us:
15 And if we know that he hear us, whatsoever we ask, we know that we have the petitions that we desired of him.

When we go to our homes, we place the key in the lock open the door and go in boldly. We do not stand at the door asking if we can enter – except if we forgot our keys. God has asked us to "come boldly unto the throne of grace." Because of God's grace, His unmerited favor towards us, we can be bold, we can be confident to go to Him with our requests. As we call on Him, we know that He hears us; there is no "call-waiting", no "busy dial tone", we have direct access to our Heavenly Father by way of His Son, our Lord and Savior, Jesus Christ.

Just as we go to a bank and write a slip for a withdrawal because we are confident the money is on our account, we go to God in confidence knowing that we can make a withdrawal on the promises He has made available for us. We can also be confident that He will not ignore us as long as our requests are according to His will. He will always grant us our petitions. How comforting!

Sunday September 19, 2021

Philippians 4:19 But my God shall supply all your need according to his riches in glory by Christ Jesus.

As children, we never doubted that our parents would feed us, or that we would have clean clothes every day to wear to school or church. We never concerned ourselves with whether or not we would have everything we needed. Maybe we would ask for something – a specific outfit for an event and were just as confident that they would provide it.

In the same way we are sure that from His bountiful, glorious, heavenly riches, God will gladly make sure all our needs are met. Note that it does not state our "greed" – overly excess, but everything we need to live the more than abundant life that He promised us, He will supply. As children ask their parents for what they need, we can ask our Heavenly Father and know beyond the shadow of a doubt that He will provide. We always ask with thanks believing that what we are asking for we will definitely receive.

Monday September 20, 2021

Mark 11:24 Therefore I say unto you, What things soever ye desire, when ye pray, believe that ye receive them, and ye shall have them.
25 And when ye stand praying, forgive, if ye have ought against any: that your Father also which is in heaven may forgive you your trespasses.
26 But if ye do not forgive, neither will your Father which is in heaven forgive your trespasses.

WOW!! This is powerful! God's promise to us His children is that whatsoever we want/desire if we believe that we have already received them, we shall have them. It is repeated more than once in the Word because God wants to reassure us that He is being serious. To be clear, we are still talking about our hearts desires that are according to the will of God.

One stipulation is that we are willing to forgive those who we have an issue with. Because God in Christ has forgiven us, we should be willing to forgive others. Will it be simple or easy? Probably not, as we have seen we were not promised "skies always blue", but with the strength of God we know can do it. As we go to God with our requests and petitions, if we have not received answers to prayer lately, we take a step back to clear our minds and hearts of any anger, hurt or hate and humbly forgive as God forgave us.

Tuesday September 21, 2021

Hebrews 4:16 Let us therefore come boldly unto the throne of grace, that we may obtain mercy, and find grace to help in time of need.

Most children can go to their parents and make a request for anything knowing that they will receive it. They have no doubt, no questions of if or maybe; they walk away confident that it is just a matter of when. Sometimes they are even as specific as to request a gift, clothes or money by a certain day and time. And in most cases, they do get whatever they ask for depending on the family's resources.

God has made it available for us to come to Him and stand righteous before Him without any sense of sin, guilt, or shortcoming. Not because of anything we could have done, but by His grace alone is this privilege ours. He forgives us, and we are justified in His sight – He does not see our sins anymore. Knowing that we can go to Him in confidence knowing that He is not holding anything against us. And it is only at the "throne of grace" we will find true love, peace, joy, and comfort. Let us accept God's invitation with humility.

Wednesday September 22, 2021

Colossians 3:1 If ye then be risen with Christ, seek those things which are above, where Christ sitteth on the right hand of God.
2 Set your affection on things above, not on things on the earth.

We take pride in who we are and our earthly family history. Someone may ask us where we are from, or the background of our family name, and we will go on and on with pride to explain where our parents or grandparents came from. Carrying on my father's last name has always been a huge deal to me. With four girls getting married and two brothers wo never did, it seemed like we would lose our identity once we gave up our father's name. Although it is long and even longer when attached to my husband's name, I keep it and carry it with pride using it on all my legal documents.

Not knowing or understanding the truth of who we are and what we have in Christ may cause many Christians to be lacking in their spiritual walk. Since we have been raised to a new life in Christ, our goal is to keep our hearts focused on the things of God. Our thinking is elevated above the worldly thoughts of our old man nature to where we are now seated in the heavenlies with Christ. We proudly identify ourselves as children of God, and are excited to talk about our Heavenly Father and all He has given us.

Thursday September 23, 2021

Colossians 3:13 Forbearing one another, and forgiving one another, if any man have a quarrel against any: even as Christ forgave you, so also do ye.
14 And above all these things put on charity, which is the bond of perfectness.

Learning to forgive was hard for me for two main reasons, one being when I was hurt, I held on to that hurt for years, trying to guard and protect my heart. The other reason was I felt like would be letting the one that hurt me off the hook – letting that person get away with it. When I was taught and understand God's Word about forgiveness, I quickly changed my thinking to forgive others. As I truly accepted God's heart to forgive me and never look at me as a sinner again, I realized I could do it too – forgive and try to forget, so as not to keep the hurt in my heart. I also realize that forgiveness was more for my healing than for the person that hurt me. I made a decision to choose to be more forgiving and since then have felt the heaviness roll off my back.

As God's representatives here on earth, our life is to bring glory to Him. One way we can do that is by being patient and tolerant of others, especially willing to forgive those who hurt us because Christ has already forgiven us. We have seen this several times already, God is making a point that He wants us to pay attention to. Show the love of God in manifestations among the household of believers, so we stay united as one.

Friday September 24, 2021

Hebrews 4:12 For the word of God is quick, and powerful, and sharper than any two-edged sword, piercing even to the dividing asunder of soul and spirit, and of the joints and marrow, and is a discerner of the thoughts and intents of the heart.

I remember a chorus we sang in Sunday School many years ago that went something like this – "be careful little hands what you do; there's a Father up above, looking down in love, so be careful little hands what you do." When I was planning something and needed to make a decision but I was not sure if it was exactly the right thing to do, that little chorus started me thinking about what the Word had to say about it.

The Word of God is alive and full of energy, and is a critic seeing right through our innermost thoughts. It cuts right through our very soul more precisely than even how a two-edged sword would be able to cut through a joint or bone. We cannot hide anything, not even our deepest innermost thoughts from God. We may be able to fool everyone, including ourselves, but never God. He sees right through the lies and our conscious will not let us rest until we make it right.

Let us be humble and honest as we go before God; He knows what we are thinking already anyway. Attempting to lie and cover up will only make things worse.

Saturday September 25, 2021

Hebrews 10:22 Let us draw near with a true heart in full assurance of faith, having our hearts sprinkled from an evil conscience, and our bodies washed with pure water.

23 Let us hold fast the profession of our faith without wavering; (for he is faithful that promised;)

Jesus Christ shed His blood to wash away our sins and we are baptized by God's gift of holy spirit. Our repentance and making a decision to confess Jesus as Lord in our lives means that we make a choice to renew our minds – no longer conformed to or behaving in the manner of the world. God wants us close to Him, in true fellowship and believing. With our conscience clear accepting His full forgiveness we are made pure and clean by the outpouring of the fire of His gift of holy spirit. We have been made whole, righteous, and able to stand in the presence of God with no sense of sin or guilt. That means that even in the face of the enemy we can stand tall and face him with no fear having no sense of condemnation and free from his clutches that bind us.

We are to be bold to make a confession of believing that as God is, "so are we in this world" as we read in 1John 4:17. We are as righteous as God Himself is righteous, (2 Corinthians 5:21), we can walk in light and shine as lights because we have God in Christ in us, and God is light. (1 John 1:5-7) We are to never waver from that belief, never doubt that God has accomplished what He said He would do in our lives. He stands by His promises.

Sunday September 26, 2021

Hebrews 10:24 And let us consider one another to provoke unto love and to good works:
25 Not forsaking the assembling of ourselves together, as the manner of some is; but exhorting one another: and so much the more, as ye see the day approaching.

As siblings we try to take care of one another, we encourage and speak kind words to build each other up. It blesses me to watch my eight-year-old grandson stop whatever he is doing to help his younger five-year-old sister. Sometimes he is totally focused on his Nintendo Switch playing a game he is trying to win, but when she comes to him pleading "Ave, please help me,' he quietly pauses the game to help her then goes right back to what he was doing. I know it blesses God's heart to see His children be kind and loving and helpful to each other. Our words should be loving and encouraging so they in turn can do the same for someone else.

Coming together as the one body in Christ is how God sees us, encouraging us to maintain that Godly fellowship in the household with love one for another. The period of getting together via zoom was a blessing in a time where social distancing was mandatory, but nothing beats coming together in person. The enthusiasm for God and His Word is more evident and can motivate others. Together we grow in unity as we pray with, have sweet fellowship and break bread with one another.

Unless it is for medical reasons, let us consider always making a way to get together in person regularly.

Monday September 27, 2021

Galatians 6:1 Brethren, if a man be overtaken in a fault, ye which are spiritual, restore such an one in the spirit of meekness; considering thyself, lest thou also be tempted.
2 Bear ye one another's burdens, and so fulfil the law of Christ.

None of us are perfect and will make mistakes as long as we are on this earth. Those of who are more spiritually mature need to be supportive, encouraging and building each other up with the Word of God and with kind, loving words. We may think we would not be tricked like the other person was, but keep in mind the adversary is like a roaring lion seeking who he may devour/destroy. It could happen to anyone of us, so we hold one another up in love.

We must not be haughty and pat ourselves on the back because we were not tricked in the same category someone else was. I may not make the same mistake someone else did, but I am as susceptible, and it could be in another area. With that in mind, I must be willing to lovingly help someone else get back on track with the truth of God's Word as I would pray someone would do for me. We stay vigilant, sharp, alert to the adversary's tricks so we can avoid them. We back off his attacks with God's Word, and the more Word we know the better equipped we will be to do so.

Tuesday September 28, 2021

Galatians 5:1 Stand fast therefore in the liberty wherewith Christ hath made us free and be not entangled again with the yoke of bondage.

The Old Testament believers kept the law to the letter, everything was governed by the rules and regulations of the law that kept them in bondage. They struggled to keep every jot and title of the law. We were made free from the curse of the law since the day of Pentecost and the ushering in of the Grace Administration.

The accomplished works of Jesus Christ gave us freedom from sin and its consequences, leading to our justification (judicial acquittal) and our righteousness (free from all sense of sin, guilt, and short comings). After we have all that, why would we risk being drawn back into that web that God rescued us from? Allowing that would seem as though we are not grateful or appreciative of all we have in Christ. Staying focused on God's Word can help us resist the adversary and keeps us from falling back into the bondage of our past sins that weigh us down. Instead we are thankful that Jesus Christ paid the price – in full, to set us free.

Wednesday September 29, 2021

Colossians 3:17 And whatsoever ye do in word or deed, do all in the name of the Lord Jesus, giving thanks to God and the Father by him.

A few years ago, I responded on one social media to someone's comments about why I was silent on a particular movement and why didn't I support it and if I could not identify with it. I responded that I chose not to be a part of it because I preferred to focus on the positives from God's Word and with my prayers, I felt I was as supportive as I could be. There was such a bitter debate with people spewing insults at one another I did not see any profit in it nor a solution to the problem.

We were recently reminded that even on social media our words and actions can be offensive to others and distract them from the truth of God's Word. Some may be perplexed as to how that could be but consider how you respond to political statements or even to other world events portrayed on the news or social media. Everyone has an opinion and yes as believers we do too, but if what we say or do might be a stumbling block to prevent someone turning to God and receiving a true knowledge of God's Word, we should be cautious of what we say and our actions. Staying thankful always can keep our hearts meek to the truth.

Thursday September 30, 2021

Hebrews 11:1 Now faith is the substance of things hoped for, the evidence of things not seen.

Hebrews 11:1 (Amplified Version) Now faith is the assurance (title deed, confirmation) of things hoped for (divinely guaranteed), and the evidence of things not seen [the conviction of their reality—faith comprehends as fact what cannot be experienced by the physical senses].

For years I heard the phrase "take a leap of faith" mainly meaning to jump into something with one's eyes closed and hope for the best. As born-again believers we believe and trust God for answers, taking believing action to see things come to past. Our believing is what helps us see past the negative situation to the end results even when it seems impossible by our five senses. That is believing action.

That is why when we pray, we thank God in advance for answering our prayer and granting our requests even though we have not seen the end result. We are so completely convinced that God will answer our prayers because He promised, and He cannot lie. When we receive the answer we give God thanks again that we have received the answer to our petitions.

OCTOBER

Friday October 1, 2021

Romans 10:13 For whosoever shall call upon the name of the Lord shall be saved.
14 How then shall they call on him in whom they have not believed? and how shall they believe in him of whom they have not heard? and how shall they hear without a preacher?
15 And how shall they preach, except they be sent? as it is written, How beautiful are the feet of them that preach the gospel of peace, and bring glad tidings of good things!

God has made a way for all men 'whosoever' it says here to be born-again. That is God's heart. Unless we as believers exercise our ministry of reconciliation, and get out of our comfort zone, how will people hear God's Word. We have the truth, the rightly divided Word of God and it has been made available for all. Those of us who have received it must step up; it is our time to move. We have been commissioned as ambassadors for Christ to make God known.

As those who take the place of the absent Christ, we have the authority and power to speak in His name and hold forth God's truth. So we go out speaking to those we meet, knocking on doors, inviting people to come and see and hear the gospel of Christ.

Saturday October 2, 2021

Romans 10:17 So then faith cometh by hearing, and hearing by the word of God.

When we first heard God's Word taught we did not immediately understand everything. We build our believing and get stronger spiritually as we hear and accept the truth of God's Word. After many years of searching for answers regarding things I was confused about in the Word, I was overjoyed to finally take a Bible class that answered every question. Since then I have repeated the class multiple times and even took the upgraded version still soaking in the truths from God's Word. Many theologians pride themselves on knowing a lot about the Bible but sadly their knowledge comes from reading books about the Bible and not from the Bible itself.

God's Word is our standard for truth and as we hear it more and more, we build our believing and confidence in it. In that way we grow and mature in our spiritual walk.

Sunday October 3, 2021

Matthew 17:20 And Jesus said unto them, Because of your unbelief: for verily I say unto you, If ye have faith as a grain of mustard seed, ye shall say unto this mountain, Remove hence to yonder place; and it shall remove; and nothing shall be impossible unto you.

There is something called 'wrong believing' and that is unbelief. We either believe right or we believe wrong, and it is not necessary to try to store up a house full of believing so to speak. We just need to be able to fully and without doubt or question believe God's Word. When we go to God's Word in prayer we should be so convinced of God's willingness and ability to give us a positive outcome that we should be able to speak to a mountain and tell it to move from one spot to another and it should - figuratively. The mountains we need removed from our lives are those of fear, doubt, worry, anger, hatred, and malice (hostility).

Consider if you are not experiencing answers to prayer that there may be evidence of 'wrong believing' that needs to be corrected. The Word of God assures us that if we believe when we pray, nothing will be impossible for us. It sure is worth it to build our believing to see things happen, to receive answers to our prayers.

Monday October 4, 2021

Colossians 3:23 And whatsoever ye do, do it heartily, as to the Lord, and not unto men;
24 Knowing that of the Lord ye shall receive the reward of the inheritance: for ye serve the Lord Christ.

Each one of my siblings and myself had chores to complete when we woke up and before we went to bed. Some chores were easier to do than others and we were not always happy to do them, but we usually were motivated by the promise from our mother to be allowed to stay up late, or attend a friend's party so we tried to get it done and done well if we wanted to be rewarded.

We are in service with God to continue to carry out the work His Son Jesus Christ started in His earthly ministry. Joyfully and gladly we choose to serve in whatever capacity there is a need because our service is to bring glory to God and not to please men. Our goal is to strive to bless others and meet needs as we endeavor to do the works of Jesus Christ and to lead others to God. We anticipate hearing God say "well done thou good and faithful servant" when we receive our reward. That is our motivation, and not earthly recognition or praise.

Tuesday October 5, 2021

Romans 8:26 Likewise the Spirit also helpeth our infirmities: for we know not what we should pray for as we ought: but the Spirit itself maketh intercession for us with groanings which cannot be uttered.
27 And he that searcheth the hearts knoweth what is the mind of the Spirit, because he maketh intercession for the saints according to the will of God.

There are times when we know we need to pray but are 'drawing a blank', we have no idea what we should be praying for. When we lost our brother several years ago, we went through something like that. My oldest niece who was more like a younger sister to us, was heartbroken and went to her neighbor with a request, "please pray for me, I don't know how to pray or what to pray for." How many of you can relate?

Sometimes our pain, grief, heart ache or despair may seem too much to bear, and we may not know "what to pray for as we ought." Many times, I have been awakened in the middle of the night and I think of someone – a family member, friend, one of my children, or grandchildren. At that time, I am just not sure what the need is. What can I do? I pray in the spirit or speak in tongues, which by-passes my understanding, communicating perfectly to God who is Spirit, by way of His gift of holy spirit in me, which is making intercession for me. Even in a situation when a medical professional may not see the healing we can pray perfectly and experience deliverance.

Wednesday October 6, 2021

Psalms 103:13 As far as the east is from the west, so far hath he removed our transgressions from us.

If we have an appliance that no longer works, and we throw it out in the dump, we never go digging for it again, do we? Once we get rid of and replace it with a new or better working one, we do not even think of it again. Look up a map and identify the north, south, east, and west. If done accurately the east and west never meet, so what does that tell us about that statement? Our past sins, transgressions, or wrong doings are removed never to be brought back up. When Jesus was crucified and died on the cross, every sin, every wrong doing was nailed on the cross with Him; when He was buried they were buried with Him, but when He rose again, He left them in the grave, never to be brought back to us. God did that – He removed every sin from us paid in full by the blood of Jesus Christ.

Praise God, hallelujah we are forgiven, we are justified – "just as if we never sinned." We believe and accept God's merciful kindness and grace. When God tells us He forgives us and remembers our sins no more He means it, so we claim it and walk out in His forgiveness and righteousness.

Thursday October 7, 2021

Romans 8:1 There is therefore now no condemnation to them which are in Christ Jesus, who walk not after the flesh, but after the Spirit.

So many Christians miss out on experiencing the true joys of salvation and living a more than abundant life because of self-condemnation. They believe they are born again but cannot shake the feelings of guilt and self-loathing when they look back at some of the mistakes they have done. They question if God really forgave them and if they experience any type of health issue will remark that it must be God's way of punishing them. We must remember that the enemy is just trying to steal our joy not allowing us to move on and making us keep thoughts of doubt and fear in our minds.

When we confess Jesus Christ as Lord in our lives and believe that God raised Him from the dead, we are born-again. We trade in our old man nature for a new man (in behavior and actions). Now that we are walking by the gift of God's holy spirit in us, He does not condemn us. Instead God put in a clause promising to forgive us and cleanse us from all unrighteousness when we confess or ask for forgiveness for our sins. (1 John 1:9) We know for a certainty that God has already forgiven us; now it is our turn to forgive ourselves and claim God's peace that passes all understanding with no condemnation.

Friday October 8, 2021

Romans 8:11 But if the Spirit of him that raised up Jesus from the dead dwell in you, he that raised up Christ from the dead shall also quicken your mortal bodies by his Spirit that dwelleth in you.

What an awesome affirmation of God's love and power in us to heal and bring us back to full health. It does not matter what the doctors, specialists, or scientists say, we claim God's promises and trust Him as we believe. Many people panic and get anxious when diagnosed with a condition the doctors may say has a "poor prognosis". They may even be told, there is nothing more medicine can do, and death is inevitable. The adversary jumps in and fills the head with fear, depression, and a sense of hopelessness, which causes people to give up. That reaction is a common one by our five senses, but we must keep in mind the power we have in Christ; we do not give up but 'prove' God as He asks us to.

The same spirit that God used when He raised Jesus Christ from the dead is what we receive when we are born again. Let us think about that for a moment! Can you see how powerful that is? Because we have God's gift of holy spirit in us, also called "Christ in you the hope of glory," we know that we have healing and new life by that same power. We believe it and claim it. Do not let the enemy steal your joy, peace of mind, or healing. Pray and believe for complete healing claiming all we have and are in Jesus Christ.

Saturday October 9, 2021

John 16:13 Howbeit when he, the Spirit of truth, is come, he will guide you into all truth: for he shall not speak of himself; but whatsoever he shall hear, that shall he speak: and he will shew you things to come.

Speaking of God's gift of holy spirit, the word 'he' should have been translated 'it'. Because it is in us, we are reminded of God's truth and by free-will choice decide to be guided by those truths. Our manifestation of the gift in us to the world governed by our five senses is our ability to speak in tongues and those meek to receive and believe the evidence will be blessed and accept that it is indeed the truth.

All born-again believers receive God's gift of holy spirit. God, our Heavenly Father, who is Spirit communicates to us via His gift of holy spirit and by revelation guides us to the 'whole truth'. When we renew our minds and listen to that still small voice, we are always blessed.

The spirit of truth guides us to speak exactly what God wants people to hear from Him when we speak in tongues. As we have been taught, it is a message for or from God and the person speaking doesn't understand what He is saying. It is however directly from God to bless those who hear it. We trust God to be meek enough to listen as His spirit in us is renewed each day by our speaking in tongues.

Sunday October 10, 2021

Romans 5:1 Therefore being justified by faith, we have peace with God through our Lord Jesus Christ:
2 By whom also we have access by faith into this grace wherein we stand, and rejoice in hope of the glory of God.

Our justification is a done deal; it is not something we are anticipating in the future. One of the sonship rights we have when we are born again is justification. God has justified us legally making us acceptable to Him, freeing us from the penalty of sin and it's consequences. When we confess Jesus Christ as Lord in our lives and believe God raised Him from the dead, we have redemption and justification by God's grace. (Romans 3:24) There is absolutely nothing we can do to make this happen; it is strictly by the grace of God.

We are declared righteous because of our believing and God gives us His peace so we can be confident in Him. We have been legally acquitted and can rest assured of our position in Christ. There is no more barrier to us coming before God, the door is wide open for us to draw near to Him face to face just as if we never sinned. What an honor! We give all praise and thanks to God.

Monday October 11, 2021

Romans 8:16 The Spirit itself beareth witness with our spirit, that we are the children of God:
17 And if children, then heirs; heirs of God, and joint-heirs with Christ; if so be that we suffer with him, that we may be also glorified together.

Usually after parents die, they leave an estate to be shared equally between their children. Some have even opted to divide things up while they are still around to ensure that each child is treated fairly. That is their inheritance as heirs of their parents. As children of God, we are heirs to His kingdom and will share in His glory with Jesus Christ.

God, who is Spirit, communicates to His children by way of His gift of holy spirit in us to announce that we are indeed His children. (1 John3:1,2) This is a legal and binding deal, paid in full by the sacrifice of His Son Jesus Christ. As God's children Jesus Christ is our brother and we share equally in all God has – eternal rewards, salvation, and His gift of holy spirit. Powerful words!

Tuesday October 12, 2021

Romans 15:13 Now the God of hope fill you with all joy and peace in believing, that ye may abound in hope, through the power of the Holy Ghost.

Joy has been described as an emotion of contentment, deep satisfaction, and fulfillment that is not dependent on events or circumstances. In comparison we have happiness based on the positive thoughts that are dependent on what is going on in our lives and around us. Peace is an "undisturbed rest" of tranquility where we can be calm. That is what we experience from God – deep contentment, and a calmness that is not affected by circumstances or people.

Whatever is going on in the world or even in our lives do not sway us or deter our relationship and sweet fellowship with our Heavenly Father. Because of our believing we are filled with joy and peace confident in our freedom and salvation in Christ. We steadfastly focus on the hope of Christ return because of God's gift of holy spirit in us and the power we have received as born-again sons of God.

Wednesday October 13, 2021

Psalms 118:1 O give thanks unto the LORD; for he is good: because his mercy endureth for ever.

Psalms 118:24 This is the day which the LORD hath made; we will rejoice and be glad in it.

As parents when our children disobey, we correct and discipline them, but we still love them. We only want the best for our children and do not want to do anything to hurt them. Many times, I will try to set the standard of what is expected of them going forward, forgive them and help them learn to do better. Other times we teach our children and withhold the punishment they probably should get.

Our Heavenly Father is loving, and He wants only what is best for His children as well, even bigger than us as parents. He has set standards in His Word for us to follow and when we are off the Word, He makes allowance for us to be forgiven and to get back on track. Every day is a new opportunity to praise God, give Him thanks and be joyful in all we have in Him. We give Him thanks for withholding judgement and punishment from us even when we deserve it. Because of God's mercy we are free from the penalty of sin forever. Let us remember to give God thanks for each and every day, let us choose to be joyful and keep an attitude of gratitude always.

Thursday October 14, 2021

Psalms 126:3 The LORD hath done great things for us; whereof we are glad.

We are reminded in Psalms 103 to not forget all of God's benefits. There are so many things to be thankful to God for, that He does not ask us to remember all of them, just not to forget all. First and foremost is God's love for us, He sent His Son to pay the price for our sins so we could be rescued from the enemy. He has given us salvation – deliverance from sin, it's consequences and the wrath to come. We have been given five sonship rights as children of God (redemption, sanctification, justification, righteousness, and the ministry of reconciliation); we received God's gift of holy spirit with the privilege of perfect prayer by speaking in tongues.

These are just a few of the blessings God has given us – the "great things" we are so glad and thankful for. Consider making a list of all the great things from God that you are thankful and that makes you happy. I will add a few to my list from above - salvation, eternal life, health, and our families, our ministry, and it's leadership. As you think about it, don't just write them down, stop and thank God for each one. Blessings.

Friday October 15, 2021

Ephesians 4:1 I therefore, the prisoner of the Lord,
beseech you that ye walk worthy of the vocation
wherewith ye are called,
2 With all lowliness and meekness, with longsuffering,
forbearing one another in love;
3 Endeavouring to keep the unity of the Spirit in the
bond of peace.

One day the phone rings and the person on the other end identifies themselves as a manager from the company you applied to work for. The person states they want to offer you the job and will send you an offer letter which will detail your job description and all that is expected of you in that position. A week, maybe two later you start your employment with that company. You will use that job-description as your guide to carry out your duties. You were called for a job and now you have to prove yourself worthy of that calling. Since the company has trusted you enough give you a job, you will want to prove that you are capable and the best person to do the job.

We are born-again, believing children of God, called to stand and live for God. As such we are encouraged to walk and live our lives in a manner of equal value to our calling. It is a calling of humility, meekness, forgiving, patient, kind, not haughty, but loving to one another. As much as possible we are to live in peace, standing like-minded, in one accord and in unity according to God's Word, keeping harmony in the household.

Saturday October 16, 2021

Hebrews 6:10 For God is not unrighteous to forget your work and labour of love, which ye have shewed toward his name, in that ye have ministered to the saints, and do minister.

Have you ever had a job where you feel like you work really hard, go above and beyond your call of duty and no one seems to care or appreciate you? Maybe it is in your family – it may seem that no matter what you do no seems to appreciate it. I watched a television show where the son was always being praised by his parents and the daughter was always being criticized. To the degree that when he did something wrong the parents were very understanding, then turned to the daughter and asked, "did you know about this; how come you did nothing to help him?"

It was a funny scenario, but we know that as children of God everything we do is important to Him and the household of believers. And there may be times we feel unappreciated, but our service is to bring glory to God, and not for worldly praise. It is a blessing to serve in God's household and we do it by our free will choice, not grudgingly but lovingly. Our heart is to bless God's people and bring glory to His name, because we know whatever we do will never be in vain. People will be blessed and turn to God as they see His love in action in our lives. God is pleased when we respond to our calling and give of a cheerful heart.

Sunday October 17, 2021

Romans 8:28 And we know that all things work together for good to them that love God, to them who are the called according to his purpose.

This is not chance or luck or wishful thinking that all things will work out. God is working to give us the positive results we are believing for. On several occasions over the years, I found myself in the position of having to make a decision about where I needed to be in my career as well as my physical location – where I would live. I remember being very torn about what I should do or where I should be. Once I got focused and prayed specifically about what I needed, I received an answer of peace which turned out to be the right decision because everything fell into place and went smoothly.

That is how we can be sure that God is working in us to make the right decision – we will be peaceful and get the best results. If we are not comfortable, but are confused, unsure or troubled, it may not be where God is directing us. We are called to do God's work, and we obey because we love Him. Even in a position of leadership, we serve God's people to bless, encourage, support, and build them up. Because we are working "according to His purpose", allowing His Word to be our guide, we are confident that all things will work together for good.

Monday October 18, 2021

Hebrews 6:18 That by two immutable things, in which it was impossible for God to lie, we might have a strong consolation, who have fled for refuge to lay hold upon the hope set before us:
19 Which hope we have as an anchor of the soul, both sure and stedfast, and which entereth into that within the veil;

It has been said many times that God does not lie, but how comforting to know that it is impossible for God to lie. God does not change, He is constant in everything – He is love, He is light, He is forgiving, and it is impossible for Him to lie. Take a look at how clearly the amplified version states these truths.

Hebrews 6:18 (Amplified) *This was so that, by two unchangeable things [His promise and His oath] in which it is impossible for God ever to prove false or deceive us, we who have fled [to Him] for refuge might have mighty indwelling strength and strong encouragement to grasp and hold fast the hope appointed for us and set before [us].*

Our confidence in God and His Word is strengthened by our understanding of His Word. Remember God does not want us to ignorant regarding His Word. We have the promise of Christ's return which is our Hope, a steadfast and unbreakable anchor that no one can destroy. It has already been cemented in place and we know that it is a done deal. We stand firm in our believing and keep our minds centered and focused on that promise coming to pass.

Tuesday October 19, 2021

Revelation 21:4 And God shall wipe away all tears from their eyes; and there shall be no more death, neither sorrow, nor crying, neither shall there be any more pain: for the former things are passed away.

When I was very young my nickname was 'cry-baby' because I cried a lot about everything. I cried if I was yelled at, if someone was getting a spanking (not necessarily me), if another kid fell and hurt themselves and/or was crying. I even cried for those I heard the adults talk about who had no food and they were discussing collecting groceries for them. That is where my longing to help others started, I think. As I got older the tears were less, but I would cry if I heard a story on the news about someone (even a stranger) in a serious accident or who died; if someone hurt me or even just told a lie about me. Well, I chose nursing as a career, and I kept crying – for and with families who lost loved ones and for sick and suffering babies. I will certainly be looking forward to the day when God will wipe away all tears.

God has promised us a time when there will be no more death; we will not have a reason to cry, sorrow, grieve or mourn. We will receive our new bodies – just like Jesus Christ and we will be perfectly healed therefore we will have no more pain either. There will be no need for doctors, pharmacies, funeral homes, or hospitals. Even our elderly will be in their new bodies and will no longer be in need of long-term care facilities. Al these things will be in the past as we will be living in the new heaven and earth. As we anticipate all what God has in store for us, we can endure through life's hardships as we look ahead to a much brighter future.

Wednesday October 20, 2021

I Thessalonians 4:13 But I would not have you to be ignorant, brethren, concerning them which are asleep, that ye sorrow not, even as others which have no hope.
14 For if we believe that Jesus died and rose again, even so them also which sleep in Jesus will God bring with him.
15 For this we say unto you by the word of the Lord, that we which are alive and remain unto the coming of the Lord shall not prevent them which are asleep.
16 For the Lord himself shall descend from heaven with a shout, with the voice of the archangel, and with the trump of God: and the dead in Christ shall rise first:
17 Then we which are alive and remain shall be caught up together with them in the clouds, to meet the Lord in the air: and so shall we ever be with the Lord.
18 Wherefore comfort one another with these words.

THIS IS OUR HOPE!! I have mentioned it a few times throughout the book, but here it is in full detail. That is what we labor for in Christ, that is what gets us up every day in anticipation. Meditate on that, soak in these truths, let the magnitude of what we have to look forward to, sink in and all that it means for us.

We will see Christ again, caught up to meet Him in the skies; and a special bonus – we will see our loves ones that we have previously lost. Without these truths, without the Hope our lives are basically lost. We would wander aimlessly; we would sink into a depression that we would never come out of. We are encouraged to "comfort one another with these words." The Word of God heals –

mentally, physically, and spiritually. In my darkest moments of grief, I reach for the Word and saturate my life with it. Getting an overdose of the truths in there has brought me through every negative, dark, sad, or hurtful situations I ever had to face. God will wipe away all our tears! We thank God for the precious hope of Christ's return

Thursday October 21, 2021

Proverbs 22:15 Foolishness is bound in the heart of a child; but the rod of correction shall drive it far from him.

Proverbs 19:18 Chasten thy son while there is hope, and let not thy soul spare for his crying.

These two are placed together because they supplement each other. These truths are worth repeating because there has been so much erroneous teaching about this topic. Children need to be taught because what is in their hearts is foolishness and so their actions will reflect that. We are all born sinners according to Romans 6:23 and until we are old enough to understand and get born-again, we need right instruction from our parents. As parents we lovingly and with Godly wisdom use the "rod of correction" not to "teach them a lesson", but to correct and teach them the rightly divided Word regarding obedience and making Godly decisions. As a child the discipline can actually help develop his character, but if left unchecked he will get to an age where your attempts to correct/discipline will fall on deaf ears. Then his negative behavior spills out into the community causing even greater problems.

Consider the truths of the Word concerning disciplining our children. In Hebrews 12:6 the Word states that God chastens/reproves/disciplines those He loves. We are reproved and corrected when we are not walking according to Godly standard from the Word and instructed in the right way. In the same way we discipline our children, with love and not in anger, to correct them and give them the necessary instruction to get them back on track

Friday October 22, 2021

I Corinthians 13:13 And now abideth faith, hope, charity, these three; but the greatest of these is charity.

I Corinthians 13:13 (Amplified Version) And now there remain: faith [abiding trust in God and His promises], hope [confident expectation of eternal salvation], love [unselfish love for others growing out of God's love for me], these three [the choicest graces]; but the greatest of these is love.

This is about "agape" the love of God in manifestations in the "church" or household of believers. Are we genuinely manifesting that love and how can we do better? When it is all said and done, what do we have left but the never ending, unconditional love of God. God will remain faithful forever, His promises will never fail. We have the Hope of Jesus Christ's return when we will be caught up to meet Him in the air. That hope gets us up each day, drives us to keep speaking the truth of God's Word and helps us endure, looking past whatever we have to go through in this life and looking instead towards the promise of eternal life and the rewards we will receive at the Bema – when we stand before God.

We show God's love to others with benevolence, a term that encompasses kindness, showing appreciation for the lives of others and giving unselfishly from a heart of thankfulness.

Saturday October 23, 2021

I Corinthians 15:51 Behold, I shew you a mystery; We
shall not all sleep, but we shall all be changed,
52 In a moment, in the twinkling of an eye, at the last
trump: for the trumpet shall sound, and the dead shall
be raised incorruptible, and we shall be changed.
53 For this corruptible must put on incorruption, and
this mortal must put on immortality.
54 So when this corruptible shall have put on
incorruption, and this mortal shall have put on
immortality, then shall be brought to pass the saying
that is written, Death is swallowed up in victory.
55 O death, where is thy sting? O grave, where is thy
victory?

This is the second place in the Bible that God speaks to us about dealing with death of loved ones and the victory we have in Jesus in spite of our sorrow, loss, and grief. (1 Thessalonians 4:13-18). The word 'sleep; here is used to euphemize the word 'death' making the reality seem less harsh and easier on us. Our loved ones who have gone before us are asleep in Christ. We are reminded of God's promise that Jesus is coming back, and believers living along with those who are 'asleep' or have died before His return, God will raise up to meet Jesus in the air.

Because Jesus Christ lives, we have the victory over death. At Christ's return we will be able to say "O death, where is thy sting? O grave, where is thy victory?" Sometimes it seems so overwhelming, and I get it, this is heavy stuff. Every time we lose someone near and dear to our hearts, we feel the pain, the sting, the loss, and incredible sadness. But thanks be to God through our Lord and Savior Jesus Christ, when we hear the sound of the trumpet, everything will change – we will be filled with joy as we meet our Lord and Savior face to face, and are reunited with our loved ones. What a glorious day to anticipate!!

Sunday October 24, 2021

I Corinthians 15:57 But thanks be to God, which giveth us the victory through our Lord Jesus Christ.

If some of you like me are not athletes, I'm sure you have witnessed many competitions – swimming, track racing, football, soccer, and more. The moment when a team wins not only they, and the coaches celebrate that victory, but all the fans as well. I remember when one of my husband's football team's won the 'Super Bowl' the excitement was palpable not only with friends but the whole city celebrated with parades and parties.

As Christians we already have the victory through our Lord and Savior. We can have victory every day as we overcome obstacles, and negative situations. Glory to God Almighty, the Creator of the heavens and earth. In Him we can claim victory in every situation, even over death. This is our future reality, for when Christ returns and claims that victory, it is ours as well. Right now, our victory is our salvation, our justification, redemption, righteousness, sanctification, and our ministry of reconciliation. Thanks, and praise to God.

Monday October 25, 2021

Romans 8:38 For I am persuaded, that neither death, nor life, nor angels, nor principalities, nor powers, nor things present, nor things to come,
39 Nor height, nor depth, nor any other creature, shall be able to separate us from the love of God, which is in Christ Jesus our Lord.

What an awesome feeling to know that no matter what our parents will not stop loving us! A parent's love goes beyond mistakes, failures, or disappointments but even they could be angry and hurt enough to stop talking to a child but probably not stop loving them.

We have seen that it is impossible for God to lie, and that He does not change. So, we can be absolutely sure that as His children we are safe in His care. He tells us there is nothing that will come between us or cause Him to stop loving us; God's love is unconditional. I am sure there have been times when we feel as if God is no longer close or not hearing us. But rest assured it is never God moving away. Two main reasons for that feeling is when we break fellowship with our Heavenly Father and/or it is an attack of the adversary.

God is determined to not even let death break His connection with us – no angels, no devil spirits, or other powers, past present or future events. When we are celebrating life on the mountaintop, successful, feeling on top of the world; when life throws us a curve-ball and we are down in the valley of despair, pain, hurt, and yes even grief, God is right there with us, helping us navigate those emotions and getting us through it. The love of God through Christ Jesus our Lord is everlasting.

Tuesday October 26, 2021

Deuteronomy 31:8 And the LORD, he it is that doth go before thee; he will be with thee, he will not fail thee, neither forsake thee: fear not, neither be dismayed.

Ah! How reassuring, how comforting! We have God in Christ in us, so that means when we pray, we do not need to ask God to go with us. Whether it's a short trip to the grocery store, to visit a friend, going for a walk around your neighborhood, God is with us. Maybe you are planning a much longer trip, such as a road trip of six to maybe 20 hours, getting on a plane to travel overseas; God is still with you. Instead of how we were taught previously to prayer "please God and if it is your will, go with us and protect us," we pray thanking God for His protection, for being with us and for our safe return.

Because we already know we have God in Christ in us, we know beyond a shadow of a doubt that He goes before, behind, beside, and even above and below us every step we take, every move we make.

Wednesday October 27, 2021

Philippians 1:27 Only let your conversation be as it becometh the gospel of Christ: that whether I come and see you, or else be absent, I may hear of your affairs, that ye stand fast in one spirit, with one mind striving together for the faith of the gospel;

I am sure many have heard of the chorus "Sermon in Shoes". People observe our lifestyles, actions, and behaviors to determine how genuine our profession of Christianity is. We may talk of being born again and living the lifestyle of a believer but until our actions show it, no one will care what we have to say.

As born-again believers and children of the most High God, our lives need to reflect that. We are to be examples so our behavior, our actions should mirror what God expects of us. That should not only be when our ministers or pastors are around watching. It is easy to be kind, loving, running to serve and being honest when we think our leadership may see or hear us. The real test of true godliness, genuine character is when they are not around, and we continue to be willing to serve and bless others.

Remembering that we are one body in Christ helps us work together, unified for the continued movement of God's Word.

Thursday October 28, 2021

James 1:5 If any of you lack wisdom, let him ask of
God, that giveth to all men liberally, and upbraideth
not; and it shall be given him.
6 But let him ask in faith, nothing wavering. For he that
wavereth is like a wave of the sea driven with the wind
and tossed.
7 For let not that man think that he shall receive any
thing of the Lord.

God is generous, loving, and giving, He is no respecter of persons and will give everyone the wisdom they need to rightly divide and understand His Word when asked in meekness and prayer. We are thankful that God does not hold a grudge, but forgives unconditionally when we turn to Him in repentance, We confess our sins, broken fellowship or where we fall short and God is ready, able, and willing to forgive and forget.

True wisdom and understanding comes from God and His Word. God will open His Word up to those who are sincere about knowing and understanding His plan for their lives. Reading books about the Bible can be helpful at times, although not always accurate and can be misleading. We can go directly to the Word with believing, prayerfully trusting that God will open it up to us. Each time we pray with believing, we are confident God hears and will answer us; any doubt causes us to waver and we will not receive the desired results.

We take a step back to renew our minds, erase doubt, worry or fear before going to God in prayer. What a difference that makes!

Friday October 29, 2021

James 1:17 Every good gift and every perfect gift is from above, and cometh down from the Father of lights, with whom is no variableness, neither shadow of turning.

If one of my children or grandchildren comes to me and says he/she is hungry, and may I please give them some bread, I will never turn them down or give them a 'mud-pie' instead. We love our children and hate to see them hungry or hurting and do everything in our power to take care of, feed them and provide for them. God is our Heavenly Father and He loved us so much He sent His Son to die for die so we could have full remission/forgiveness of sins. How much greater is His love for us than our earthly parents.

He is not only all present, but all powerful and all knowing. He knows what we need before we even ask. And because He loves us, every time He answers our prayer requests it will be perfect – exactly what we need at the right time. God is light and there is no darkness in Him so we know the answers will always be the best. In everything He remains constant and is never dishonest in any situation. We can trust and rely fully in all God has for us.

Saturday October 30, 2021

James 3:17 But the wisdom that is from above is first pure, then peaceable, gentle, and easy to be intreated, full of mercy and good fruits, without partiality, and without hypocrisy.

So many people work hard to get into the most prestigious and well-known colleges and universities around the world. They want to have degree after degree and study for years to boast about their education and everything they know. While there is nothing wrong with obtaining a wealth of education, we value the wisdom we receive from God and His Word as the highest degree. Earthly education will benefit us for a while, but Godly wisdom is eternal.

The wisdom we receive from God above is morally and spiritually clean, undefiled, respectful, and considerate. When we are filled with all the wisdom of God, we are gentle, loving, kind, patient, willing to listen, and compassionate, because that is what the Word of God teaches us. We are meek, remain humble, not thinking ourselves better than others, we are not self-righteous, or hypocritical, but willing and ready to help, support, encourage and build up others in the Word.

Sunday October 31, 2021

Romans 4:17 (As it is written, I have made thee a father of many nations,) before him whom he believed, even God, who quickeneth the dead, and calleth those things which be not as though they were.
18 Who against hope believed in hope, that he might become the father of many nations, according to that which was spoken, So shall thy seed be.

Abraham was convinced of God's promise to make him a "father of many nations". When he was almost a hundred years old and his wife Sara was also "past her childbearing years", Abraham could still picture the promise coming to pass. It may have seemed impossible by their five senses, but nothing is impossible with God, who raised people from the dead. Would we be able to do that? Can we see the answer clearly as if it has already happened?

Maybe you are believing for a job and you have heard the company has a freeze on hiring, but you start preparing for the call to interview. If the company has a dress code, you could possibly go as far as purchasing the specific outfit you will need. Or maybe you have applied to go to a specific college and you do not have the funds yet, but you keep doing everything you know to do, expecting the acceptance letter and the scholarships to cover it.

We need to be so convinced of God's willingness and ability to answer prayer and give us the desires of our hearts that we have no room for doubt. We get a clear picture in our head of the deliverance we are praying for and wait with expectation knowing that is coming. We can even start making plans based on the answer we are anticipating.

NOVEMBER

Monday November 1, 2021

Psalms 25:9 The meek will he guide in judgment: and the meek will he teach his way.
10 All the paths of the LORD are mercy and truth unto such as keep his covenant and his testimonies.

We need to be humble to the teachings of the truths in God's Word. That is the only way we will be able to renew our minds. It means we need to be "coachable". You may have heard employers use that word referring to new employees or maybe business partners, meaning that you must be willing to listen, learn and adapt as necessary to be able to succeed.

God will open up His Word to us and guide/direct us as we stay meek, 'coachable' willing to listen, learn and adapt (change our thinking.) I have heard so many people say, "I've been taught and believed 'so and so' all my life; not sure I can or want to change that." But once we've been taught the rightly divided Word and see that what we've been taught and/or believed all our life is not Word-based, we need to be meek enough to change our thinking to what the Word of God says. Knowing God's Word is all truth, we should want to be meek to believe.

Tuesday November 2, 2021

Psalms 55:22 Cast thy burden upon the LORD, and he shall sustain thee: he shall never suffer the righteous to be moved.

Most of my jobs have required long hours and hard work, and from the time I walk through the doors until I leave to go home, I am on the go, non-stop. I remember the relief when on the rare occasion I got help to get through the tasks that seemed to overwhelm me. When my workday was over, I would walk out, sit in my car for several minutes in peace and quiet to relax and shed some of the days tension. There have been times when going through a rough time, I would cling on to a dear friend for support – just needing that care, love and understanding just to feel like I am not carrying everything alone. What a tremendous blessing that has been!

God knows sometimes we need that break; that some problems just weigh us down. We take some time to go to His Word, spending time in meditation with Him, feeling Him lift the load off our backs. God will take those burdens of grief, pain, hurt, sadness, and anything else while He holds us gently in His arms.

How comforting that we can give all our troubles, cares, whatever we are going through, to God. Let God's strength replace our weakness, in times when we feel unable to cope. And knowing it is not a bother to Him, makes it feel even better, doesn't it? We are not forcing our burdens on God. He sincerely wants to take over so we can focus on the movement of His Word.

Wednesday November 3, 2021

James 1:21 Wherefore lay apart all filthiness and superfluity of naughtiness, and receive with meekness the engrafted word, which is able to save your souls. ***22*** But be ye doers of the word, and not hearers only, deceiving your own selves.

There is so much distraction in the world, and it may be easy to let ourselves be drawn in by whatever is happening around us, follow the trends or fads. As born- again believers God's Word takes precedence in our hearts and lives. No matter how tempted we may be to jump on whatever 'band wagon' is the trend for that time, we stay meek, focused on the truths of God's Word that we have been taught. We allow it to be implanted in our hearts as it is what has brought us salvation.

If we are to walk as God's children, shining as lights for Him in this world, we let go of all uncleanness, any old, wicked ways, and any appearance of evil. Whatever old habits that have become a part of our lives must go as we renew our minds to God's Word. We have been called and set apart, so we do not allow ourselves to be tricked. Instead we set the example by taking a stand, speaking the truth, and living according to the standards set forth in the Word of God. God will reward us as we stay faithful.

Thursday November 4, 2021

Matthew 5:16 Let your light so shine before men, that they may see your good works, and glorify your Father which is in heaven.

We recently heard a teaching of an example of walking into a dark room, not being able to see clearly and bumping into everything. In the same way, I may be looking into my purse for my lipstick and search around in there not able to find it. Depending on how deep the purse is, things sink to the bottom and it is too dark in there to find anything. When I shine a flashlight into the purse, I can find my lipstick right away. That is how simple it is for light to dispel darkness.

Since we take the place of the absent Christ, one of our responsibilities is to represent Him. We do so by being a reflection of God's light. In first John we read that God is light so as people look at us, they should be able to see the light that is God reflecting from us in everything we do. We are to walk the walk, not just talk it; what we say should be a mirror of how we walk. In that way we bring glory to our Heavenly Father. We do not leave any doors open to allow any negatives to be attributed to God or His Word.

Friday November 5, 2021

Matthew 7:1 Judge not, that ye be not judged.

Matthew 7:5 Thou hypocrite, first cast out the beam out of thine own eye; and then shalt thou see clearly to cast out the mote out of thy brother's eye.

This is not meant to be condemning or critical but to give some degree of reproof and correction if needed. We may not like how someone dresses or the way they speak or how they raise their kids. As long as it is not directly contrary to the Word of God, our goal is to be encouraging, speak the truth in love and pray with/for others. We are exhorted to not judge, but to carefully examine our own lives. Is there something we are doing or saying that could be a stumbling block? Then, because we are meek and renew our minds, we get rid of the negatives in our thoughts and lives before we reach out to others.

This may explain it a little clearer. When I travel by plane the flight attendance always says if the use of oxygen masks or life vests, are required at any time, the adult has to put theirs on first, then turn to help a child or someone else who needs assistance. Contrary to what many Christians think, we are our brother's keeper. We look out for one another to bless, build up and support. We can be a listening ear, a shoulder to cry on, or to rejoice with in celebration.

Saturday November 6, 2021

Matthew 18:3 And said, Verily I say unto you, Except ye be converted, and become as little children, ye shall not enter into the kingdom of heaven.
4 Whosoever therefore shall humble himself as this little child, the same is greatest in the kingdom of heaven.

We are to have the same simplicity of love, trust, and believing that children do. A child loves unconditionally and trusts wholeheartedly. Children feel safe and secure in their parents care confident that they will not allow any harm to come to them. They believe whatever their parents say, no matter how strange it sounds. Children accept that Santa Claus and the Easter Bunny are real because that is what they were taught. They accept and believe the stories because they trust what their parents tell them without question.

That is the kind of humility, trust and believing that God requires of us. Unless we can become that humble, trusting, and confident towards God and His Word our spiritual growth is hindered. I have spoken to many people who think that debating or arguing about and questioning the accuracy of God's Word makes them somehow seem more intelligent or intellectual. After being a nurse for over forty-five years with experience in every area of nursing, I feel completely confident in debating any topic and winning any argument related to it. As far as the Word of God goes, I accept what it says without question and if something still seems a little unclear after research and study, I believe the issue is with my understanding and never with the accuracy of God's matchless Word.

Sunday November 7, 2021

Matthew 21:21 Jesus answered and said unto them, Verily I say unto you, If ye have faith, and doubt not, ye shall not only do this which is done to the fig tree, but also if ye shall say unto this mountain, Be thou removed, and be thou cast into the sea; it shall be done. ***22*** And all things, whatsoever ye shall ask in prayer, believing, ye shall receive.

This promise is repeated multiple times in God's Word because our believing is such a big deal. The key is to trust and not doubt that God is able and willing to perform what He says He will do in your life. Imagine moving a mountain from one spot to another just because you believe to do so! Well Jesus was setting the stage for the statement that would follow. All things would mean all things!!

Many years ago, several medical doctors told my parents one of my sisters would be a vegetable and would never learn due to her serious medical condition. Most people would accept it and probably say it is God's will. Thank God for a believing, praying mother who did not accept the diagnosis, but "called the elders in the church" to pray for her. After missing months of school, my sister returned and thrived, skipping classes, graduating valedictorian, went on to earn a degree with a very successful career, married with three very well-educated, successful children. God worked a miracle to move that mountain proving the doctors wrong and He can do it for anyone who believes.

When we go to God in prayer with a believing heart and

knowing for a certainty that He will come through for us, He will – 100% of the time.

Monday November 8, 2021

Matthew 5:18 For verily I say unto you, Till heaven and earth pass, one jot or one tittle shall in no wise pass from the law, till all be fulfilled.

God's Word stands forever; every word in the Bible is yay and amen. So many powerful people, including kings and government leaders have tried to get rid of the Word of God. It was banished, burned, and destroyed in any way they could, but thousands of years later, it is still here. All the prophecies in there, everything that has been foretold and forthtold will stand until it has all come to pass. It is a sure word, a faithful word that we can rely on when everything and everyone else fails us. So saith the Word of the Lord!!!

As born-again believers God's Word is our only true standard for truth to help us understand God's will for our lives. It is our life and for our lifestyle, not just a devotional tool. And yes, we it is very useful for a student of the Word and in our personal daily devotional time, but it does not end there. We study and learn all that God has in His Word for us, apply it to our lives and share it with others. The Word of God is all truth and is the will of God.

Tuesday November 9, 2021

Matthew 22:36 Master, which is the great commandment in the law?
37 Jesus said unto him, Thou shalt love the Lord thy God with all thy heart, and with all thy soul, and with all thy mind.
38 This is the first and great commandment.
39 And the second is like unto it, Thou shalt love thy neighbour as thyself.
40 On these two commandments hang all the law and the prophets.

The book of Exodus outlines what has been known for many years as the 'Ten Commandments." Churches and other religious bodies live their lives by every single word contained in the ten commandments. These have truly been are still are God's standard for right living. The Word of God says that to love Him with everything we have – heart, soul, and mind (passionately, prayerfully and intellectually) and just as important we are to love others as we would love ourselves, is the foundation of His commandments.

We are not to erase the original ten commandments; on the contrary, when we fully embody these two commandments, all the other commandments, which include the ten commandments and others that were outlined thousands of years ago, are all encompassing.

Wednesday November 10, 2021

Psalms 127:1 Except the LORD build the house, they labour in vain that build it: except the LORD keep the city, the watchman waketh but in vain.

We see people spend hundreds of thousands and maybe even millions of dollars to build their perfect home. Maybe it is on a hillside, or with an ocean view and includes every amenity you can imagine. One day a hurricane or tornado hits the area, and in a few minutes, all is gone – the roof blown away and/or the whole house is leveled. No matter how secure you think you've built your house, no matter how much you've spent to build it, it can so easily be gone.

Unless we are trusting God to protect us and our families, if God is not a part of our lives and believing we do not fully have his protection. Through prayer and fellowship, with the Word of God as our standard we can keep a strong, healthy, united family. God is first in our homes and lives we teach His Word to your children, spend time in prayer and thankfulness to experience God's mighty blessing and protection on your lives.

Thursday November 11, 2021

Matthew 7:7 Ask, and it shall be given you; seek, and ye shall find; knock, and it shall be opened unto you: ***8*** For every one that asketh receiveth; and he that seeketh findeth; and to him that knocketh it shall be opened.

How many of us have searched for years for answers to things that perplexed us in life? I remember as a very young child wanting to know why did people have to die, and what happened then – after we die, how come the Bible says Jesus was dead and buried three days and three nights but we were taught He died on Good Friday and rose on Easter Sunday morning? That was only two nights. The Bible seemed so confusing to my young, uneducated mind coupled with the fact that different churches had different philosophies, doctrines, and teachings? How was I to know or believe which one was accurate?

Well, I talked to God a lot about it, asking Him if I would ever understand or did I have to wait until I got to heaven to know what He required of me? I prayed and asked God to direct me to where I would learn and understand the Bible and be able to 'rightly-divide' it like it says in II Timothy 2:15. And He led me to the right place where I learned how to read, study, and understand the Bible, the interpretations and even how to know that I had the accuracy of God's Word. What a blessing to know that God will show us how to "find Him" as we "seek" or look for Him in His Word by diligent study.

Friday November 12, 2021

Matthew 7:11 If ye then, being evil, know how to give good gifts unto your children, how much more shall your Father which is in heaven give good things to them that ask him?

Parents may ask their children to make a list of what they would like for their birthdays or for Christmas. If the child asks for a doll or a fire-truck or for more technology-inclined kids they may ask for a tablet, X-box, or a Nintendo Switch, no parent will say "I cannot afford any of it, so I'll just get him/her a piece of coal from the fireplace." Now, I understand there are many parents who may say these requests are way above their budget and there is no way to afford such expensive gifts. But they will not give the child something useless like maybe a rock. As a child, I was not given an option to ask for what I might have wanted; it just was not affordable. But we were quite creative – we would either make something or each child (six of us) was given a $1.00 bill to go 'shopping'. That way everyone got something, and no matter what it was we were always happy and thankful.

If we as humans (man and woman of body and soul) know how to give our kids presents to bless them, how much more our Heavenly Father who gave us life? According to the book of James "every good and perfect gift" comes from God.

What are you believing for, what have you asked God for? Rest assured when you get the answer it will be even better than you expected.

Saturday November 13, 2021

Matthew 5:44 But I say unto you, Love your enemies, bless them that curse you, do good to them that hate you, and pray for them which despitefully use you, and persecute you;

The hardest thing to do by our five senses is to be kind, forgiving, or to love those who have hurt us or done us wrong in any way. Growing up in a house with five siblings and having to share rooms, there was always a fight over something. As a Christian woman my mother was always telling us to love and forgive each other as God forgave us. It took us a while to calm down and say, "I'm sorry" and actually mean it; and we were siblings. Mama did not let us get away with it though. We were not off the hook until we could say it and sound like we meant it. Even having been taught that standard after I grew up, it was hard for me to let go of hurts and disappointments. Although I was able to readily forgive, I held on to and nursed my hurts for a long time.

Since I have started studying God's Word and understanding His heart for His people, I have really worked hard to practice forgiving and praying for those who have wronged me. God also asks us to bless them that curse us and do good to them even if they persecute us or are spiteful. Tough pill to swallow? Yes indeed, but consider what God's only begotten Son, Jesus Christ went through for us. He was tortured, spat upon, degraded, and a whole lot more before He was crucified, dying on the cross so we can have salvation. And He forgave them, asking God to "forgive them for they know not what they do." And yes God forgave them as well. Who am I not to do the same when I feel slighted, hurt, or persecuted? Because I am forgiven, I can forgive also.

Sunday November 14, 2021

Mark 16:15 And he said unto them, Go ye into all the world, and preach the gospel to every creature.

Matthew 16:17 And these signs shall follow them that believe; In my name shall they cast out devils; they shall speak with new tongues;
18 They shall take up serpents; and if they drink any deadly thing, it shall not hurt them; they shall lay hands on the sick, and they shall recover.

Jesus Christ commissioned His disciples to go and preach to all who would listen. He said, "into all the world" and to "every creature" or to the whole creation. God's heart is that all men come to a true knowledge of His Word, so as the time of Jesus's earthly ministry was coming to an end, He instructed His disciples to continue the work He had started. All born-again believers living in this Grace Administration, have been given the ministry and the Word of reconciliation; we are sent forth as representatives of Christ to continue His great work.

The prophecy spoken to the disciples then is for us today as well. Signs, miracles and wonders will follow us, and people will believe; in the name of Jesus Christ we can bring healing to people, casting out devils as they receive healing mentally. No matter what we face we are covered by God's protection and the adversary's attacks will not be able to stop us. We have the added benefit of God's gift of holy spirit and we can manifest it in the external realm by speaking in tongues.

Monday November 15, 2021

Luke 6:38 Give, and it shall be given unto you; good measure, pressed down, and shaken together, and running over, shall men give into your bosom. For with the same measure that ye mete withal it shall be measured to you again.

It has been said that "we can never out-give God;" because as we give, we always receive back double. All my life I have always really enjoyed giving – to friends, family or anyone who was in need. Once I learned and understood the principles of tithing and abundant sharing, I am even more excited to give back to the continued movement of God's Word. We do not give because we want to get anything back, but it is so fulfilling to think about working together with God every time we give. Because we are in a partnership with God, He always blesses us back for giving. God first gave by giving us His Son for our salvation, showing us He loves us unconditionally – John 3:16. We love God and in return we give to others the truths from His Word to bless and build them up spiritually.

We help others as we give of our natural abilities, talents, and time. We also can give of our excess - things we no longer need or use. God's promise is that when we give out of a cheerful heart, we receive back more than we give. God wants us to prove Him to see how much He will do for us as we faithfully tithe and give of our abundance.

Tuesday November 16, 2021

Zephaniah 3:17 The LORD thy God in the midst of thee is mighty; he will save, he will rejoice over thee with joy; he will rest in his love, he will joy over thee with singing.

When Paul and Silas were thrown in jail, the situation seemed hopeless, but they never despaired. Instead they were heard singing and praising God and refused to allow their circumstances from make them angry and bitter. The angel of the Lord opened the prison gates, and they could have just walked away but they did not. The prison guard was surprised and thankful asking, "Sirs what must I do to be saved?" Paul and Silas were a testimony of God's love, care, and protection, and the jailor and his whole family believed in God and were saved. (Acts 16)

God Almighty is in the midst of us; He is never so far away that He cannot hear or answer us when we call. God heard Paul and Silas while they were in prison. His Word tells us He is "a very present help in trouble." (Psalms 46:1) to be our place of shelter, rescue, and protection. When we are weak, we can draw from God who is our strength to renew our energy and keep going. God wants to see His people blessed and happy, confident in His care. We can rejoice and relax in His love because it is constant. Circumstances around us cannot shake our trust in God nor take away our joy as we are content in our innermost being.

Wednesday November 17, 2021

Luke 21:13 And it shall turn to you for a testimony.
14 Settle it therefore in your hearts, not to meditate
before what ye shall answer:
15 For I will give you a mouth and wisdom, which all
your adversaries shall not be able to gainsay nor resist.

On the day of Pentecost after the everyone heard the disciples speak in their tongues "the wonderful works of God," people were questioning what did it all mean. Peter stood up boldly, faced the multitude and preached his first sermon. He most likely did not plan out what he would say or prepare a teaching in case someone asked them what they were doing. Peter trusted God to give Him the right words to reach the hearts of as many as were meek to hear and receive it. By the end of his teaching about three thousand of those who heard it were saved/ born-again. (Acts 2). When Jesus was tempted, He responded with "it is written", and satan had to flee. (Matthew 4)

When we are confronted or questioned about our stand for God and what we believe, we are not afraid because we keep God's Word in our hearts. (memorize/ retemorize). We are bold and confident in answering because God's Word speaks for itself. Our responses will be directly from God as they will be the words we already have stored in our hearts and minds. We will see men and women repent and turn to God when we share the truths of His Word. That is the power we have in God and His Word.

Thursday November 18, 2021

Matthew 6:28 And why take ye thought for raiment? Consider the lilies of the field, how they grow; they toil not, neither do they spin:
30 Wherefore, if God so clothe the grass of the field, which to day is, and to morrow is cast into the oven, shall he not much more clothe you, O ye of little faith?
31 Therefore take no thought, saying, What shall we eat? or, What shall we drink? or, Wherewithal shall we be clothed?
33 But seek ye first the kingdom of God, and his righteousness; and all these things shall be added unto you.
34 Take therefore no thought for the morrow: for the morrow shall take thought for the things of itself. Sufficient unto the day is the evil thereof.

These verses have been taught together and separately; I think they belong together. It is so easy to get anxious about what may or may not happen in the days or weeks ahead. The year 2020 was filled with so much confusion and uncertainty. Every day the news reminded us of how terrible the pandemic was, what people were most likely to get and die from COVID-19. Businesses were shutting down, people were losing their jobs, and so many were dying. That has been the reality – there did not even seem to be a solution, no cure or treatment in sight and the vaccines that were coming out had side effects that were too risky.

What were we as Christians supposed to do; how were we to handle the uncertainty when so many around us seemed to be paralyzed by fear? Well, the Word tells us worrying will do nothing. We can worry about the possibility of losing our jobs and having no food, but would that stop us from losing our jobs? God in His infinite wisdom takes care of the birds and plants and flowers. How much more would He take care of those who trust in Him? The solution is to put our trust completely in our Heavenly Father knowing that He will provide for and take care of us. No matter what the situation, if it is another pandemic or maybe a health issue, maybe you need a car to get to work, or clothes for the kids. Trust in God; He knows our needs and wants to bless us.

Friday November 19, 2021

Isaiah 32:18 And my people shall dwell in a peaceable habitation, and in sure dwellings, and in quiet resting places;

How beautiful it is to live in a 'nice' peaceful environment! I have seen people move several times looking for the perfect place to settle and call home, only to find they do not like the place. I remember relocating to a different state and moving into what we thought was a really nice neighborhood. We were in a lovely ranch with a deck and yard – just the right size. We just had our first grandchild and loved having her over to play on the deck or run around in the yard. Until one day in the middle of the night, I believe it was around two am we were awakened by the loud roar of a motorcycle going up and down our small, quiet, road (actually a 'lane'.) After a while we fell asleep and figured they were out of town and had made a wrong turn. When it happened again for several nights, we still gave them the benefit of the doubt – they were visiting family and would soon leave. But no, it went on for weeks, months and we decided after much discussion to move out. We had lived there now for almost six years and really enjoyed it because of the peaceful atmosphere and pleasant neighbors, but we were not blessed by the nightly disturbances that got worse and did not seem like it would end.

God is a God of peace and even when the world around us is in chaos and in an uproar, when we trust Him, He keeps us peaceful. Our rest will always be content and undisturbed because He assures us that our habitation will be peaceful. Just like we had to move away from the nightly disturbances our God will lead us away from situations, places or people that might disturb our rest and try to steal our peace.

Saturday November 20, 2021

John 6:63 It is the spirit that quickeneth; the flesh profiteth nothing: the words that I speak unto you, they are spirit, and they are life.

God's gift of holy spirit in each and every born-again believer restores us and gives us new life spiritually. The 'flesh' spiritually refers to our old man nature – our behavior before were born again. Think back about the time before you heard the truth of God's Word and decided to confess Jesus Christ as Lord in your life and believe that God raised Him from the dead. I can still vividly remember the change that took place in my life. Things I thought were 'no big deal' suddenly seemed unacceptable, and I recognized them as things God would not approve of. Some were little things – like going to work late or not being faithful with my tithe and abundant sharing.

The Word of God opened my eyes, revived me, making me alive spiritually. I saw the world in a whole different light. Living by my five senses (the flesh) was of no benefit or profit to me. The words of Jesus Christ outlined in the Bible were given to those holy men of God by revelation and is that life from God's holy spirit that energizes us.

Sunday November 21, 2021

Psalms 138:1 I will praise thee with my whole heart: before the gods will I sing praise unto thee.
2 I will worship toward thy holy temple, and praise thy name for thy lovingkindness and for thy truth: for thou hast magnified thy word above all thy name.

This brings to mind the beautiful words of one of my favorite songs – "mighty God, I praise your name; O Holy One I worship you, cause you are God all by yourself." We bow down and worship, praise and honor the name of God, whether we call Him Heavenly Father, Holy Spirit, Almighty, Elohim, Jehovah or even Dad. We respect and reverence Him because He is the omnipotent one (all-powerful and supreme).

God tells us that He magnified or elevated His Word above all His name. He wants us to know the power that we have in His Word when we study it, make it our own and share it to others. People are saved, made whole, delivered from any kind of bondage by having an accurate knowledge of God's matchless Word. In Psalms 107:20, we read that "God sent His Word and healed". That definitely makes it clear why He would magnify His Word about His very name? As powerful as the name of God is, His Word is elevated about it. Take a moment, and let that sink in.

Monday November 22, 2021

Psalms 139:14 I will praise thee; for I am fearfully and wonderfully made: marvellous are thy works; and that my soul knoweth right well.

Every year around the same time in the Fall we celebrate Thanksgiving Day, a day we have set aside when we bring to mind all we are thankful for. To name a few – family, health, food, a roof over our heads, our jobs, friends, pets, the ocean, mountains, tress, gardens, and so much more. Have you ever thanked God for you – your life, who you are, what you have accomplished, your body? I don't know about you, but I can honestly say, I never have. When I was younger, and everyone commented on my body I was too shy, embarrassed, and never truly took time to appreciate it. As I got older, and life's changes happened I started to miss the younger body that I took for granted and never appreciated. It has been a difficult adjustment to the changes, but God's Word has reassured me that I am fearfully (awesomely) and wonderfully made. So, no matter what changes I am faced with, I remind myself of these truths and give thanks to God.

God's Word says we are remarkably, awesomely, and wonderfully made. Just looking into the mirror, I am in awe of all God thought of when He put the human body together. This is what I plan to do and encourage you reading this page to try it. Find a full-length mirror (buy one, go to a friend's, or even to a mall), take a good look at yourself from head to toe and give God thanks for how He put your body together. Take a quick minute to focus on a part you do not particularly like, and thank Him for it, then quickly move on.

It is not just about the outward appearance, think about the internal organs, how your brain works, your heart, lungs, stomach, blood vessels and lymphatic system. Think about what a blessing it is to be able to see, hear, smell, eat, speak. Your hands, fingers, legs, feet toes and the intricacy of how they function are all very significant in how we function and move.

Let us tell our Heavenly Father how thankful we are that He made us awesomely and wonderfully and give Him praise.

Tuesday November 23, 2021

Psalms 145:17 The LORD is righteous in all his ways, and holy in all his works.
18 The LORD is nigh unto all them that call upon him, to all that call upon him in truth.
19 He will fulfil the desire of them that fear him: he also will hear their cry, and will save them.

God is righteous (worthy, upright, and just) in everything He has done, and still does. His works of creation sets Him apart from everything and everyone. Many people, particularly scientists love to boast about things they have created. But have they really created anything from scratch? That is what to create would mean – to make something out of nothing. Whatever man makes, builds, or develops, He needed some kind of matter which God had already created in Genesis chapter one.

That is why we set Him apart in our hearts and lives as well, allowing nothing or no one to take God's place of being first in everything we do. When we reach out to Him, He is never too far away from our reach, and He responds immediately. As we trust God and give Him the reverence and respect due Him, He rewards us fulfilling our hearts desires. What have you been calling out to God for, what is that need that seems like it will not be answered? Do not stop believing, praying, and trusting until you get that result. God promises to fulfill your heart's desires.

Wednesday November 24, 2021

II Corinthians 2:14 Now thanks be unto God, which always causeth us to triumph in Christ, and maketh manifest the savour of his knowledge by us in every place.

It was just two weeks since I had accepted the position of 'Assistant Director' at a facility. The staff were challenging, and everything was disorganized and out of order. I set to work to correct some areas that stood out as some of the main causes of the disarray. I immediately addressed some staff issues where no one seemed to be team-players, several had serious issues with punctuality and had difficulty following the dress code. By the middle of the second week the Chief Executive Officer (CEO) called me at home stating the board of directors were very impressed with all I had accomplished in that short time and wanted to offer me the position of Director. I was stunned, excited, and petrified all at the same time. After I took some time to talk to God I was reassured that I could do it, so I accepted. God worked mightily in me to do a great job there – causing me to 'triumph' (be very successful) in that role for several years.

It is through us that the knowledge of God and His Son Jesus Christ is spread all over the world. It is though the accomplished works of Jesus Christ that God causes us to be victorious. The love of God that Christ came to make known has a rippling effect. God so wants to bless our lives and wants the world to see us succeed in every aspect of our lives. He reminds us of how precious, sweet, and satisfying His Word is and our role in sharing it with others.

Thursday November 25, 2021 -THANKSGIVING DAY

I Thessalonians 5:18 In everything give thanks: for this is the will of God in Christ Jesus concerning you.

HAPPY THANKSGIVING. As we get together with our families, and remember all the things we are thankful for, keep in mind everything we have because of what God accomplished for us through His Son Jesus Christ. Because of Jesus Christ's free-will choice to obey His Father and give His life for us, we have new life, we have salvation, we have God's gift of holy spirit. We legally belong to God's family and everything He has we have as joint heirs with Christ. We have power in the name of Jesus Christ and can do the works and greater ones that Jesus Christ did while He was here on earth.

We have also been given legal rights as sons of God, some of which are our sonship rights? They are, sanctification (been set apart), justification (just as if we never sinned), righteousness (the ability to stand in the very presence of God without any sense of sin, guilt or short-coming), redemption (legally bought back, delivered free from sin), and the ministry and Word of reconciliation (we get to be representatives for God by taking the place of the absent Christ.)

So, along with our thanks for the food, family, friends, health, life, clothes, transportation, a house, pets, and everything else, we take time to give thanks for all we have in Christ.

Friday November 26, 2021

John 1:1 In the beginning was the Word, and the Word was with God, and the Word was God.
2 The same was in the beginning with God.
3 All things were made by him; and without him was not any thing made that was made.
4 In him was life; and the life was the light of men.
5 And the light shineth in darkness; and the darkness comprehended it not.

It was very exhilarating for me to get a clear picture of what these verses mean. Jesus Christ was the Word made flesh, sent to dwell among us. This cannot mean that He was literally words on paper, but He made known God by opening up the truths of God's Word. In the beginning when God created the heavens and the earth, Jesus Christ and the written Word were only with God in His fore-knowledge, as He begin to formulate the plan of man's redemption and of bringing His Word to pass.

God made the world all by Himself, bringing light into the world by speaking it forth (Genesis 1:3), and breathing life into Adam's nostril when He created man. When Jesus Christ began His earthly ministry, the words He spoke helped people understand God's heart and brought light to a world lost in darkness brought on by the adversary.

As representatives of Jesus Christ we now do the same by continuing to speak the truths of God's Word.

Saturday November 27, 2021

John 8:31 Then said Jesus to those Jews which believed on him, If ye continue in my word, then are ye my disciples indeed;
32 And ye shall know the truth, and the truth shall make you free.

We have ability to be free by what God accomplished for us by way of His Son Jesus Christ. But we must accept and believe these truths to actually be set free. Just reading the Word is clearly not enough, we have to live by the standards put in place for us and know (truly understand and believe) the Word of God. Until then we are still in bondage by our thoughts, fears, worries, cares, doubt, and confusion brought on by the adversary.

A hurricane or tornado is bearing down on your town. The news is horrifying because you witness what devastation it has caused already in its path. We listen to the news media and they state all the things that could possibly go wrong, which could lead to even more fear if we let it. What is the plan, what can we do? We pray! We are not bound by fear of what may or may not happen if/when it hits us. The same spirit of God that worked in Jesus Christ when He spoke to the storm and said "peace, be still," works in us today and we can do the same. We are truly free when these truths become a reality in our lives.

Sunday November 28, 2021

John 4:24 God is a Spirit: and they that worship him must worship him in spirit and in truth.

Thousands of years ago, on the day of Pentecost man first received God's gift of holy spirit and spoke in tongues. This was a new era – nothing like it had ever been seen or heard previously. Man was able to have direct communication with God, our Heavenly Father. Water baptism was no longer necessary as receiving God's gift was to be baptized with His spirit. (Acts 1:5)

The verse should accurately read, God is Spirit since the 'a' is left out of most critical Greek texts. In that form we cannot see or touch Him, since He has no flesh, bones, or blood. God cannot speak directly to us as humans but communicates to us by way of His gift of 'holy spirit' in us only when we are born again. It is a law – that God can only communicate to what He is – Spirit. So, when we go to God in prayer to make request, praise, and/or worship, we must be able to speak by God's spirit in us, which is speaking in tongues.

Monday November 29, 2021

John 7:38 He that believeth on me, as the scripture hath said, out of his belly shall flow rivers of living water.
39 (But this spake he of the Spirit, which they that believe on him should receive: for the Holy Ghost was not yet given; because that Jesus was not yet glorified.)

This was a prophecy regarding the receiving of God's gift of holy spirit. God's gift of holy spirit in the born-again believer is energized supernaturally when one speaks in tongues. (Acts 2:2-4) Speaking in tongues only became available on the day of Pentecost at the initial outpouring when people were first able to be born-again and receive God's gift of holy spirit.

The words that pour out are overflowing like a river because we have no control of what we speak, because the words we speak are not ours but given to us by God. We do however have control of that we speak. When we open our mouths to speak in tongues, God's spirit in us is edified enabling us to bring forth the message for or from God at the specific moment to a specific person(s). We make the decision to speak in tongues believing to receive and deliver the message God has for His people at that specific time.

Tuesday November 30, 2021

Psalms 147:3 He healeth the broken in heart, and bindeth up their wounds.

Losing a loved one can be very devastating, sad, and even a bit confusing. We may question why, because we are just at a loss as to why it had to happen. Some teachings tell us that we should not question what God has done and He takes people for a reason. This teaching is clearly not rightly dividing the Word of God, since it tells us that it is the devil who has the power of death – (Hebrews 2:14). God is love and He cares for us. Instead we are comforted by the hope of Christ's return. Many times, it may seem that He is so far away and could not possibly hear us, but this is not true. No matter how badly our heart is broken God can put it back together, we just need to reach out and let Him do it. Obviously, God does not want us in pain, sad, hurting, depressed or He would not say that He heals those who are of a broken heart.

Hearts can be broken by hurt, loss of a relationship, a broken marriage, or death of a loved one. In any of these situations, God understands our pain and wants to bring healing if we will let Him. No amount of therapy can do what God and His Word can do to heal completely.

God is the healer of broken hearts, weaving back together the threads that were torn apart, He will bring back the peace and joy that was destroyed and stay by our side through it all.

DECEMBER

Wednesday December 1, 2021

John 3:16 For God so loved the world, that he gave his only begotten Son, that whosoever believeth in him should not perish, but have everlasting life.
17 For God sent not his Son into the world to condemn the world; but that the world through him might be saved.

When Adam and Eve sinned and lost their spiritual connection with God, they allowed satan to take control of everything that God had given them. To take that power back from the devil (our adversary), and free man from the bondage of sin, God immediately started putting a plan in motion to re-connect with man.

God made man to fellowship with Him and He wanted that back. His plan of salvation was to send His "only begotten Son" Jesus Christ to be our Savior. Jesus Christ paid the legal price as the sacrifice for the sin of all mankind. The main purpose of Jesus Christ's life, death, resurrection, and ascension was to make salvation available. Man's only responsibility is to confess Jesus as Lord in our lives and believe that God raised Him from the dead to receive that gift of everlasting life.

Thursday December 2, 2021

Jeremiah 10:23 O Lord, I know that the way of man is not in himself; it is not in man that walketh to direct his steps.

When I relocated many years ago, I knew nothing of the place I was moving to and had no idea what to expect. Everything I had planned was thrown out when I settled down and realized that my plans did not fit into anything in that new location. By our five senses we can make plans for our future as best as we can keeping in mind that things can happen to change those plans. We do not have control over how our lives turn out; we have no idea what will happen later in a day, a week, or a month. Our best laid plans are turned upside down at times by circumstances beyond our control. We have no charge of our destiny, only God knows what lies ahead and can see what is coming long before we do. The only smart thing to do is to allow God by way of His Word be our guide in this life.

The only way we can guarantee success in every situation or challenge that arises is by trusting God to direct/guide our every decision. God wants to be with us and help us navigate this life, we just need to trust Him to do that.

Friday December 3, 2021

John 15:16 Ye have not chosen me, but I have chosen you, and ordained you, that ye should go and bring forth fruit, and that your fruit should remain: that whatsoever ye shall ask of the Father in my name, he may give it you.

This is interesting that God would put in His Word that we did not choose Him, but that He chose us. He wants us to know that He purposely appointed us a place in His household to carry out our ministry of reconciliation. This is a powerful, awesome privilege. Wherever we are is exactly where God wants us to be. When things did not work out like I wanted them or how I had planned I really questioned why I was not where I had anticipated. But God has told us He knows the plans He has for us.

And just so we are clear, God has called us and for those who have responded to His call He has commissioned to go share His Word to all who will receive it. We are to do 'good' works that will reflect the life of Christ. We are to be kind, giving, loving, hospitable, and generous; these are the attributes that will show God's love to others and what will remain in their hearts. I decided to stop fighting it and surrender to God's plan for my life; it is a much more peaceful place to be. As long as we continue to follow and live His Word, sharing it with others, we are promised to receive whatever we ask of God in the name of His Son Jesus Christ. What a beautiful promise!

Saturday December 4, 2021

James 5:16 Confess your faults one to another, and pray one for another, that ye may be healed. The effectual fervent prayer of a righteous man availeth much.

I read a true story some time ago about this Christian family who was praying for healing for their son. The young man was a believer and was praying as well, claiming all the promises he could remember from God's Word. His father was a minister and his mother faithfully prayed day after day; they wrote Bible verses on sticky notes and had them pasted all over the wall in his hospital room. The doctors stated there was nothing more they could do and that the family and patient needed to prepare for the end. They did not accept this and kept on praying. One day the doctors walked in the room with a hospital chaplain and told him he had no more than ten hours to live, suggesting he allow the chaplain to pray for his last hours and for a peaceful demise. He politely thanked them and asked the chaplain to leave and not come back because he still believed God would heal him.

When they left the room, he began to talk to God about what was happening. He had done everything he needed to do as a believer, and it seemed (by his five senses) that healing was not coming. It was then he heard God say that he needed to forgive. At first, he was thinking there was no one he was holding a grudge against, but soon two maybe three names came to mind. He called his parents and asked that they reach out to these people and tell them he needed to see them right away. They went to see him, thinking they were going to say their good-byes. The young man reminded them of whatever each specific situation was and asked for forgiveness for holding on to it and told them he forgave them. They cried and prayed together (one by one), and after the last one left the young man had the best night sleep he'd had since being admitted. By the next morning, his temperature of 105 had gone down to 100, he was more alert and awake, and the staff found him walking from the bathroom. Stunned they called the doctors who ran some tests and by the end of the day stated they could only call it a miracle because he was completely cured of his illness/ disease.

The key here is that if we are praying and believing for something and particularly healing and it doesn't seem like it will happen, think back on any one you need to forgive or ask for forgiveness. Holding on to anger, hurt, and disappointment can hinder our full recovery. Let go and let God work a miracle for you today.

Sunday December 5, 2021

John 20:21 Then said Jesus to them again, Peace be unto you: as my Father hath sent me, even so send I you.
22 And when he had said this, he breathed on them, and saith unto them, Receive ye the Holy Ghost:
23 Whose soever sins ye remit, they are remitted unto them; and whose soever sins ye retain, they are retained.

When Jesus was about to leave this earth to be with His Father, He commissioned His disciples to continue His work. He reassured them that they had nothing to worry about, that they could be free from anxiety or fear because they would have Christ in them. On the day of Pentecost, that became a reality and still today that is the reality of all born-again believers everywhere. That was the first time it was available for people to be born-again and receive God's gift of holy spirit. The power of that gift in every believer allows us to lead others into the new birth, teaching them how to receive God's gift and how to manifest it in the sense's realm.

When we are born-again and receive God's gift of holy spirit, we are also filled with God's peace – a sense of undisturbed, untroubled rest in our minds. We are no longer tossed about mentally or physically nor filled with anxiety when difficulties arise because we can speak in tongues and remain joyful and thankful.

Monday December 6, 2021

Acts 1:8 But ye shall receive power, after that the Holy Ghost is come upon you: and ye shall be witnesses unto me both in Jerusalem, and in all Judaea, and in Samaria, and unto the uttermost part of the earth.

The power of the gift of holy spirit in each and every believer makes it possible to do the works of Jesus Christ and greater. Since the manifestation of the gift of holy spirit was not available while Jesus Christ was here on earth, (not even to Him) only those born again on and after the day of Pentecost are able to receive it and lead others into receiving it as well. As Jesus Christ commissioned His disciples so many years ago, we are being commissioned to go “to the uttermost part of the earth” to teach Gods Word to others. We have been given the ministry and the Word of reconciliation and are fully equipped/prepared to do so.

As Christians we represent the absent Christ; the Bible says we are ambassadors for Christ. An ambassador is an accredited official who represents a country or sovereign power; he/she would speak for that country, king, or queen. That is how significant our role as ambassadors/ representatives for Christ is. And we should not take it lightly; our lives illuminate and brings attention to God and His Son Jesus Christ everywhere we go. Let us be the best representatives that we can be.

Tuesday December 7, 2021

Romans 14:19 Let us therefore follow after the things which make for peace, and things wherewith one may edify another.

We belong to the family of God and are one body in Christ. One of the things, the Word says is that "a house divided against itself cannot stand." (Mark 3:25) We want to always keep things undisturbed, and tranquil so that there is peace among God's household of believers. If there is always division, strife, disagreements and fighting, the household will be dismantled; we will no longer be examples that can lead others to God.

With six of us children growing up together we would fight, argue, and disagree many times. I remember wrestling with my younger sister over something none of us remember, but her hand was under her and her wrist got dislocated at some point. She was screaming in pain and when I took a look at her wrist I was also screaming. Thankfully, it was an easy fix – one trip to the emergency room and she was as good as new. Well, guess what, we never wrestled again, because I was so full of dread of a similar thing happening again. I could not apologize enough, and I am also thankful that she forgave me, she knew I did not do it on purpose, and definitely did not mean to hurt her. Once we decided that was it for our 'wrestling' days, things were much more peaceful at home and we remained great friends over the years.

As God's children there will be disagreements and

arguments, and maybe even ‘wrestling matches’ (not literally of course), but as long as we can acknowledge our faults, ask for forgiveness and forgive each other, the household will be a peaceful place. Let us strive to encourage, support, and build up one another to keep peace in the household of God.

Wednesday December 8, 2021

I Corinthians 10:13 There hath no temptation taken you but such as is common to man: but God is faithful, who will not suffer you to be tempted above that ye are able; but will with the temptation also make a way to escape, that ye may be able to bear it.

In Matthew chapter four, we read of Jesus Christ's temptations from the adversary. And again, in Hebrews 4:15, we read that Jesus Christ was faced with similar temptations that we have. So, He gets it; He understands our struggles with wanting something and being tempted so badly to just throw caution to the wind and go for it. Hebrews tells us He was tempted "yet without sin." That means that whatever temptation He faced, Jesus Christ refused to give in – that was His free-will choice. We also have a choice to make – the easy way and give in or handle it like our Savior and big brother Jesus Christ. Remember what He said in Matthew chapter 4 – "it is written"; and that is how we handle our temptations as well – with the Word.

God's Word reassures us that we will not be tempted above or more than we can bear, but that God has already made the way for us to overcome, to be victorious. What is your decision? Let us decide to face things like Jesus Christ did.

Thursday December 9, 2021

Acts 2:38 Then Peter said unto them, Repent, and be baptized every one of you in the name of Jesus Christ for the remission of sins, and ye shall receive the gift of the Holy Ghost.
39 For the promise is unto you, and to your children, and to all that are afar off, even as many as the LORD our God shall call.

God is no respecter of persons; He wants all men to be born again. It is available to all, but only by choice, He will not force anyone to be born-again against their will. When we accept God's invitation to be confess Jesus Christ as Lord in our lives and believe that God raised Him from the dead, we are saved/born-again and receive God's gift of holy spirit by being baptized "not of water but of the Word."

Many Christians erroneously believe that the gift of holy spirit was only meant for those who believed on the day of Pentecost. Others believe that it has been given to a few select, chosen believers. God's promise of His gift of holy spirit and the power to speak in tongues was not just for a select few, nor did it end with the believers of the first century church. It is still available for every man, woman, boy, and girl who has and will believe and are born again. If you have confessed Jesus Christ as Lord in your life and believe that God raised Him from the dead, you are born again and have received God's free gift of holy spirit. Each of us has the free will choice to operate it. If you are not yet speaking in tongues, it is not God's will, something is holding you back; it is your choice. Why not let your doubts go, let go of the wrong teaching you have been holding on to, trust God and His Word and make the decision to manifest His gift of holy spirit in your life? You will experience such a spiritual uplifting such as you have never known before.

Friday December 10, 2021

Exodus 15:26 And said, "If thou wilt diligently hearken to the voice of the Lord thy God, and wilt do that which is right in His sight, and wilt give ear to His commandments and keep all His statutes, I will put none of these diseases upon thee which I have brought upon the Egyptians; for I am the Lord that healeth thee."

Jehovah-Ropheka/Rapha: The Lord that healeth. God is the ultimate source of all health, our solution for sickness, disease, injury, weakness, and instability. He promised the Israelites that they would never experience any poor health as long as they were obedient to His Word. God was able to get them out of Egypt with not one "feeble person" among them. (Psalms 105:37) We are fully aware that medical science has its place and the work they do to assist in the healing process is remarkable, but God is the ultimate healer. Many times, when physicians have acknowledged that there is nothing more they can do, we have seen God step in and work a miracle. There have been so many documented examples of this taking place both in the Bible, in my own experience and around the world. A very inspiring true story turned into a movie that I would highly recommend on the topic is "Breakthrough".

God's heart is always physical and spiritual health and healing for His people. As believers our preventative measures include doing God's will and going to Him first when things seem off in any category. We trust God and believe His Word and see signs, miracles and wonders come to pass.

Saturday December 11, 2021

Acts 2:46 And they, continuing daily with one accord in the temple, and breaking bread from house to house, did eat their meat with gladness and singleness of heart,
47 Praising God, and having favour with all the people. And the Lord added to the church daily such as should be saved.

The believers in the first-century church met 'daily' with one purpose in mind that was to give God praise and to spend time with each other. What a great example for us; we too should be excited to spend time together with like-minded believers. That does not necessarily mean we get together every single day and not always in a church service or Bible study group. They were 'breaking bread', meeting at a coffee house maybe, going to each other's homes, maybe each person bringing a dish. They were happy, thankful, and humble, blessed to be sharing one with another. We can call another believer to share the Word, pray with or share an outreach goal. In doing so, we can encourage, support and build each other up.

We are always being watched, maybe even scrutinized for our stand as Christians so we want our lives to be examples, shining lights so others can see Christ in us. Like the first century believers, we will be respected, and people will want what we have – whatever is giving us the joy they will see in our lives each day. God will send the meek hearts to us who want to know more about Him and His Word.

Sunday December 12, 2021

Acts 4:12 Neither is there salvation in any other: for there is none other name under heaven given among men, whereby we must be saved.
Acts 4:13 Now when they saw the boldness of Peter and John, and perceived that they were unlearned and ignorant men, they marvelled; and they took knowledge of them, that they had been with Jesus.

Your level of education does not matter, you may or may not have a degree, but God has called you to be His light shining to dispel the darkness overshadowing the world. Our message is that the only source of our salvation, the only way to be born-again and receive God's gift of holy spirit is through His Son Jesus Christ. For years many have neglected to teach this maybe because they think it is too easy, there has to be more to it and so they keep searching for more, maybe get confused and miss out on the simple truths of God's Word. Romans 10:9 and 10 spells it out. God made it simple so we can teach it to our children.

Peter and John in the book of Acts were not educated, "unlearned and ignorant men" it states, but they stood out because of the power of God's gift of holy spirit in them. They spoke as well-educated and knowledgeable men. We are bold, no matter our level of education, because God has promised to give us the words we need to speak when we need it. If we are speaking to kids, we will have the appropriate words and examples to help them understand the Word, if we are among professors, doctors, lawyers etc. we have no need to feel less than. God will provide the words so that these highly educated people will be in awe of the accuracy of the Word of God that we speak. Be bold, be courageous, trust God.

Monday December 13, 2021

Acts 4:19 But Peter and John answered and said unto them, Whether it be right in the sight of God to hearken unto you more than unto God, judge ye.
20 For we cannot but speak the things which we have seen and heard.

When we sit around at lunch time, maybe going for a walk or even out shopping, I find myself in a position to have to answer questions regarding my belief or stand on the Word. Have you ever been told, "O, so you are very religious?" My reply each time is "actually no, I'm not religious, I'm spiritual." The next question is "what's the difference?" Well, to me being religious means I am involved in a particular religion or that I embrace doctrines from specific religious denominations. I used to think that it really did not matter what religious organization I was affiliated with but one day came to the realization that it mattered which ones taught God's Word accurately or rightly divided. I knew that I wanted and needed a closer relationship with God and a better understanding of His Word and that is what I believe to be spiritual – an intimate relationship with my Heavenly Father who is Spirit. As I got older and got involved in Biblical research and Bible study, I know that my standard of truth is the Word of God and it takes precedence over everything and everyone else in this world.

When I am questioned on specific topics and I am able to give the chapter and verse, I am satisfied that it is the rightly divided Word of God, and there is no room for argument. My stand is "that is what the Word says," it doesn't matter if people do not agree; that does not change the truth, and I can only speak what the Word of God says."

Are we so convinced and persuaded about the truths of God's Word that nothing or no one will sway us or stop us from speaking it? That is where we need to be in our spiritual walk.

Tuesday December 14, 2021

Acts 10:34 Then Peter opened his mouth, and said, Of a truth I perceive that God is no respecter of persons:
35 But in every nation he that feareth him, and worketh righteousness, is accepted with him.

It has been said by some Christians that God wants one person to have His gift of holy spirit and not another; or that maybe He prefers not to answer their prayers for whatever reason. They may mention someone they know, maybe a praying mother or minister and say something about that person having a special connection with God, because He answers their prayers. We have addressed this topic and looked at these words in different forms, because I believe it is a very significant and important message that we all need to hear and accept.

God's Word says right here that he is not partial to anyone specifically, He does not think one person is better than another or have a favorite child, like maybe some of our earthly parents. When we become born-again, we each receive God's gift of holy spirit and are able to manifest it in our lives by speaking in tongues. It is not just for a select few. If for some reason, someone is not able to speak in tongues, it is never God's fault, something in that person's heart or life is holding them back. As long as we open our mouths and believe for God to give us the words it will happen. That we speak is our free will choice. God just requires love and respect for Him and His Word, and a life pleasing to Him by staying in fellowship with Him.

Consider what may be holding you back from receiving all God has in store for you. You are special to Him and each one of us is His favorite child.

Wednesday December 15, 2021

II Corinthians 4:16 For which cause we faint not; but though our outward man perish, yet the inward man is renewed day by day.
17 For our light affliction, which is but for a moment, worketh for us a far more exceeding and eternal weight of glory;

We will all age and may get disheartened when we realize that we are no longer as healthy, strong, or maybe no longer as physically beautiful as we used to be. I remember when I was about to turn sixty, I found myself starting to get depressed. Where have the years gone, I pondered? My health was no longer like it was, physically I had changed so much, I hardly recognized myself, and now I was almost sixty? One early morning lying in bed and thinking about my upcoming birthday, I heard that still small voice. Almost ignoring it, I rolled over starting to plan a "pity party" in my head, but we know our Heavenly Father is persistent when He wants to get a point across. He started reminding me of all I had accomplished in the past fifty-nine years. I was married, had two amazing children and three beautiful, smart, and loving grandchildren. Yes, I had also experienced sadness, grief, and loss - lost triplets born too early to survive, had thyroid surgery, survived domestic, physical, and sexual abuse. But I had also answered my calling being a nurse for forty plus years and my wealth of experience in that field is unparalleled to many of my profession. My education went from diploma registered nurse to bachelors, masters, and doctorate degree programs; I became a

Certified Health Minister, Master Herbalist, a graduate of several biblical research classes, run a Bible Study Fellowship with my husband in our home and am a published author. What was I complaining or feeling depressed about? I HAVE LIVED LIFE!!

I got out of bed with a spring in my steps, ran down the stairs to declare to my husband that I wanted an 'epic' sixtieth birthday celebration. No longer feeling sorry for myself but seeing the possibilities that lay ahead I was thankful to God for all He had brought me through. We do not get discouraged or lose heart no matter what our situation looks like, because it is fleeting, and lasts but a moment. We have a life to live to glorify God and our eternal rewards to look forward to at Christ's return when we will be like Him and live eternally with our Heavenly Father. Let us look past the earthly troubles, not focusing on what we do not have, but instead let us focus on what awaits us in God's glory.

Thursday December 16, 2021

Acts 17:28 For in him we live, and move, and have our being; as certain also of your own poets have said, For we are also his offspring.

We are children of God and we exist because of Him; everything we are and have is from God. God created man to fellowship with and worship Him; our very existence, and everything we do including our limitations are determined by Him. And when we are born again we are legally adopted into God's family spiritually.

That should keep us in awe, not fear of this almighty, all powerful, all knowing Spirit called God. With reverence and respect we acknowledge His holiness, and power, His sovereign rule, and His heart to love unconditionally. He loves so deep, so all-encompassing that He refused to give up when man sinned and allowed the adversary, God's archenemy to take over rulership of man and the world that He (God) created. Instead He set in motion a plan to legally buy back man's freedom and secure man's forever place with Him in the heavenlies.

What a God! What a loving Father; we owe Him everything and yes all He asks back is love for one another, love for Him, trust, and fellowship. That we can do!

Friday December 17, 2021

Acts 28:31 Preaching the kingdom of God, and teaching those things which concern the Lord Jesus Christ, with all confidence, no man forbidding him.

The apostle Paul had a checkered past, as he has mentioned in his writings with regret. One day he was confronted by Jesus who basically encouraged him to give up that life and stop fighting against the truth of God's Word. Renewing his mind, and believing Jesus' words regarding Himself and God's plan for man, Paul turned away for his life of crime, gave it up 'cold-turkey' and immediately began to study the Word and teach everyone what he knew about the truth.

Paul learned that Jesus Christ was indeed the Son of God, that He was born of man and because it was a man's sin that destroyed the lines of communication between God and man, God needed a man to pay the price for man's sin. God showed Paul that Jesus was the sacrificial Lamb, our Passover as symbolized in the Old Testament, who came to take away the sins of the world. The religious rulers of the day, that Paul used to work for when he tortured and killed so many Christians, were angry that now Paul taught salvation through Jesus Christ who they still despised. Paul was arrested and imprisoned several times, and while on house arrest continued to speak of the truths of God's Word regarding His Son Jesus Christ and that salvation was only available in His name.

We as believers are as convinced and determined as Paul to speak the truth of God's Word, not allowing anyone to hinder us as we reconcile men and women back to God. There are still many believers around the world that do not have freedom of speech or religion and suffer for speaking or teaching God's Word. We are privileged and thankful that God has placed us where we can still freely share the true gospel of His Son Jesus Christ and salvation from sin.

Saturday December 18, 2021

Romans 1:4 And declared to be the Son of God with power, according to the spirit of holiness, by the resurrection from the dead:

Jesus Christ is the only man who God raised from the dead, to die no more. That is the proof we have that He is indeed the true and only begotten Son of God. That is God's way of setting Jesus Christ apart from others who have been raised from the dead; they have all died since but Jesus Christ is alive seated at the right hand of God.

Take a look at how the Amplified version states this verse, making it clearer.

Romans 1:4 (Amplified) and [as to His divine nature] according to the Spirit of holiness was openly designated to be the Son of God with power [in a triumphant and miraculous way] by *His* resurrection from the dead: Jesus Christ our Lord.

And that same power that God used when He raised Jesus Christ from the dead is in every born-again believer. What power we have in our Savior as we receive and confess Him as Lord in our lives. It is "Christ in us the hope of glory" – Colossians 1:27, and as Jesus Christ is seated in the heavenlies at God the Father's right hand, so will we, in eternity with Him. What a day to look forward to!

Sunday December 19, 2021

Romans 1:16 For I am not ashamed of the gospel of Christ: for it is the power of God unto salvation to every one that believeth; to the Jew first, and also to the Greek.

On many occasions we see crowds of people on the streets in protests, some peaceful and others leading to violence. No one is backing down from what they believe in, walking the streets, holding signs, chanting maybe but wanting their voice heard regarding whatever they stand for. In most of these cases, their cause may be legitimate or hold some merit, others make no sense and may appear to some of us as a waste of time. To the person taking a stand for and demanding more be done for some type of cancer or wanting a specific holiday recognized, it means a lot to them and they are bold, even facing ridicule to do it.

How much more those of us who stand for God and speak the truths of His Word. Do we bow down the minute someone questions what we believe; or do we only speak about God and Jesus Christ behind closed doors – maybe in a church setting or in our homes? Absolutely NOT! We want to be bold and courageous when speaking God's Word as we are His representatives, we speak for Him. There is power in the 'word of reconciliation' regarding what God accomplished in Jesus Christ for us, so we are not ashamed to take a stand and speak for God.

Monday December 20, 2021

Psalms 139:12 Yea, the darkness hideth not from thee; but the night shineth as the day: the darkness and the light are both alike to thee.

Recently I listened to a teaching and heard this verse which caused me to ponder its true meaning. At first it seemed a bit perplexing as to what it really was saying about God as the Creator. As we remember in Genesis 1:3, God spoke light into being and then later on the fourth day (verses 14 to 18) He divided that light into day and night. For years I never felt comfortable being out walking in the dark because I could not see clearly. From dawn to dusk, there is still light out and I can clearly see where I am walking, if there is a puddle or ice on the ground. When I am not able to decipher what's in my path, I tend to walk more gingerly and less confidently which also takes much longer.

Some people tend to behave differently after dark – most crimes occur at night when people believe they will not be seen. Or some may more readily sneak around when they think they will not be caught. It may be difficult to capture everything that goes on after dark by our five senses, but not to God. We cannot hide from Him.

God sees everything clearly no matter how much light or how dark it is; the night to Him is as clear as if it were day. Once I understood that, I realized that I can trust God to make a clear path for me as I walk, so I don't fall into a puddle of water or slip on ice. I thank Him for his protection and safety and if I head off for a walk and it is dark, I trust that my Heavenly Father will take care of me just as much in the dark as in the day light. In the same way we want our behavior to remain Godly whether it is day - light or night - dark I like the amplified version.

Psalms 139:12 (Amplified) Even the darkness is not dark to you and conceals nothing from you; but the night shines as bright as the day; darkness and light are alike to you.

Tuesday December 21, 2021

Psalms 34:8 O taste and see that the LORD is good: blessed is the man that trusteth in him.

The analogy here is as one would taste a dish to find out if he/she would like it, so we go to God's Word, read it, study it and make it our own. Once we develop a true understanding, we determine it is as sure a Word as it says we build our trust in it, and are blessed, satisfied, happy. I would not read many passages in the Word when I was still searching and asking questions regarding the meaning of certain topics such as Job's story. Once I was able to understand the clear reference of the goodness of God versus the 'badness' of the devil, the passage was more enjoyable to me.

From Genesis to Revelation, we see God's goodness outlined in many scenarios. There were situations where people disobeyed His commandments, where they worshiped false gods, and even blasphemed/cursed God. God was always patient, loving, and forgiving when they turned from their evil ways back to Him. When we trust God, put our trust and confidence in His Word, we are blessed by Him providing for us, protecting us, and healing us.

As we examine God's Word and make it our own, starting with one verse, we can memorize it and savor it, and we can document the blessings that will start pouring in.

Wednesday December 22, 2021

Romans 11:33 O the depth of the riches both of the wisdom and knowledge of God! how unsearchable are his judgments, and his ways past finding out!

God's ways are mysterious; so many have tried and still are trying to figure it out. Scientists try to prove or disprove the Word of God trying to make sense of all God has done or is doing. They have studied everything they can about how God functions and have written books on what they believe to be their understanding of God's ways.

Medical doctors accepted to be some of the most brilliant minds of our day are confused by miracles when they have no explanation why someone who they were so sure was as good as dead, is healed. Man has studied the human body and its workings for centuries but will never fully grasp the full understanding of the details God 'wonderfully and marvelously' made.

We will never be able to measure the wealth and depth of God's knowledge until maybe when we are together with Him in eternity. It is deeper than anything our finite minds can comprehend. We stand in awe of the vast expanse, complexity, and depth of what is our Heavenly Father's wisdom.

Thursday December 23, 2021

Romans 12:1 I beseech you therefore, brethren, by the mercies of God, that ye present your bodies a living sacrifice, holy, acceptable unto God, which is your reasonable service.
2 And be not conformed to this world: but be ye transformed by the renewing of your mind, that ye may prove what is that good, and acceptable, and perfect, will of God.

God made our bodies – every intricate detail of it and He is not asking for a literal sacrifice, but that we live in obedience to His Word. As sons of God, we are sanctified/ set apart and our lives should show that we are a 'peculiar people' (special and chosen by God Himself – 1 Peter 2:9.) By our free-will choice we make a dedicated, decision to devote our lives in service to the movement of God's Word. We do not allow our minds to be fashioned after the pattern of the world but according to the true standards of God's Word. To renew the mind takes discipline to make a conscious effort to turn away from our old ways of living, of reacting or dealing with people or situations that hurt us or caused us to harbor anger or grudges. Instead we go to God's Word for answers to handle every situation.

We keep in mind that God has already placed everything we need that pertains to "life and godliness" in His Word, so whatever we need, the answer is in there.

Friday December 24, 2021

Luke 1:35 And the angel answered and said unto her, The Holy Ghost shall come upon thee, and the power of the Highest shall overshadow thee: therefore also that holy thing which shall be born of thee shall be called the Son of God.

Luke 1:46 And Mary said, My soul doth magnify the Lord,
47 And my spirit hath rejoiced in God my Saviour.

Biblical research has proven that Jesus was not born on a cold December day or night thousands of years ago. This is a time that many Christians around the world set aside to celebrate His birth and it is a blessing to celebrate that He was born. God had set a plan in motion, making the decision to have His Son born of a woman to fulfill the prophecy of a Savior to redeem man from the clutches of the adversary. It took many years until God found the perfect woman to be the mother of His Son, a woman who would trust God completely and say with no doubt in her heart "be it unto me according to thy Word."

Mary was humbly glorifying God for having chosen her and for what a privilege it was to be called the mother of the Savior of all mankind. Her praise went to God, she did not allow her ego to take over. One of the amazing works of research that clearly documents the facts surrounding Jesus Christ birth can be found in the book "Jesus Christ our Promised Seed" by V.P. Wierwille.

Saturday December 25, 2021 – CHRISTMAS DAY

Luke 2:7 And she brought forth her firstborn son, and wrapped him in swaddling clothes, and laid him in a manger; because there was no room for them in the inn.

Remembering all we have in Christ, it is significant that we set aside time to recognize His humble beginnings in a manger (an animal feeding box). He grew up to be called 'King of the Jews (Judeans), but He never had a castle, a throne or any riches. His mother wrapped Him warmly in a blanket and thanked God for the precious gift that was His Son.

We can take some time today to read the whole story surrounding this verse in Luke 2: 1- 6, 8 -18

Luke 2:19 But Mary kept all these things, and pondered them in her heart.
21 And when eight days were accomplished for the circumcising of the child, his name was called JESUS, which was so named of the angel before he was conceived in the womb.

The name Jesus was a fulfillment of prophecy, that He would be called Jesus because He would save God's people from sin. Let us be thankful for the precious gift God sent to make salvation available, redeem and justify us and that we could be born-again of His spirit.

Sunday December 26, 2021

Romans 16:25 Now to him that is of power to stablish you according to my gospel, and the preaching of Jesus Christ, according to the revelation of the mystery, which was kept secret since the world began,

From the beginning of time after the first sin of mankind, God put a plan in motion to rescue man from the power of the adversary. His written Word along with Jesus Christ existed in the fore knowledge of God and He kept it a secret from there until it was revealed after Jesus Christ's death and resurrection. The mystery was that although God had initially sent His Son to rescue the children of Israel from the bondage of sin, He was then making it available for the Gentiles to have the same privilege to be called God's children. As long as we make the confession of Jesus Christ as Lord in our lives and believe that God raised Jesus from the dead, we are legally adopted into the family of God. Jesus Christ is our brother, and we will share fully in God's inheritance.

We are strengthened and established by the power of God in us by way of His Son Jesus Christ. The gospel and preaching of what we have and what is available to all who choose to believe is our ministry of reconciliation.

Monday December 27, 2021

I Corinthians 1:10 Now I beseech you, brethren, by the name of our Lord Jesus Christ, that ye all speak the same thing, and that there be no divisions among you; but that ye be perfectly joined together in the same mind and in the same judgment

Brothers and sisters in Christ, we belong to the 'one body' of Christ; we have all been called to do the works of Jesus Christ. As children of God, we need to be united in the common goal to bring men and women back to God. When we became born again, we receive five sonship rights, one of which is the ministry of reconciliation. Our job description is to speak God's Word and reconcile men and women back to God. God alone is the author of the Bible from Genesis to Revelation; His Son Jesus Christ is the subject of the Bible from Genesis to Revelation. Our message to the world is regarding God's love for us and the sacrifice He made to send His only begotten Son to be the Savior of the world. Through Jesus Christ, we have access to our Heavenly Father – God, and it is in His name we pray. Because of all God accomplished for us by way of His Son Jesus Christ, we can now be called children of God, we have God's gift of holy spirit and the ability to manifest power from on high.

That is what joins us together as one, like-minded with the same word/message, and in unity. We should not be divided in our teachings, our stand, or our lifestyle. As one in the Lord Jesus Christ, we shine together as lights for God, to lead others to Him.

Tuesday December 28, 2021

I Corinthians 1:30 But of him are ye in Christ Jesus, who of God is made unto us wisdom, and righteousness, and sanctification, and redemption:

It is through God we have salvation by His Son Jesus Christ because He planned this from the very beginning. When we became born-again, we were given legal rights as His children. We were given wisdom to understand and have a full knowledge of His Word and His plan of salvation that was a mystery until the Grace Administration; righteousness which makes us acceptable and in right standing before God, whereby we can stand in the presence of God without any sense of sin, guilt or shortcomings. Sanctification is our 'consecration' by which God declares us holy in His eyes and sets us apart for Him; and redemption is the ransom paid in full by Jesus freeing us from the power of the adversary, sin and the consequences and penalty of sin.

My heart fills with joy and my eyes with tears every time I remember the magnitude of all God has done for me and all I have in Christ. What unconditional love and what complete forgiveness from our Heavenly Father. God desires love and fellowship from us which I believe is not too much to ask.

Wednesday December 29, 2021

Romans 4:17 (As it is written, I have made thee a father of many nations,) before him whom he believed, even God, who quickeneth the dead, and calleth those things which be not as though they were

God's ways and thoughts are not like ours; He sees things way into the future that we cannot even begin to comprehend. He promised Abraham to make him a father of many nations and the years went by and nothing. Then one day God spoke to Abraham reminding him of that promise and that He was absolutely still going to make that happen. Abraham took note of the fact that he was now ninety-nine years old and his wife Sarah was ninety years old, both well way past child-bearing years. Abraham had to see past those five-senses facts to believe that God was able to make that happen, which He did.

When we go to God in prayer, we must develop a similar mindset to see 'things that are not as though they are.' The doctors say there is nothing they can do, and the prognosis is poor. We do not just give up but trust God that His promise of "by the stipes of His Son Jesus Christ we were healed." It is a done deal – we picture ourselves well, healthy, healed, walking, and leaping and praising God. What are you praying and believing for? It does not have to be just about health or healing, maybe it is your finances, to get out of debt, for a child, school, marriage, whatever the request, claim God's promise that if we ask anything according to His will, He will give it to us. Picture the answer is already received despite how impossible or bleak the situation looks, see ‘things that are not as though they are.’ Trust God; He really does want to bless us His kids.

Thursday December 30, 2021

Ephesians 3:14 For this cause I bow my knees unto the Father of our Lord Jesus Christ,
16 That he would grant you, according to the riches of his glory, to be strengthened with might by his Spirit in the inner man;
17 That Christ may dwell in your hearts by faith; that ye, being rooted and grounded in love,
18 May be able to comprehend with all saints what is the breadth, and length, and depth, and height;
19 And to know the love of Christ, which passeth knowledge, that ye might be filled with all the fulness of God.

My prayer for each of you who embarked on and completed this journey with me, is that you continue to spend every day practicing the presence of God. Embrace all you have in Christ, it is God's free gift, there is absolutely nothing we can do to deserve it so let us stop trying to work for it. God gave us His gift of holy spirit when we confessed Jesus Christ as Lord in our lives and believed in our heart that God raised Him from the dead. As we must build up our physical bodies by proper nourishment and exercise, we build up the spirit in our innermost being by manifesting it and speaking in tongues. That is our proof that we are born again, and heaven bound. Do not let doubts, worries, fears, thoughts of unworthiness or anxiety bring us down, keep building your believing in God and His rightly divided Word.

The Phillips version has such a beautiful summary, I will let it speak to you the words that I pray for you as well.

Ephesians 3:14-19 (Phillips) When I think of the greatness of this great plan I fall on my knees before God the Father (from whom all fatherhood, earthly or heavenly, derives its name), and I pray that out of the glorious richness of his resources he will enable you to know the strength of the spirit's inner re-enforcement - that Christ may actually live in your hearts by your faith. And I pray that you, firmly fixed in love yourselves, may be able to grasp (with all Christians) how wide and deep and long and high is the love of Christ—and to know for yourselves that love so far beyond our comprehension. May you be filled through all your being with God himself!

How beautiful!! God bless you.

Friday December 31, 2021 – NEW YEAR'S EVE

Ephesians 3:20 Now unto him that is able to do exceeding abundantly above all that we ask or think, according to the power that worketh in us,

As we close out the year 2020, and move into a New Year, I am reminded of the apostle Paul's words in II Corinthians 1:2 "Grace be to you and peace from God our Father, and from the Lord Jesus Christ."

Now unto God who alone is able by His power in us to do infinitely more than we could ever ask or think or even imagine, unto Him we give all glory by Christ Jesus. Let us claim all God's promises, they are in His Word for us, let us keep believing His Word, never doubting and let us be bold and courageous as we take a stand for God and speak the truths in His Word.

Numbers 6:24 The Lord bless thee, and keep thee:

25 The Lord make his face shine upon thee, and be gracious unto thee:

26 The Lord lift up his countenance upon thee, and give thee peace.

And in the Amplified Classic Version:

Numbers 6:24 The Lord bless you and watch, guard, and keep you;

25 The Lord make His face to shine upon and enlighten you and be gracious (kind, merciful, and giving favor) to you;

26 The Lord lift up His [approving] countenance upon you and give you peace (tranquility of heart and life continually).

GOD BLESS YOU!

YOU ARE GOD'S BEST!

About The Author

Candia grew up attending an Evangelical Church and at the age of five asked her mother what she should do to be 'saved.' She spent years after that searching for answers to questions that continued to perplex her about the Bible, only to be told by pastors, deacons, and Sunday school leaders that she asked too many questions. Her continued quest to learn and understand the accuracy of God's Word, led Candia to a non-denominational Christian bible fellowship, research and teaching ministry, and after years of foundational, intermediate, and advanced class level studies she along with her husband continue to study and teach the Bible in their home fellowship under the leadership of the President and ministers of the ministry.

In 2020, Candia was recognized by the President and Board of Directors for thirty years of her faithful stand with the ministry. What an honor and blessing to be part of such a wonderful group with fellowships around the world which continues to teach those interested in learning more about God, His Word, His will for their lives and how to practically incorporate those teachings into our daily lives. We believe and teach that God wants us to manifest that "more than abundant life" that Jesus Christ came to make available for us. John 10:10(b)" ... I (Jesus Christ), am come that they might have life and that they might have it more abundantly."

In this role, as in many others during her life, Candia has been a counselor, mediator, advocate, educator, communicator, and change agent for many.

In 2009, she started a small women's group called 'Women of Virtue' (WOV) with a goal to bless, encourage, support, empower as many women as possible. They hold several women's events throughout the year – some planned, some spontaneous.

After over forty-five years of nursing Candia has completely transitioned from the traditional bedside nursing and has been more focused on Natural Health and Healing endeavoring to help herself as well as any who are interested to realize a better quality of life, by following the standards set forth in God's word. God made the body to heal itself and as we tap into that knowledge, we can achieve improved health and healing naturally. Candia is extremely proud of her extensive career as a nurse and is in no way trying to ignore conventional medicine but compliment it.

Candia is a Certified Health Minister, Master Herbalist, MHA/RN and has published several books, a few being collaborations with some family, friends, and colleagues. Having just started her business, 'Healing and Comforting Hearts' Candia sees her life continue to move in the direction that God is leading her.

Her latest book, In the Garden Devotionals - A Daily Walk and Talk with God is a tool to complement your meditation and quiet time with God to bless and uplift you in your spiritual growth. Candia's believing is that you will utilize it daily, use the empty pages/spaces to document your thoughts and welcomes anyone who wants to reach out to her to share what has blessed them.

NOTES

NOTES

.

Made in the USA
Middletown, DE
16 February 2021

33862781R00247